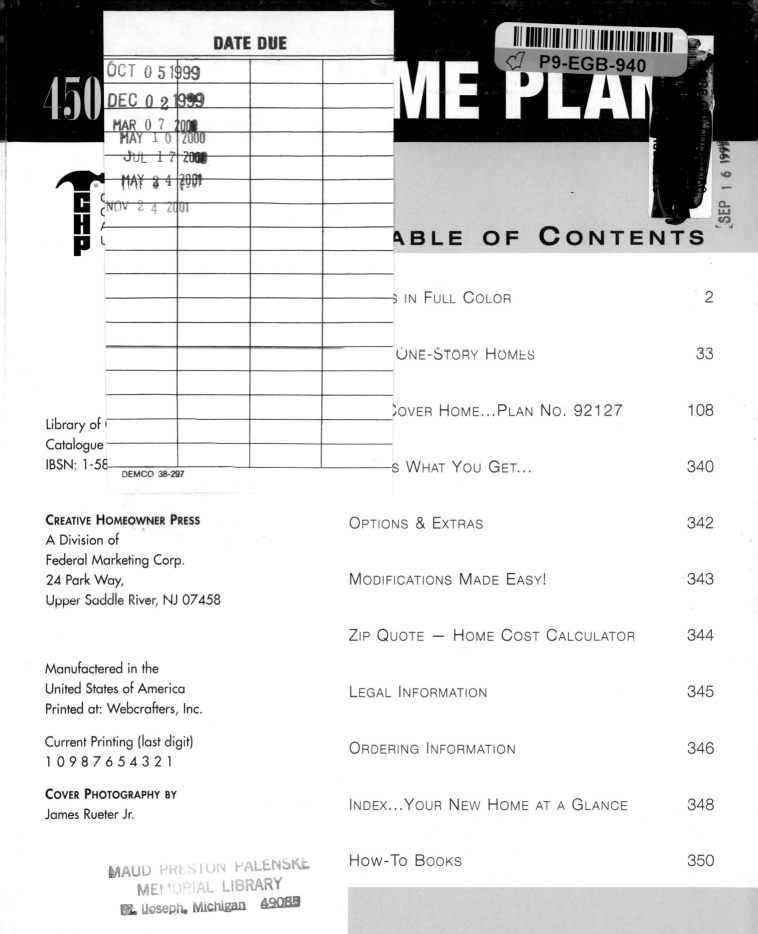

450 ...ME PLAN

P9-EGB-940

SEP 1 6 1998

CHP

TABLE OF CONTENTS

...S IN FULL COLOR   2

...ONE-STORY HOMES   33

...COVER HOME...PLAN NO. 92127   108

...S WHAT YOU GET...   340

OPTIONS & EXTRAS   342

MODIFICATIONS MADE EASY!   343

ZIP QUOTE — HOME COST CALCULATOR   344

LEGAL INFORMATION   345

ORDERING INFORMATION   346

INDEX...YOUR NEW HOME AT A GLANCE   348

HOW-TO BOOKS   350

Library of C...
Catalogue...
IBSN: 1-58...

CREATIVE HOMEOWNER PRESS
A Division of
Federal Marketing Corp.
24 Park Way,
Upper Saddle River, NJ 07458

Manufactered in the
United States of America
Printed at: Webcrafters, Inc.

Current Printing (last digit)
1 0 9 8 7 6 5 4 3 2 1

COVER PHOTOGRAPHY BY
James Rueter Jr.

price code **B**

total living area: 1,738 sq. ft.

Perfect For A View

plan no.

**1
0
8
3
9**

Photography by John Ehrenclou

Perfect for a sloping lot and lakeside property, this home's simple streetside facade contrasts with it's expansive, breathtaking rear views

This Ranch home features a large sunken Great room, centralized with a cozy fireplace. The master bedroom has an unforgettable bathroom with a super skylight. The huge three-car plus garage can include a work area for the family carpenter. In the center of this home, a kitchen includes an eating nook for family gatherings. The porch at the rear of the house has easy access from the dining room. One other bedroom and a den, which can easily be converted to a bedroom, are on the opposite side of the house from the master bedroom. The photographed home may have been modified to suit individual tastes.

plan info

Main Floor	1,738 sq. ft.
Basement	1,083 sq. ft.
Garage	796 sq. ft.
Bedrooms	Two
Baths	2(full)
Foundation	Crawl Space/ Slab or Basement/ Crawl Space Combo

The Great room is bathed in natural light from a wall of windows and French doors, which draw you outside to the spacious deck with an impressive viewpoint.

Overlooking the expansive Great room is an open, raised kitchen, providing exciting views from outside while preparing meals for guests and family.

Crawl / Slab Option

66'-0"

Optional Deck

Master Br
11-6 x 16-0

Great Rm
22-5 x 15-0

Screened
Porch
9-9 x 9-9

Brkfst Bar

Dining Rm
15-0 x 9-6

Kitchen
11-4 x 9-0

Foyer

Br
9-0 x 11-0

Air-Lock

Breakfast
11-0 x 8-0

Pantry

Garage
32-0 x 28-0

Porch

52'-0"

Den
15-0 x 10-0
8'-6" Clg.

main floor

Away from streetside distractions, you'll enjoy many hours of quiet repose, and sweeping views on this wonderful full length deck.

Simple Elegant Lines

plan no.

3
4
1
5
0

Photography by John Ehrenclou

Simple, elegant roof lines and special window treatments add to this charming, compact design

plan info

Main Floor	1,492 sq. ft.
Basement	1,486 sq. ft.
Garage	462 sq. ft.
Bedrooms	Three
Baths	2(full)
Foundation	Basement, Slab or Crawl Space

Consider this plan if you work at home and would enjoy a homey, well-lit office or den. The huge, arched window floods the front room with light. This house offers a lot of other practical details for the two-career family. Compact and efficient use of space means less to clean and organize. Yet the open plan keeps the home from feeling too small and cramped. Other features like plenty of closet space, step-saving laundry facilities, easily-cleaned kitchen, and a window wall in the living room make this a delightful plan. The photographed home may have been modified to suit individual tastes.

◀ Modify the kitchen to suit your cooking style...here the eating bar counter has been turned into an island.

main floor

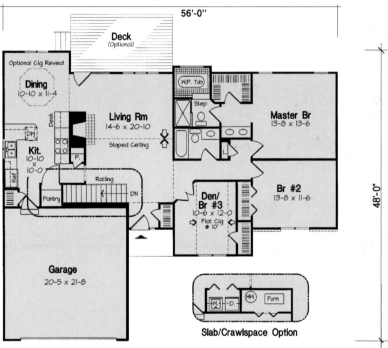

56'-0"

Deck (Optional)

Optional Clg Reveal

Dining 10-10 x 11-4

Desk

DW

Kit. 10-10 x 10-0

Ref.

P.

Living Rm 14-6 x 20-10

Sloped Ceiling

W.P. Tub

Step

Master Br 13-8 x 13-6

Pantry

Railing

DN

Br #2 13-8 x 11-6

Den/ Br #3 10-6 x 12-0

Flat Clg @ 10'

Garage 20-5 x 21-8

48'-0"

HW D. HW Furn

Slab/Crawlspace Option

An EXCLUSIVE DESIGN *By Karl Kreeger*

The view from the den hints at the marvelous, high sloped ceiling in the living room, with a dramatic floor to ceiling brick fireplace! ▶

total living area: 1,737 sq. ft.

Exciting Ranch Design

plan no.

201000

Photography by John Ehrenclou

Stacked windows fill the front bedroom of this home with natural light and sophisticated style.

plan info

Main Floor	**1,737 sq. ft.**
Basement	**1,727 sq. ft.**
Garage	**484 sq. ft.**
Bedrooms	**Three**
Baths	**2(full)**
Foundation	**Basement/ Crawl Space or Slab**

Stacked windows fill the wall in the front bedroom of this one-level home, creating an attractive facade and a sunny atmosphere inside. Around the corner, two more bedrooms and two full baths complete the bedroom wing, set apart for bedtime quiet. Notice the elegant vaulted-ceiling in the master bedroom, the master tub and shower illuminated by a skylight, and the double vanity in both baths. Active areas enjoy a spacious feeling. Look at the high, sloping ceilings in the fireplaced living room, the sliders that unite the breakfast room and kitchen with an adjoining deck, and the vaulted ceilings in the formal dining room off the foyer. The photographed home may have been modified to suit individual tastes.

Dramatic ceiling treatment, extra tall windows and recessed lighting create a master bedroom that's very appealing.

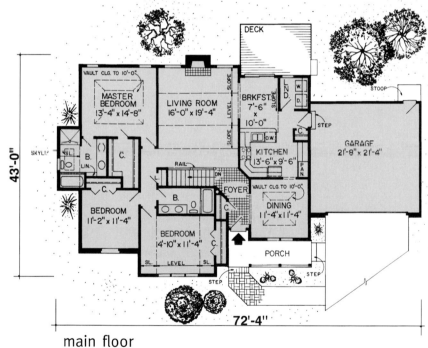

main floor

An EXCLUSIVE DESIGN
By Karl Kreeger

Escape from it all in this exquisite master bath with a tiled, step-up spa tub.

Skylit Ranch Design

plan no.

1 0 5 7 0

Photography by Bob Shimer of Hedrich Blessing Photography

Arched entry shelters visitors, and creates beautiful sparkle and curbside appeal.

plan info

Main Floor	2,450 sq. ft.
Basement	2,450 sq. ft.
Garage	739 sq. ft.
Bedrooms	Four
Baths	2(full)
Foundation	Basement

A partial stone veneer front makes this large ranch design very inviting. Inside, a vestibule entry serves as an airlock. A large library/den next to the foyer shares a two-way fireplace with the living room and has a sloped ceiling, as does the living room. The living room leads to a deck or a screened porch. A very large kitchen has a hexagonal island with a connecting dining room. The dining room also has skylights adding warmth and additional lighting to the room. Also in the dining room, a door leads out to the veranda. This spacious design has four bedrooms and plenty of ample closet space. The photographed home may have been modified to suit individual tastes.

Airy island kitchen is sure to be a family gathering spot as meals are prepared and the daily adventures of school and work are exchanged.

main floor

96'-0"

PATIO

DECK

SCREENED PORCH

M. BEDROOM
14'-6"
X
17'-4"

DINING
13'-0"
X
10'-0"

LIVING RM.
26'-0"X 17'-4"

SKYLT.

ROOF WIND.

KITCHEN
ISLAND
15'-0"X 9'-6"

BEDROOM 4
10'-2"
X
9'-8"

BOOKS

BOOKS

FOYER

STUDY ALCOVE
8'-4"
X
9'-4"

LIBRARY/DEN
15'-4"X 20'-6"

VESTIBULE

BEDROOM 2
10'-0"
X
11'-10"

BEDROOM 3
11'-8"
X
10'-8"

SHOP AREA

GARAGE
23'-4"
X
29'-4"

60'-6"

An
EXCLUSIVE DESIGN
By Karl Kreeger

A sloped ceiling, a one and a half story brick fireplace, recessed lighting and a ceiling fan come together to create this beautiful living and dining space.

Porch Adds Charm

plan no.

3 4 0 2 9

Photography by John Ehrenclou

You'll be charmed by this country porch and inspired to create your own front garden and creative landscaping.

plan info

Main Floor	1,686 sq. ft.
Basement	1,676 sq. ft.
Garage	484 sq. ft.
Bedrooms	Three
Baths	2(full)
Foundation	Basement/ Slab or Crawl Space

Keep dry during the rainy season under the covered porch entry way of this gorgeous home. A foyer separates the dining room with a decorative ceiling from the breakfast area and the kitchen. Off the kitchen is the laundry room, conveniently located. The living room features a vaulted beamed ceiling and a fireplace. A full bath is located between the living room and two bedrooms, both with large closet. On the other side of the living room is the master bedroom. The master bedroom has a decorative ceiling, and a skylight above the entrance of its private bath. The double vanity bathroom features a large walk-in closet. For those who enjoy outdoor living, an optional deck is offered, accessible through sliding glass doors off of this wonderful master bedroom. The photographed home may have been modified to suit individual tastes.

Beamed, Cathedral ceiling with fan adds plenty of impact in the fireplaced living room.

An
EXCLUSIVE DESIGN
By Karl Kreeger

Slab/Crawl Space Option

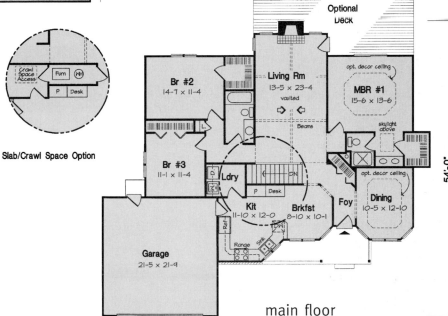

main floor

Roomy bedrooms include options for decorative ceiling treatments, and sliders.

Dogleg counter opens up the kitchen, and flows into a comfortable, windowed breakfast room.

Decorative Windows

plan no.

94923

Photography Supplied by Design Basics, Inc.
Builders — E&G Construction Unlimited

© design basics, inc.

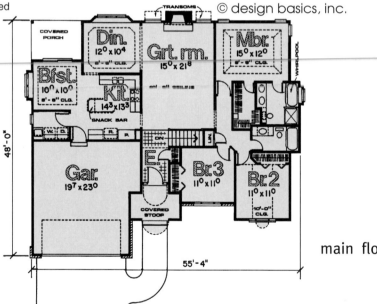

main floor

plan info

Main Floor	**1,666 sq. ft.**
Basement	**1,666 sq. ft.**
Garage	**496 sq. ft.**
Bedrooms	**Three**
Baths	**1(full), 1(half)**
Foundation	**Basement**

Brick and stucco enhance this dramatic front elevation showcased by sleek lines and decorative windows. The inviting entry has a view into the Great room. The fireplace in the Great room is framed by sunny windows with transoms above. The dining room, accented by a bay window, is nestled between the Great room and the superb kitchen/breakfast area. The design of sleeping areas places a buffer between secondary bedrooms and the master suite. The peaceful master suite enjoys a vaulted ceiling, roomy walk-in closet and a sunlit master bath with a double vanity and a whirlpool tub. The photographed home may have been modified to suit individual tastes.

Roomy Stucco & Stone

plan no.

9 2 6 5 7

Photography Supplied by Studer Residential Design

main floor

70' - 8"

64' - 4"

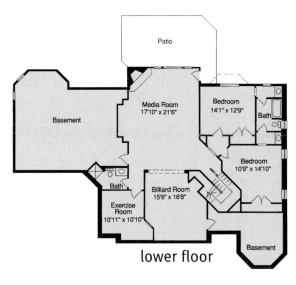

lower floor

plan info

Main Floor	2,582 sq. ft.
Lower Floor	1,746 sq. ft.
Basement	871 sq. ft.
Bedrooms	Three
Baths	2(full), 1(half), & 1(three-quarter)
Foundation	Basement

Stucco and stone accents provide character to the exterior of this expansive one-level home. An arched entry leads inside, where welegant window styles and dramatic ceiling treatments create impact. The extra large gourmet kitchen and breakfast room offer a spacious area for chores and family gatherings; and a striking view through the Great room to the fireplace wall. A butler's pantry is located off the sunken dining room. An extravagant master bedroom suite and library with built-in book shelves round out the main floor. Two bedrooms with a tandem bath, a media room, billiard room and exercise room complete the floor. No materials list is available for this plan. The photographed home may have been modified to suit individual tastes.

Great for Young Families

plan no.

99805

Photography by Jon Riley of Riley & Riley Photography

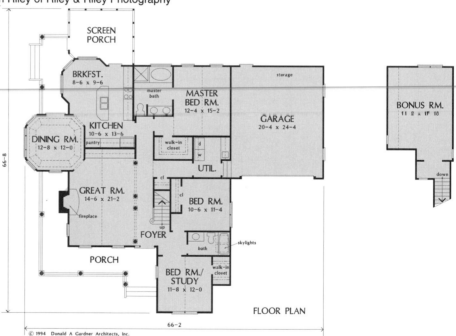

SCREEN PORCH

BRKFST.
8-6 x 9-6

master bath

MASTER BED RM.
12-4 x 15-2

storage

GARAGE
20-4 x 24-4

BONUS RM.
11-2 x 17-18

KITCHEN
10-6 x 13-6

DINING RM.
12-8 x 12-0

pantry

walk-in closet

d
w

UTIL.

down

66-9

GREAT RM.
14-6 x 21-2

fireplace

cl

cl

BED RM.
10-6 x 11-4

up

FOYER

PORCH

bath

skylights

BED RM./ STUDY
11-8 x 12-0

walk-in closet

FLOOR PLAN

66-2

© 1994 Donald A Gardner Architects, Inc.

plan info

Main Floor	1,787 sq. ft.
Bonus Room	326 sq. ft.
Garage	521 sq. ft.
Bedrooms	3
Baths	2(full)
Foundation	Basement/ Crawl Space

This exciting three bedroom country home is perfect for the active young family. The Great room features a fireplace, cathedral ceiling, and built-in bookshelves. The kitchen is designed for efficient use with its food preparation island and pantry. The master suite with cathedral ceiling, walk-in closet, and a luxurious bath provides a welcome retreat. Two additional bedrooms, one with a cathedral ceiling and walk-in closet, share a skylit bath. A second floor bonus room makes a perfect study or play area. This plan is available with a crawl space or a basement foundation. Please specify when ordering. The photographed home may have been modified to suit individual tastes.

Grand First Impression

plan no.

99807

Photography by Jon Riley of Riley & Riley Photography

basement plan

crawl space plan

plan info

Main Floor	**1,879 sq. ft.**
Bonus Room	**360 sq. ft.**
Garage	**485 sq. ft.**
Bedrooms	**Three**
Baths	**2(full)**
Foundation	**Basement/ Crawl Space**

Dormers cast light and interest into the foyer for a grand first impression that sets the tone in a home full of today's amenities. The Great room, articulated by columns, features a cathedral ceiling and is conveniently located adjacent to the breakfast room and kitchen. Tray ceilings and picture windows with circle tops accent the front bedroom and dining room. A secluded master suite, highlighted by a tray ceiling in the bedroom, includes a bath with skylight, garden tub, separate shower, double vanity, and spacious walk-in closet. This plan is available with a basement or crawl space foundation. Please specify when ordering. The photographed home may have been modified to suit individual tastes.

price code **C**

total living area: 1,832 sq. ft.

Classic Country

plan no.

99808

Photography by Jon Riley of Riley & Riley Photography

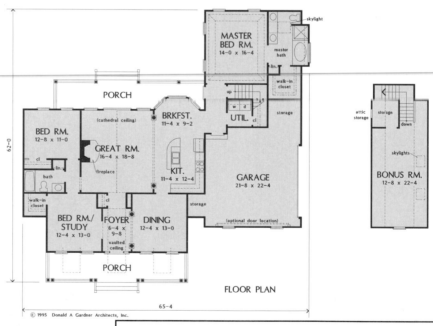

MASTER BED RM.
14-0 x 16-4

skylight

master bath

walk-in closet

PORCH

BRKFST.
11-4 x 9-2

UTIL.

storage

attic storage

storage

BED RM.
12-8 x 11-0

(cathedral ceiling)

GREAT RM.
16-4 x 18-8

fireplace

KIT.
11-4 x 12-4

GARAGE
21-8 x 22-4

skylights

BONUS RM.
12-8 x 22-4

bath

walk-in closet

BED RM./ STUDY
12-4 x 13-0

FOYER
6-4 x 9-8

DINING
12-4 x 13-0

storage

vaulted ceiling

(optional door location)

PORCH

62-0

65-4

FLOOR PLAN

© 1995 Donald A Gardner Architects, Inc.

plan info

Main Floor	1,832 sq. ft.
Bonus Room	425 sq. ft.
Garage	562 sq. ft.
Bedrooms	Three
Baths	2(full)
Foundation	Basement/ Crawl Space/Slab

Dual porches, gables, and circle-top windows give this home its special country charm. The foyer, expanded by a vaulted ceiling, introduces a formal colonnaded dining room. The open kitchen features columns and an island for easy entertaining. The vaulted Great room is always bright with light from the circle-top clerestory. Extra room for growth is waiting in the skylit bonus room. The front bedroom doubles as a study for versatility. A tray ceiling adds volume to the private master suite that has a bath with skylight, garden tub, double vanity, and both linen and walk-in closets. Plan includes a crawl space foundation. The photographed home may have been modified to suit individual tastes.

Executive Home

plan no.

99803

Photography by Jon Riley of Riley & Riley Photography

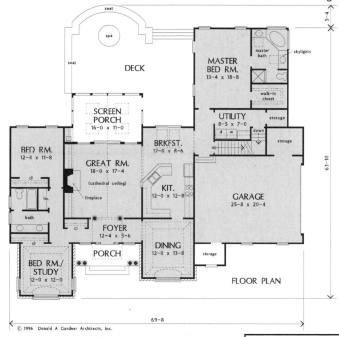

Don't like the Brick.

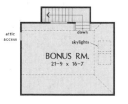

© 1996 Donald A Gardner Architects, Inc.

plan info

Main Floor	1,977 sq. ft.
Bonus area	430 sq. ft.
Garage	610 sq. ft.
Bedrooms	Three
Baths	2(full)
Foundation	Basement/ Crawl Space

Elegant exterior and lively interior spaces, make this three bedroom executive home make life a breeze. A palladian window provide light for a dramatic entrance. Prepare gourmet meals in the well-planned kitchen while chatting with family and friends in the large Great room with cathedral ceiling, fireplace, and built-in cabinets. The screened porch, breakfast area, and master suite access the deck with optional spa. The large, private master suite features a luxurious skylit bath with separate shower, corner whirlpool tub, and separate vanities. A skylit bonus room above the garage adds space when needed. This plan is available with a basement or crawl space foundation. Please specify when ordering. The photographed home may have been modified to suit individual tastes.

Exterior/Interior Style

plan no.

92630

Photography by Rob & Donna Kolb of Exposures Unlimited

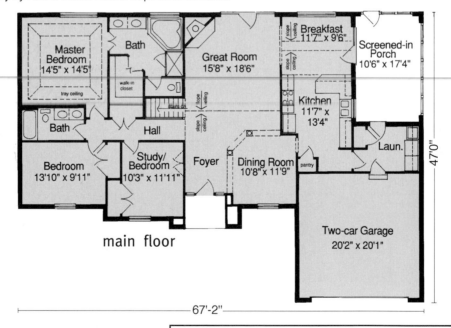

main floor

67'-2"

47'0"

plan info

Main Floor	1,782 sq. ft.
Basement	1,735 sq. ft.
Garage	407 sq. ft.
Bedrooms	Three
Baths	2(full)
Foundation	Basement/ Crawl Space/ Slab

The appeal of this ranch style home is not only in its charm and exterior style. The Great room and the dining room, accented by a sloped ceiling, columns and custom moldings, work together with the corner fireplace, to create an outstanding space. People will naturally want to gather in this breakfast area where the sloped ceiling continues, and the light permeates through the rear windows and the French doors, which leads to the spacious screened porch. Convenience was the order of the day when this kitchen was designed. Relaxing in the master bedroom suite is enhanced by the ultra bath with a whirlpool tub, a double vanity and a large walk-in closet. There is no materials list available for this plan. The photographed home may have been modified to suit individual tastes.

C price code

Brick Beauty

plan no.

22004

Photography by John Ehrenclou

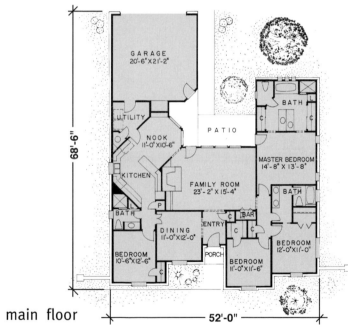

main floor

68'-6"

52'-0"

GARAGE
20'-6" X 21'-2"

UTILITY

NOOK
11'-0" X 10'-6"

PATIO

BATH

KITCHEN

MASTER BEDROOM
14'-8" X 13'-8"

FAMILY ROOM
23'-2" X 15'-4"

BATH

BATH

P

BAR

DINING
11'-0" X 12'-0"

ENTRY

BEDROOM
10'-6" X 12'-6"

PORCH

BEDROOM
11'-0" X 11'-6"

BEDROOM
12'-0" X 11'-0"

View of the eating nook from the beautiful, dynamic living room.

plan info

Main Floor	2,070 sq. ft.
Garage	474 sq. ft.
Bedrooms	Four
Baths	3(full)
Foundation	Basement/Slab/ Crawl Space

Four bedrooms, one a spectacular master suite with an extra large bath, equip this plan for a large family or overnight guests. The centrally located family room merits a fireplace, a wetbar, and access to the patio, and a dining room is provided for formal entertaining. An interesting kitchen and a nook, as well as two and one-half baths, are featured. The photographed home may have been modified to suit individual tastes.

Elegant Convenience

plan no.

24701

Alternate Foundation Plan

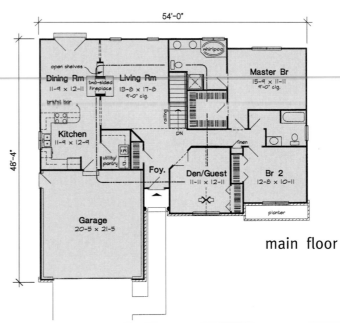

main floor

plan info

Main Floor	1,625 sq. ft.
Basement	1,625 sq. ft.
Garage	455 sq. ft.
Bedrooms	Three
Baths	2(full)
Foundation	Basement/ Crawl Space or Slab

This home features a well designed floor plan, offering convenience and style. The roomy living room includes a two-sided fireplace shared with the dining room. An efficient U-shaped kitchen, equipped with a peninsula counter/breakfast bar, is open to the dining room. An entrance from the garage into the kitchen eliminates tracked in dirt an affords step-saving convenience when unloading groceries. The private master suite includes a whirlpool tub, a double vanity and a step-in shower. A large walk-in closet adds ample storage space to the suite. The secondary bedroom and the den/guest room share use of the full hall bath.

C price code

Country Cottage

plan no.

99804

© 1994 Donald A. Gardner Architects, Inc.

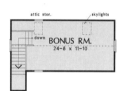

FLOOR PLAN

GARAGE
21-0 x 21-4

storage

attic stor.   skylights

down BONUS RM.
24-8 x 11-10

PORCH   skylights

MASTER
BED RM.
14-8 x 15-4

BRKFST.
10-4 x 8-6

UTIL.
8-8 x
11-0

GREAT RM.
17-4 x 19-0
(cathedral ceiling)
fireplace

KITCHEN
11-8 x 10-6

master
bath

walk-in
closet

linen

bath

DINING
11-4 x 12-8

FOYER
8-8 x 8-0

BED RM.
12-2 x 12-4

BED RM.
10-10 x 12-4

PORCH

70-2

70-8

pantry?
Basement?

plan info

Main Floor	**1,815 sq. ft.**
Bonus Space	**336 sq. ft.**
Garage	**522 sq. ft.**
Bedrooms	**Three**
Baths	**2(full)**
Foundation	**Basement/ Crawl Space/Slab**

We hardly wasted an inch creating a spacious interior for this dormered and gabled country cottage that lives much bigger than it looks. The front bedroom, master bedroom, and open Great room/kitchen gain vertical space from cathedral ceilings while the open foyer pulls the dining room and Great room together visually. The wrap-around front porch, breakfast bay window, and a skylit back porch add charm and expand living space. The master bath pampers the owner with a whirlpool tub, separate shower and dual vanity. A bonus room adds flexibilty to the plan.

price code **C**

Ideal for a Narrow Lot

plan no.

96437

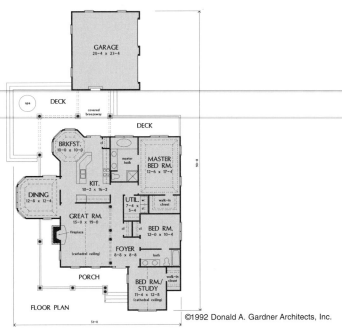

GARAGE
20-4 x 23-4

spa DECK

covered breezeway

DECK

BRKFST.
10-0 x 10-0

master bath

MASTER BED RM.
12-6 x 17-4

KIT.
10-2 x 16-2

DINING
12-8 x 12-4

UTIL.
7-4 x 5-4

walk-in closet

GREAT RM.
15-0 x 19-0

BED RM.
12-0 x 10-4

fireplace

(cathedral ceiling)

FOYER
8-6 x 8-8

bath

PORCH

BED RM./ STUDY
11-4 x 12-8
(cathedral ceiling)

walk-in closet

FLOOR PLAN

©1992 Donald A. Gardner Architects, Inc.

plan info

Main Floor	1,858 sq. ft.
Garage & Storage	504 sq. ft.
Bedrooms	Three
Baths	2(full)
Foundation	Basement/Slab /Crawl Space

Perfect for a narrow lot, this cozy plan possesses more elegance and openness than many houses twice its size. Columns open the interior for circulation and spaciousness. The Great room with fireplace and the bedroom/study reach great heights with cathedral ceilings, while the dining room, breakfast area, and master bedroom gain stature from tray ceilings. The open kitchen and dining room access the porch and deck area, while the master suite features a walk-in closet, dual vanity, shower, and whirlpool tub.

Dramatic Ranch

plan no.

2 0 1 9 8

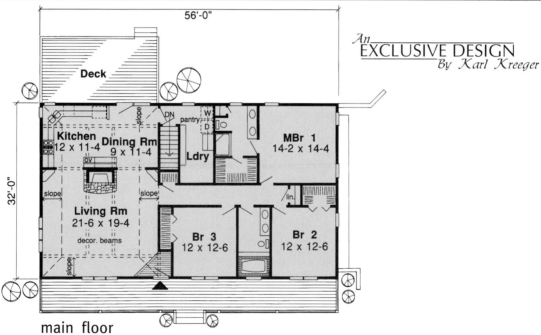

56'-0"

An EXCLUSIVE DESIGN
By Karl Kreeger

Deck

32'-0"

Kitchen 12 x 11-4
Dining Rm 9 x 11-4
pantry
Ldry
MBr 1 14-2 x 14-4
DN
W D

slope slope
slope

lin.

Living Rm 21-6 x 19-4
decor. beams

Br 3 12 x 12-6
Br 2 12 x 12-6

slope

main floor

plan info

Main Floor	1,792 sq. ft.
Basement	818 sq. ft.
Garage	857 sq. ft.
Bedrooms	Three
Baths	2(full)
Foundation	Basement

The exterior of this ranch home is all wood with interesting lines. More than an ordinary ranch home, it has an expansive feeling to drive up to. The large living area has a stone fireplace and decorative beams. The kitchen and dining room lead to an outside deck. The laundry room has a large pantry, and is off the eating area. The master bedroom has a wonderful bathroom with a huge walk-in closet. In the front of the house, there are two additional bedrooms with a bathroom. This house offers one floor living and has nice big rooms.

Easy Living

plan no.

20164

An
EXCLUSIVE DESIGN
By Karl Kreeger

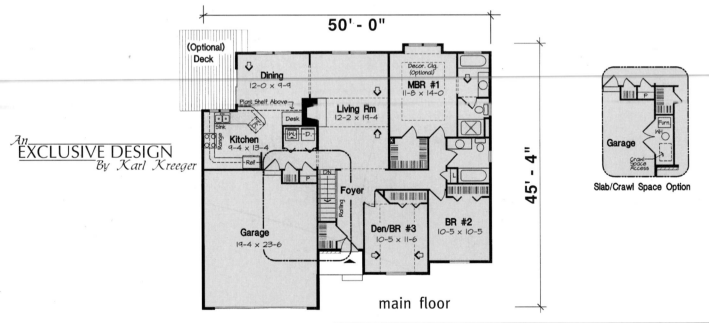

50'- 0"

45'- 4"

(Optional) Deck

Dining
12-0 x 9-9

Plant Shelf Above

Decor. Clg. (Optional)

MBR #1
11-8 x 14-0

Living Rm
12-2 x 19-4

Desk

Sink

Range

Kitchen
9-4 x 13-4

Ref.

Foyer

P

DN

Garage
19-4 x 23-6

Railing

Den/BR #3
10-5 x 11-6

BR #2
10-5 x 10-5

main floor

Garage

P

Furn.

WH

Crawl Space Access

Slab/Crawl Space Option

plan info

Main Floor	1,456 sq. ft.
Basement	1,448 sq. ft.
Garage	452 sq. ft.
Bedrooms	Three
Baths	2(full)
Foundation	Basement/ Crawl Space or Slab

Here's a pretty, one-level home designed for carefree living. The central foyer divides active and quiet areas. Enjoy the fireplaced living room with dramatic, towering ceilings and a panoramic view of the backyard. The adjoining dining room features a sloping ceiling crowned by a plant shelf, and sliders to an outdoor deck. A handy, U-shaped kitchen features abundant cabinets, a window over the sink overlooking the deck, and a walk-in pantry. You'll find three bedrooms tucked off the foyer. Front bedrooms share a handy full bath, but the master suite boasts its own private bath with both shower and tub, a room-sized walk-in closet, and a bump-out window that adds light and space.

One-Level Classic

plan no.

34043

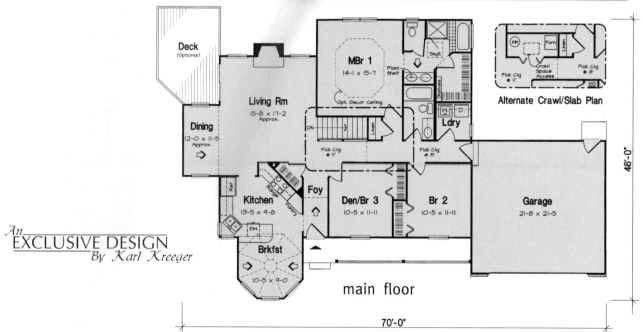

Deck (Optional)

Living Rm
15-8 x 17-2
Approx.

MBr 1
14-1 x 15-7

Plant Shelf

Skylit

Dining
12-0 x 11-5
Approx.

Opt. Decor Ceiling

DN

Linen

Flat Clg
@ 11'

Ldry

Flat Clg
@ 8'

Ref

Kitchen
13-5 x 9-8

Foy

Den/Br 3
10-5 x 11-11

Br 2
10-5 x 11-11

Garage
21-8 x 21-5

DW

Brkfst
10-5 x 9-0

main floor

An
EXCLUSIVE DESIGN
By *Karl Kreeger*

Alternate Crawl/Slab Plan

Crawl Space Access

Flat Clg @ 11'

Furn

Linen

Flat Clg @ 8'

46'-0"

70'-0"

plan info

First Floor	1,583 sq. ft.
Basement	1,573 sq. ft.
Garage	484 sq. ft.
Bedrooms	Three
Baths	2(full)
Foundation	Basement/ Crawl Space or Slab

This convenient, one-level plan is perfect for the modern family with a taste for classic design. Traditional Victorian touches in this three-bedroom beauty include a romantic, railed porch and an intriguing breakfast tower just off the kitchen. You will love the step-saving arrangement of the kitchen between the breakfast and formal dining rooms. Enjoy the wide-open living room with sliders out to a rear deck, and the handsome master suite with its skylit, compartmentalized bath. Notice the convenient laundry location on the bedroom hall.

Detailed Charmer

plan no.

20161

An EXCLUSIVE DESIGN
By Karl Kreeger

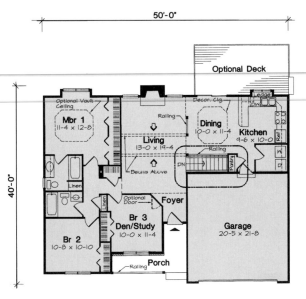

Optional Deck

50'-0"

40'-0"

Optional Vault Ceiling

Mbr 1
11-4 × 12-8

Living
13-0 × 19-4

Railing

Decor. Clg.

Dining
10-0 × 11-4

ledge

Kitchen
9-6 × 10-0

Beams Above

Railing

DN

Ref

Linen

Optional Door

Foyer

Br 3 Den/Study
10-0 × 11-4

Br 2
10-8 × 10-10

Garage
20-5 × 21-8

Railing **Porch**

main floor

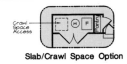

Crawl Space Access

Slab/Crawl Space Option

plan info

Main Floor	1,307 sq. ft.
Basement	1,298 sq. ft.
Garage	462 sq. ft.
Bedrooms	Three
Baths	2(full)
Foundation	Basement/ Crawl Space or Slab

Notice by the exciting, spacious living room, complete with high sloping ceilings and a beautiful fireplace flanked by large windows. The large master bedroom shows off a full wall of closet space, its own private bath, and an extraordinary decorative ceiling. Two bedrooms and another full bath conveniently located. Take advantage of the accessibility off the foyer and turn one of these rooms into a den or office space. The dining has decorative ceiling details, and a full slider out to the deck. The kitchen includes a double sink and an attractive bump-out window. The adjacent laundry room, optional expanded pantry, and a two-car garage make this Ranch a charmer.

Quaint and Cozy

plan no.

9
9
8
7
8

© 1993 Donald A. Gardner Architects, Inc.

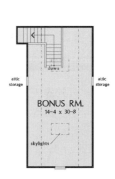

main floor

© 1993 Donald A Gardner Architects, Inc.

plan info

Main Floor	1,864 sq. ft.
Bonus area	420 sq. ft.
Garage & Storage	614 sq. ft.
Bedrooms	Three
Baths	2(full), 1(half)
Foundation	Basement/ Crawl Space

Quaint and cozy on the outside with porches front and back, this three-bedroom country home surprises with an open floor plan featuring a large Great room with cathedral ceiling. Nine foot ceilings add volume throughout the home. A central kitchen with angled counter opens to breakfast area and Great room for easy entertaining. The privately located master bedroom has cathedral ceiling and nearby access to the deck with optional spa. Operable skylights over the tub accent the luxurious master bath. A bonus room over the garage makes expanding easy. This plan is available with a basement or crawl space foundation. Please specify when ordering.

total living area: 1,685 sq. ft.

Dramatic Dormers

plan no.

99810

© 1996 Donald A. Gardner Architects, Inc.

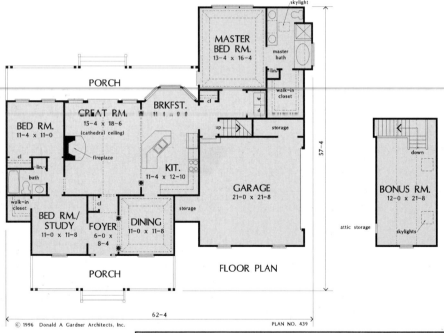

skylight

MASTER BED RM.
13-4 x 16-4

master bath

walk-in closet

PORCH

GREAT RM.
15-4 x 18-6
(cathedral ceiling)

BRKFST.
11-0 x 9-0

BED RM.
11-4 x 11-0

fireplace

KIT.
11-4 x 12-10

up

storage

GARAGE
21-0 x 21-8

walk-in closet

bath

BED RM./ STUDY
11-0 x 11-8

FOYER
6-0 x 8-4

DINING
11-0 x 11-8

storage

PORCH

FLOOR PLAN

57-4

62-4

down

BONUS RM.
12-0 x 21-8

attic storage

skylights

© 1996 Donald A Gardner Architects, Inc.   PLAN NO. 439

plan info

Main Floor	1,685 sq. ft.
Bonus Room	331 sq. ft.
Garage	536 sq. ft.
Bedrooms	Three
Baths	2(full)
Foundation	Basement/Slab/ Crawl Space

The foyer is open to the dramatic dormer and is defined by elegant columns, while the dining room is augmented by a tray ceiling. The front room does double duty as a bedroom or a study. A cathedral ceiling and a clerestory accentuating the rear porch opens the Great room. The Great room is further expanded into the open kitchen and breakfast room by a cased opening with accent columns. The private master suite features a tray ceiling in the bedroom. A garden tub with a picture window is the focal point of the master bath. Two bedrooms on the other side of the home share a full bath and linen closet.

total living area: 2,211 sq. ft.   Great Roof Line   D

price code

plan no. 96449

This three-bedroom executive home does it all. The open kitchen draws family and guests together. The Great room has a cathedral ceiling, fireplace, and arched window. Notice the sky-lights over the breakfast area. Nine foot ceilings add volume, and a tray ceiling in the front bedroom adds impact. The plan includes a skylight bonus room.

plan info

Main Flr.	2,211 sq. ft.
Bonus Rm.	408 sq. ft.
Garage	700 sq. ft.
Bedrooms	Three
Baths	2(full)
Foundation	Basement/Slab /Crawl Space

©1994 Donald A. Gardner Architects, Inc.

---

total living area: 1,568 sq. ft.   Traditional Ranch   B

price code

plan no. 20220

The large front palladium window gives great curb appeal. The living room has a vaulted ceiling. A built-in pantry, double sink and break-fast bar highlight the kitchen. The private master suite has a large walk-in closet and a private bath with a double vanity. The two additional bedrooms share the full hall bath. No materials list available for this plan.

An EXCLUSIVE DESIGN
By Karl Kreeger

plan info

Main Flr.	1,568 sq. ft.
Basement	1,568 sq. ft.
Garage	509 sq. ft.
Bedrooms	Three
Baths	2(full)
Foundation	Basement/Slab Crawl Space

Extras Add Style

plan no.

24700

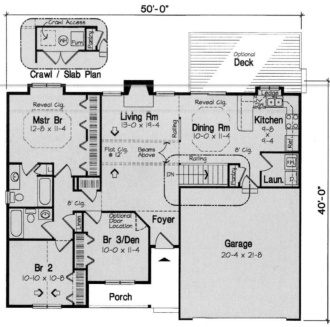

main floor

plan info

Main Floor	1,312 sq. ft.
Basement	1,293 sq. ft.
Garage	459 sq. ft.
Bedrooms	Three
Baths	2(full)
Foundation	Basement/ Crawl Space or Slab

You don't have to sacrifice style when buying a smaller home. Notice the palladian window with a fan light above at the front of the home. The entrance porch includes a turned post entry. Once inside, the living room is topped by an impressive vaulted ceiling. A fireplace accents the room. A decorative ceiling enhances both the master bedroom and the dining room. Efficiently designed, the kitchen includes a peninsula counter and serves the dining room with ease. A private bath and double closet highlight the master suite. Two additional bedrooms are served by a full hall bath.

plan no. 20083

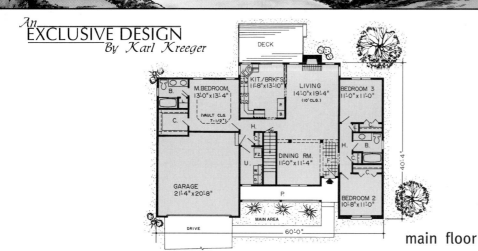

Active living areas are open and centrally located. From the foyer, you'll enjoy a full view of the spacious dining, living, and kitchen areas in one sweeping glance. You can even see the deck adjoining the breakfast room. Two bedrooms share a full bath and the quiet atmosphere that results from intelligent design. The master suite features a full bath with double sinks.

An EXCLUSIVE DESIGN *By Karl Kreeger*

main floor

plan info

Main Flr.	1,575 sq. ft.
Basement	1,575 sq. ft.
Garage	475 sq. ft.
Bedrooms	Three
Baths	2(full)
Foundation	Basement/Slab Crawl Space

---

plan no. 20156

The half-round windows flanking the clapboard-faced chimney add style. The dining room combines with ten-foot ceilings to make the sunny living room seem even more spacious. Glass on three sides enahnces the dining room. Bedrooms are tucked away for privacy. The master suite has a window seat, compartmentalized bath and walk-in closet.

An EXCLUSIVE DESIGN *By Karl Kreeger*

main floor

plan info

Main Flr.	1,359 sq. ft.
Basement	1,359 sq. ft.
Garage	501 sq. ft.
Bedrooms	Three
Baths	2(full)
Foundation	Basement/Slab Crawl Space

Basic Ranch Design

plan no.

34054

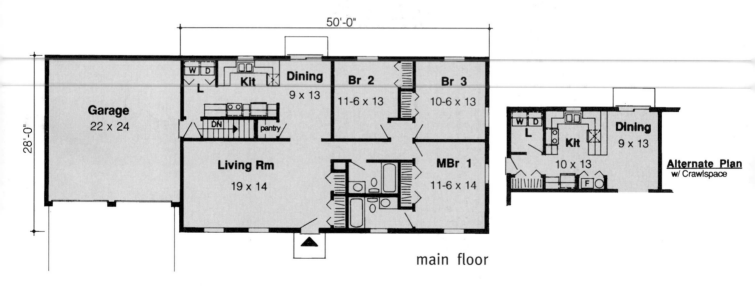

50'-0"

28'-0"

| Garage | | |
| 22 x 24 | | |

W D
L
Kit
Dining
9 x 13
Br 2
11-6 x 13
Br 3
10-6 x 13

DN
pantry

Living Rm
19 x 14

MBr 1
11-6 x 14

W D
L
Kit
10 x 13
Dining
9 x 13
F

Alternate Plan
w/ Crawlspace

main floor

plan info

Main Floor	1,400 sq. ft.
Basement	1,400 sq. ft.
Garage	528 sq. ft.
Bedrooms	Three
Baths	2(full)
Foundation	Basement/ Crawl Space or Slab

There's a lot of convenience packed into this affordable design. Flanking the kitchen to the right is the dining room which has a sliding glass door to the backyard, and to the left is the laundry room with an entrance to the garage. The master bedroom boasts its own full bathroom and the additional two bedrooms share the hall bath. An optional two-car garage plan is included.

Split Bedroom Plan

No. 94057

This plan features:

— Three bedrooms

— Two full baths

■ Covered porch entry leads to formal Living Room with a fireplace

■ Efficient U-shaped Kitchen opens into the Dining Room and features a double sink

■ The large Family Room opens to the rear sundeck and is accessible to the Kitchen

■ These active family living spaces are in the center of the house which lends privacy to the Master Bedroom and bath

■ Two additional bedrooms share a full bath and two linen closets

■ Laundry area is conveniently located near the Master Bedroom

■ No materials list is available for this plan

Main floor — 1,403 sq. ft.
Width 50'-0"
Depth 54'-0"

Total living area 1,403 sq. ft. ■ *Price Code A*

MAIN FLOOR

Country Trimmings

No. 24715

This plan features:

— Two bedrooms

— Two full baths

■ The covered Porch and detailed accents create a country atmosphere

■ The Breakfast bay overlooks the porch and is open to the Kitchen which includes a built-in desk and a pantry

■ Step down into the Great room, accented by a fireplace with windows on either side

■ The Master bath with skylight highlights the Master suite which includes two walk-in closets

■ A cozy window seat and a vaulted ceiling enhance the private Den

■ A screened Porch off the formal Dining room and an expansive rear deck expand living space to the outdoors

■ No materials list is available for this plan

Main floor — 1,771 sq. ft.
Basement — 1,194 sq. ft.
Garage — 517 sq. ft.

Total living area 1,771 sq. ft. ■ *Price Code B*

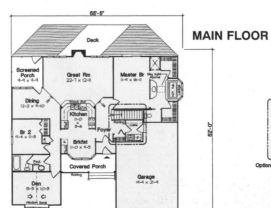

MAIN FLOOR

Optional Slab / Crawl Space Plan

Compact Ranch Loaded with Living Space

No. 34328

This plan features:

— Three bedrooms

— One full bath

■ A central entrance, opening to the Living Room with ample windows

■ A Kitchen, featuring a Breakfast area with sliding doors to the backyard and an optional deck

Main area — 1,092 sq. ft.
Basement — 1,092 sq. ft.

Total living area 1,092 sq. ft. ■ *Price Code A*

ALTERNATE FLOOR PLAN
for Crawl Space

MAIN AREA

Skylit Master Bath

No. 94926

This plan features:

— Two bedrooms

— Two full baths

■ A covered front stoop leads to a tiled formal entry inside the home

■ The Great Room has a large rear wall fireplace that is centered between windows

■ The Living Room or third bedroom has a 10' ceiling and a large front window

■ The Dining Room has a built-in hutch

■ The Kitchen is laid out in a convenient manner and has a snackbar for quick meals

■ The bright Breakfast nook has a rear wall bay and another 10' ceiling

■ The Master bedrooms has a decorative ceiling, two walk-in closets and a full bath

■ Two-car garage with a third bay in the rear

Main floor — 1,996 sq. ft.
Garage — 683 sq. ft.

Total living area 1,996 sq. ft. ■ *Price Code C*

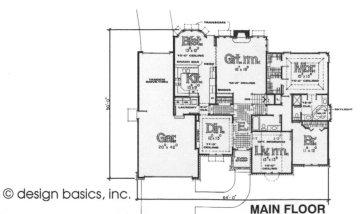

© design basics, inc.

MAIN FLOOR

■ *Total living area 1,393 sq. ft.* ■ *Price Code A* ■

No. 90680 ✖

■ This plan features:

— Three bedrooms

— Two full baths

■ A covered Porch leading into an open Foyer and Living/Dining Room with skylights and front to back exposure

■ An efficient Kitchen with a bay window Dinette area, a walk-in Pantry and adjacent to the Mud Room, Garage area

■ A private Master Bedroom with a luxurious Master Bath leading to a private Deck complete with a pampering Hot Tub

■ Two additional bedrooms with access to a full hall bath

Main floor — 1,393 sq. ft.
Basement — 1,393 sq. ft.

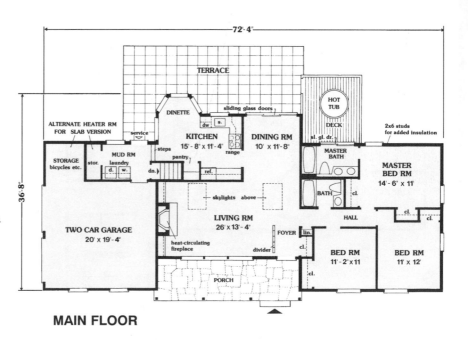

MAIN FLOOR

Comfortable and Charming

■ *Total living area 1,964 sq. ft.* ■ *Price Code C* ■

MAIN FLOOR

Patio

Dining Room
14' x 13'6"
sloped ceiling

Great Room
16'1" x 21'5"
11' ceiling height

Dressing

Master Bedroom
15'11" x 12'1"
sloped ceiling

walk-in closet

Breakfast
19'9" x 12'

Kitchen

Bedroom
12'4" x 10'1"

linen

Laun.

pantry

wood rail

Foyer
9' ceiling height

walk-in closet

Hall

stairs dn

Two-car Garage
22'4" x 20"

Porch

Bath

Bedroom
12'4" x 10'

55'-8"

55'-2"

No. 92660

■ **This plan features:**

— Three bedrooms

— Two full baths

■ Great Room with massive fireplace and lots of windows with Patio access

■ Formal Dining Room with sloped ceiling and expansive view of back yard

■ Cooktop island and pantry in Kitchen efficiently serve Breakfast area and Dining Room

■ Corner Master Bedroom offers a sloped ceiling, walk-in closet and pampering bath with whirlpool tub and two vanities

■ No materials list is available for this plan

Main floor — 1,964 sq. ft.
Basement — 1,809 sq. ft.
Garage — 447 sq. ft.

Easy One-Level Living

No. 20104

This plan features:

— Three bedrooms

— Two full baths

■ A sky-lit Kitchen

■ Ample closet space

■ Built-in storage areas in the Kitchen

■ A Master bath with twin vanities, a raised tub, and a walk-in shower

Main area — 1,686 sq. ft.
Basement — 1,677 sq. ft.
Garage — 475 sq. ft.

■ *Total living area 1,686 sq. ft.* ■ *Price Code B* ■

MAIN AREA

An EXCLUSIVE DESIGN
By Karl Kreeger

Wrapping Porch and French Doors

No. 93421

This plan features:

— Three bedrooms

— Two full baths

■ The wrapping front porch and the rear patio provide places for outdoor entertaining

■ The foyer opens into the Family room that features a 10' ceiling and a fireplace

■ The Dining room has a pantry, a 9' ceiling, and a built in china cabinet for your best dishes

■ The Kitchen is arranged in a convenient L-shape and has a center island

■ The large Master bedroom has a 9' ceiling, a walk in closet and a private full bath

■ Two secondary bedrooms have ample closet space and share a bath in the common hall

■ A detached two-car garage is located in the rear

■ No materials list is available for this plan

Main floor — 1,507 sq. ft.
Garage — 484 sq. ft.

■ *Total living area 1,507 sq. ft.* ■ *Price Code B* ■

An EXCLUSIVE DESIGN
By Greg Marquis

37

Luxurious Single Level

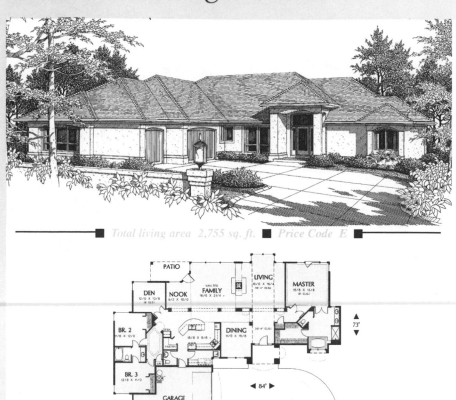

Total living area 2,755 sq. ft. ■ Price Code E

MAIN FLOOR

No. 91590

■ This plan features:

— Three bedrooms

— Two full and one half baths

■ This sprawling home features an Entry with a 13' ceiling that extends into the Living Room

■ The secluded Master Suite spans the width of the home and includes a private bath

■ The Living Room and the Family Room share a see-through fireplace

■ A cozy Den is located in the back corner of this home

■ The large Kitchen includes an angled island with a double sink, plus a walk-in pantry

■ Two additional bedrooms and a bath are in the hall with the decorative ceiling treatment

■ This plan has a three-car garage

■ There is no materials list available for this plan

Main floor — 2,755 sq. ft.
Garage — 816 sq. ft.

Impressive Brick and Wood Facade

Total living area 1,651 sq. ft. ■ Price Code B

MAIN FLOOR

No. 94921

■ This plan features:

— Two or three bedrooms

— Two full baths

■ Covered front and rear Porches expand living space outside

■ Handy Serving area located between formal Dining Room and expansive Great Room

■ Transom windows frame hearth fireplace in Great Room and highlight Breakfast Room

■ Hub Kitchen with built-in pantry, snackbar and adjoining laundry/Garage entry

■ French doors lead into Den with wetbar that can easily convert to third bedroom

■ Exclusive Master Bedroom includes a decorative ceiling, walk-in closet, twin vanities and a corner whirlpool tub

Main floor — 1,651 sq. ft.
Basement — 1,651 sq. ft.
Garage — 480 sq. ft.

© design basics, inc.

Economy at It's Best

■ *Total living area 1,717 sq. ft.* ■ *Price Code B* ■

No. 91746 ⚒

■ **This plan features:**

— Three bedrooms

— Two full and one three quarter baths

■ A vaulted ceiling topping the Entry, Living and Dining Rooms

■ A lovely bay window in the Living Room, which includes direct access to a side deck

■ A Master Suite with a private compartmented bath with an oversized shower

■ Two additional bedrooms share a full hall bath topped by a skylight

■ A vaulted ceiling topping the Dining area

■ A walk-in pantry adds to the storage space of the cooktop island Kitchen

Main area — 1,717 sq. ft.
Garage — 782 sq. ft.

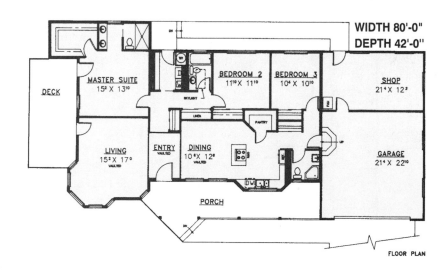

WIDTH 80'-0"
DEPTH 42'-0"

DECK

MASTER SUITE
15² X 13¹⁰

BEDROOM 2
11¹⁰ X 11¹⁰

BEDROOM 3
10⁴ X 10¹⁰

SHOP
21⁴ X 12²

LIVING
15² X 17⁰
VAULTED

ENTRY
VAULTED

DINING
10⁸ X 12²
VAULTED

PANTRY

GARAGE
21⁴ X 22¹⁰

PORCH

FLOOR PLAN

Ranch with Handicapped Access

■ *Total living area 1,734 sq. ft.* ■ *Price Code B* ■

No. 20403

■ **This plan features:**

— Three bedrooms

— One full and one three quarter baths

■ Ramps into the front Entry from the Porch; the Utility area and the Kitchen from the Garage; and the Family Room from the Deck

■ An open area topped by a sloped ceiling for the Family Room, the Dining Room, the Kitchen and the Breakfast alcove

■ Kitchen with a built-in pantry and an open counter

■ A Master Bedroom suite accented by a sloping ceiling above a wall of windows, offering access to the Deck

■ Two front bedrooms with sloped ceilings sharing a full hall

Main floor — 1,734 sq. ft.
Garage — 606 sq. ft.

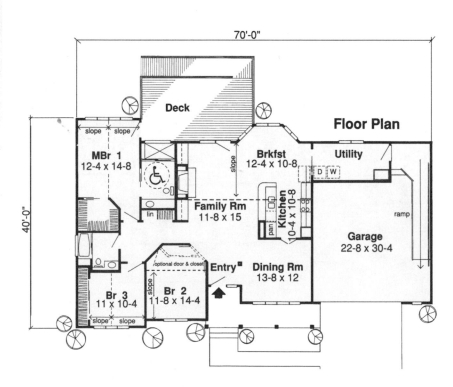

Floor Plan

70'-0"

40'-0"

Deck

MBr 1
12-4 x 14-8

Br 3
11 x 10-4

Br 2
11-8 x 14-4

Family Rm
11-8 x 15

Brkfst
12-4 x 10-8

Kitchen
10-4 x 10-8

Utility

D W

Garage
22-8 x 30-4

ramp

Dining Rm
13-8 x 12

Entry

optional door & closet

slope

Unusual Tile Roof

No. 10601

This plan features:

— Three or four bedrooms

— Three full baths

■ Stone arched Porch accesses tiled Entry with sloped ceiling and Parlor through French doors

■ Spacious Living Room with sloped ceiling, tiled hearth fireplace, and access to brick Patio

■ Convenient Dining Room enhanced by arches and a double window

■ Hub Kitchen with large pantry, a breakfast bar and glass eating Nook

■ Comfortable Family Room offers another fireplace with wood storage, a wetbar and access to Laundry/Garage

■ Den/Guest Room provides many options

■ Expansive Master Bedroom with a bay window, Patio access, walk-in closet, dressing area and private bath

■ Two additional bedrooms have private access to a full bath

Main floor — 3,025 sq. ft.
Garage — 722 sq. ft.

Total living area 3,025 sq. ft. ■ Price Code E

MAIN FLOOR

Columned Classic

No. 96521

This plan features:

— Four bedrooms

— Three full and one half baths

■ Grand columns featured both on the front Porch and in the Entry way

■ The formal Living room has a corner fireplace

■ The U-shaped Kitchen has a convenient eating bar

■ The Master bedroom in rear of home over looks Courtyard

■ Three additional large Bedrooms share two and a half Baths

Main floor — 3,084 ft.
Bonus — 868 sq. ft.
Garage — 672 sq. ft.

Total living area 3,084 sq. ft. ■ Price Code E

OPTIONAL ROOM

Dignified Facade

Total living area 1,829 sq. ft. ■ Price Code C

Basement? (handwritten)

FLOOR PLAN

No. 96492

This plan features:

— Three bedrooms

— Two full baths

■ A grand hip roof and four front facing gables, a dual columned entry with transoms, and graceful keystone arches

■ Single front dormer lighting the Foyer, while two rear dormers bring plenty of light into the Great Room

■ A cathedral ceiling adding space to the open Great Room with built-in bookshelves on either side of the fireplace

■ Master Suite, topped by a tray ceiling, having his-n-her walk-in closets and a spectacular bayed bath with garden tub, separate shower, dual vanity and an enclosed toilet

■ Secondary bedrooms sharing the full, double vanity bath in the hall

Main floor — 1,829 sq. ft.
Bonus room — 424 sq. ft.
Garage & Storage — 660 sq. ft.

Big On Style

Total living area 1,405 sq. ft. ■ Price Code A

Floor Plan

No. 98505

This plan features:

— Three bedrooms

— Two full baths

■ The Living room has a bright front window wall and a fireplace

■ The Dining room is defined by columns and opens out onto a covered patio

■ The Kitchen has a desk, a pantry and a counter serving bar

■ The Master bedroom is topped by a vaulted ceiling and features a triangular shaped walk-in closet and a private bath

■ Two other bedrooms have ample closet space and share a bath in the hall

■ Pass through the Utility room to the two-car garage

■ There is no materials list available for this plan

Main floor — 1,405 sq. ft.
Garage — 440 sq. ft.

Arched Windows Accent Sophisticated Design

■ *Total living area 2,551 sq. ft.* ■ *Price Code E* ■

No. 92509 ✖

■ This plan features:

— Four bedrooms

— Two full and one half baths

■ Graceful columns and full-length
windows highlight front Porch

■ Spacious Great Room with
decorative ceiling over hearth
fireplace between built-in cabinets

■ Kitchen with peninsula counter
and Breakfast alcove

■ Secluded Master Bedroom suite
offers access to back Porch, and
has a decorative ceiling and plush
bath

■ Three additional bedrooms with
loads of closets space share double
vanity bath

■ An optional crawl space or slab
foundation — please specify when
ordering

Main floor — 2,551 sq. ft.
Garage — 532 sq. ft.

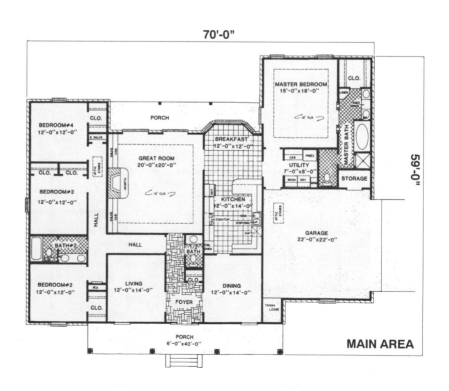

Comfort and Style

■ *Total living area 1,423 sq. ft.* ■ *Price Code A* ■

An
EXCLUSIVE DESIGN
By Westhome Planners, Ltd.

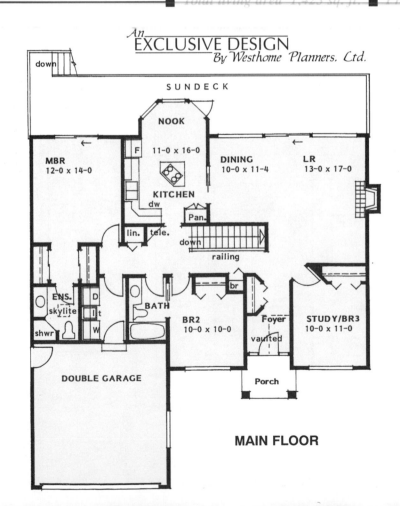

MAIN FLOOR

down

SUNDECK

NOOK
11-0 x 16-0

DINING
10-0 x 11-4

LR
13-0 x 17-0

MBR
12-0 x 14-0

F

KITCHEN
dw

Pan.

lin.   tele.

down

railing

ENS.
skylite

D
t

br

BATH

BR2
10-0 x 10-0

Foyer
vaulted

STUDY/BR3
10-0 x 11-0

shwr

W

DOUBLE GARAGE

Porch

No. 90990

■ This plan features:

— Two bedrooms with possible third bedroom/den

— One full and one three quarter baths

▨ An unfinished daylight basement, providing possible space for family recreation

▨ A Master Suite complete with private bath and skylight

▨ A large Kitchen including an eating nook

▨ A sundeck that is easily accessible from the Master Suite, Nook and the Living/Dining area

Main floor — 1,423 sq. ft.
Basement — 1,423 sq. ft.
Garage — 399 sq. ft.
Width — 46'-0"
Depth — 52'-0"

Vacation Retreat or Year Round Living

No. 1078

■ This plan features:

— Two bedrooms

— One full bath

■ A long hallway dividing bedrooms and living areas assuring privacy

■ A centrally located utility room and bath

■ An open Living/Dining Room area with exposed beams, sloping ceilings and optional fireplace

Main floor — 1,024 sq. ft.
Carport & Storage — 387 sq. ft.
Deck — 411 sq. ft.

■ *Total living area 1,024 sq. ft.* ■ *Price Code A* ■

MAIN FLOOR

Entry Boasts Sweeping Views

No. 99308

■ This plan features:

— Three bedrooms

— Two full baths

■ Traditional exterior with soaring interior spaces

■ Vaulted entry allows access to the Great Room ahead, staircase and breakfast area to the right and bedroom to the left

■ Cooktop island Kitchen open to the Breakfast Room

■ Mudroom entrance from the garage into the Kitchen for ease in unloading groceries

■ Master Suite with vaulted ceiling in the bedrooms and a walk-in closet

■ Two additional bedrooms sharing the full bath in the hall

Main floor — 1,560 sq. ft.

■ *Total living area 1,560 sq. ft.* ■ *Price Code B* ■

MAIN FLOOR

Porches Expands Living Space

No. 96529

This plan features:

— Three bedrooms

— Two full and one half baths

- Porches on the front and the rear of this home expand the living space to the outdoors

- The rear porch is accessed directly from the Great Room

- The spacious Great Room is enhanced by a 12' ceiling and a fireplace

- The well-appointed kitchen has an extended counter/eating bar and easy access to the Dining Room

- Secondary bedrooms have a full bath located between the rooms

- The Master Suite is enhanced by his-n-her walk-in closets, a whirlpool tub and a separate shower

- A Bonus Room for the future expansion

Main floor — 2,089 sq. ft.
Bonus room — 497 sq. ft.
Garage — 541 sq. ft.

■ Total living area 2,089 sq. ft. ■ Price Code C ■

MAIN FLOOR

Tremendous Curb Appeal

© 1995 Donald A Gardner Architects, Inc.

No. 99806

This plan features:

— Three bedrooms

— Two full baths

- Wrap-around porch sheltering entry

- Great Room topped by a cathedral ceiling and enhanced by a fireplace

- Great Room, Dining Room and Kitchen open to each other for a feeling of spaciousness

- Pantry, skylight and peninsula counter add to the comfort and efficiency of the Kitchen

- Cathedral ceiling crowns the Master Suite and has many amenities; walk-in and linen closet, a luxurious private bath

- Swing room, Bedroom or Study, topped by a cathedral ceiling

- Skylight over full hall bath naturally illuminates the room

Main floor — 1,246 sq. ft.
Garage — 420 sq. ft.

■ Total living area 1,246 sq. ft. ■ Price Code B ■

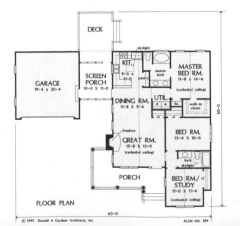

FLOOR PLAN

© 1995 Donald A Gardner Architects, Inc.   PLAN NO. 389

Total living area 2,387 sq. ft. ■ *Price Code E* ■

No. 92546 ✖

■ **This plan features:**

— Four bedrooms

— Two full and one half baths

■ Dining Room accented by an arched window and pillars

■ Decorative ceiling crowns the Den which contains a hearth fireplace, built-in shelves and large double window

■ Kitchen with a peninsula serving counter and Breakfast area, adjoining the Utility room and Garage

■ Master Bedroom suite with a decorative ceiling, two vanities and a large walk-in closet

■ Three additional bedrooms with double closets share a full bath

■ An optional slab or crawl space foundation — please specify when ordering

Main floor — 2,387 sq. ft.
Garage — 505 sq. ft.

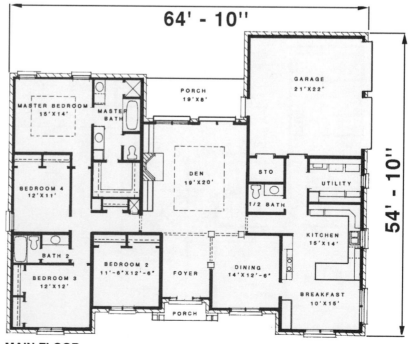

MAIN FLOOR

For Today's Sophisticated Homeowner

Total living area 1,500 sq. ft. ■ Price Code A

No. 93027

■ **This plan features:**

— Three bedrooms

— Two full baths

■ A formal Dining Room that opens off the foyer and has a classic bay window

■ A Kitchen notable for it's angled eating bar that opens to the Living Room

■ A cozy fireplace in the Living Room that can be seen from the Kitchen

■ A Master Suite that includes a whirlpool tub/shower combination and a walk-in closet

■ 10' ceilings in the major living areas, including the Master Bedroom

■ No materials list is available for this plan

Main area — 1,500 sq. ft.
Garage — 437 sq. ft.

WIDTH 59-10

DEPTH 44-4

MASTER BATH

PORCH

BRKFST
8-0 X 11-6
10 FT CLG

FP

LIVING RM
16-0 X 13-8
10 FT CLG

KITCHEN
10-6 X 14-0

GARAGE

MASTER BEDRM
11-4 X 14-6
10 FT CLG

SLOPE

BATH 2

ENTRY

PAN

BEDRM 2
12-0 X 13-0

BEDRM 3
11-0 X 13-6
10 FT COFFERED CLG

PORCH

DINING RM
10-6 X 12-0

MAIN AREA

Compact One Level Home

No. 92685

■ This plan features:

— Three bedrooms

— Two full baths

■ Great Room combines with the Breakfast area to form a spacious gathering place

■ Sloped ceiling tops Great Room and reaches a 12' height

■ Windows across the rear of home provide a favorable indoor/outdoor relationship

■ Step-saving Kitchen with surplus counter space, cabinets and a pantry

■ Master Suite includes a walk-in closet and a full bath

■ Two additional bedrooms share the full bath in the hall

■ No materials list is available for this plan

Main floor — 1,442 sq. ft.
Basement — 1,442 sq. ft.
Garage — 421 sq. ft.

Total living area 1,442 sq. ft. ■ Price Code A

MAIN FLOOR

Very Versatile

No. 91104

■ This plan features:

— Three bedrooms

— Two full baths

■ The Dining room that is located off the Foyer is punctuated by columns

■ The L-shaped Kitchen features a center island, a snackbar, and a pantry

■ The cozy nook is located convenient to the Kitchen

■ The Great room has a fireplace, built-in shelves, and a vaulted ceiling

■ The spacious Master bedroom has a vaulted ceiling, a walk-in closet and a private bath

■ Two secondary bedrooms each have walk-in closets, and share a full hall bath

■ This plan features a multi-purpose room that can be used as an office or sitting room

■ There is no materials list available for this plan

Main floor — 2,126 sq. ft.
Garage — 443 sq. ft.

Total living area 2,126 sq. ft. ■ Price Code D

MAIN FLOOR

Stylish Single-Level

No. 93100

This plan features:

— Three bedrooms

— Two full and one half baths

- A well-appointed, U-shaped Kitchen separated from the Dining Room by a peninsula counter

- A spacious Living Room, enhanced by a focal point fireplace

- An elegant Dining Room with a bay window that opens to a screen porch, expanding living space

- A Master Suite with a walk-in closet and private Master Bath

- Two family bedrooms that share a full hall bath

Main area — 1,642 sq. ft.
Garage — 591 sq. ft.
Basement — 1,642 sq. ft.

■ *Total living area 1,642 sq. ft.* ■ *Price Code B* ■

WIDTH 57'-0''
DEPTH 66'-0''

MAIN FLOOR

An
EXCLUSIVE DESIGN
By Ahmann Design Inc.

Sprawling Ranch

No. 98424

This plan features:

— Three bedrooms

— Two full and one half baths

- Foyer with a 12' high ceiling and flows into the Dining and Living rooms

- Family Room in rear of home with a fireplace and radius windows on either side

- The Kitchen is L-shaped and has a center island with a cooktop

- The Breakfast bay area includes a walk-in pantry

- The Master Suite is beyond belief with a tray ceiling, a sitting area, a walk in closet and a luxurious bath

- Two other bedrooms are large in size and share access to a full bath

- An optional basement or crawl space foundation — please specify when ordering

Main floor — 2,236 sq. ft.
Basement — 2,236 sq. ft.
Garage — 517 sq. ft.

■ *Total living area 2,236 sq. ft.* ■ *Price Code D* ■

WIDTH 63'-0''
DEPTH 67'-0''

MAIN FLOOR

■ Total living area 1,454 sq. ft. ■ Price Code A ■

No. 90412

■ This plan features:

— Three bedrooms

— Two full baths

■ A centrally located Great Room with a cathedral ceiling, exposed wood beams, and large areas of fixed glass

■ The Living and Dining areas separated by a massive stone fireplace

■ A secluded Master Suite with a walk-in closet and private Master Bath

■ An efficient Kitchen with a convenient laundry area

■ An optional basement, slab or crawl space foundation — please specify when ordering

Main area — 1,454 sq. ft.

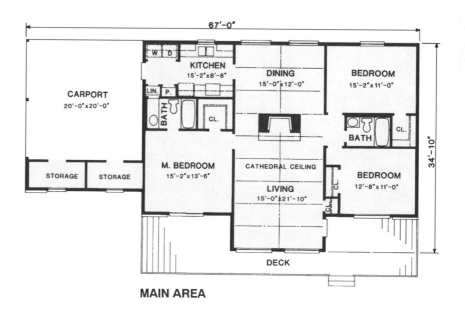

MAIN AREA

Luxurious Masterpiece

■ *Total living area 3,818 sq. ft.* ■ *Price Code F* ■

No. 92265

Main Floor

■ **This plan features:**

— Four bedrooms

— Three full and one half baths

■ An elegant and distinguished exterior

■ An expansive formal Living Room with a 14' ceiling and a raised hearth fireplace

■ Informal Family Room offers another fireplace, wetbar and a cathedral ceiling

■ A hub Kitchen with a cooktop island, peninsula counter, and a bright breakfast area

■ Private Master Bedroom with a pullman ceiling, lavish his-n-her baths and a garden window tub

■ Three additional bedrooms with walk-in closets and private access to a full bath

■ No materials list is available for this plan

Main floor — 3,818 sq. ft.
Garage — 816 sq. ft.

Distinctive European Design

No. 92516 🛠

This plan features:

— Three bedrooms

— Two full baths

■ A spacious Foyer leading into a grand Living Room, topped by a vaulted ceiling, with a fireplace between built-in cabinets and a wall of glass leading to a covered Porch

■ A gourmet Kitchen with a peninsula counter/snackbar and a built-in pantry, that is central to the Dining Room, the bay window Breakfast area, the Utility Room and the Garage

■ A large Master Bedroom, crowned by a raised ceiling, with French doors leading to a covered Porch, a luxurious bath and a walk-in closet

■ Two additional bedrooms with decorative windows and over-sized closets share a full hall bath

■ An optional crawl space or slab foundation — please specify when ordering

Main floor — 1,887 sq. ft.
Garage & Storage — 524 sq. ft.
Width — 57'-10"
Depth — 54'-5"

Total living area 1,887 sq. ft. ■ Price Code D ■

MAIN FLOOR

High Ceilings Add Volume

No. 98456 🛠

This plan features:

— Three bedrooms

— Two full baths

■ A covered entry gives way to a 14' high ceiling in the foyer

■ An arched opening greets you in the Great Room that also has a vaulted ceiling and a fireplace

■ The Dining Room is brightened by triple windows with transoms above

■ The Kitchen is a gourmet's delight and is open to the Breakfast Nook

■ The Master Suite claims a tray ceiling, vaulted sitting area and private bath

■ Two bedrooms on the opposite side of the home share a bath in the hall

■ An optional basement, slab, or crawl space foundation — please specify when ordering this plan

Main floor — 1,715 sq. ft.
Basement — 1,715 sq. ft.
Garage — 450 sq. ft.

Total living area 1,715 sq. ft. ■ Price Code B ■

MAIN FLOOR

European Styling

■ Total living area 2,290 sq. ft. ■ Price Code D ■

BONUS ROOM ABOVE GARAGE

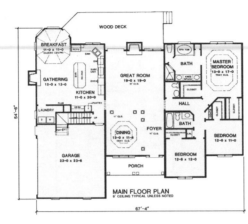

MAIN FLOOR PLAN
9' CEILING TYPICAL UNLESS NOTED

No. 90467

■ **This plan features:**

— Three bedrooms

— Two full and one half baths

■ The large foyer leads to the open Living and Dining rooms

■ A large informal area includes the Kitchen, Gathering, and Breakfast rooms

■ The Kitchen features an island bar, double sink, pantry, desk, and a wall oven

■ The home has two fireplaces, one in the Great room the other in the Gathering room

■ Decorative ceiling can be found in the Dining room, the Master suite, and the Breakfast nook

■ The Master suite features dual walk-in closets and a five piece bath

■ Two additional bedrooms share a linen closet and a full bath

■ An optional basement or crawl space foundation — please specify when ordering

Main floor — 2,290 sq. ft.
Basement — 2,290 sq. ft.
Bonus — 304 sq. ft.
Garage — 544 sq. ft.

Contemporary Drama

■ Total living area 1,553 sq. ft. ■ Price Code B ■

Floor Plan

No. 84505

■ **This plan features:**

— Three bedrooms

— Two full baths

■ The covered front porch leads into the Foyer

■ Living Room with a cathedral ceiling, a wetbar and an optional fireplace

■ Past the sliding doors in the rear of the Living Room is a screened porch

■ Dining Room with windows that overlooking the rear yard

■ Kitchen laid out in an efficient U-shape, with a laundry closet nearby

■ Master bedroom located in the rear of the home and has a full bath

■ Two secondary bedrooms share a full bath

■ Two-car garage

■ No materials list is available for this plan

Main floor — 1,553 sq. ft.
Garage — 526 sq. ft.

■ *Total living area 1,040 sq. ft.* ■ *Price Code A* ■

No. 1074 Ɽ ✗

■ **This plan features:**

— Three bedrooms

— One full and one three quarter baths

■ Active living areas centrally located between two quiet bedroom and bath areas

■ A Living Room that can be closed off from bedroom wings giving privacy to both areas

■ A bath located behind a third bedroom

■ A bedroom complete with washer/dryer facilities

Main floor — 1,040 sq. ft.
Storage — 44 sq. ft.
Deck — 258 sq. ft.
Carport — 230 sq. ft.

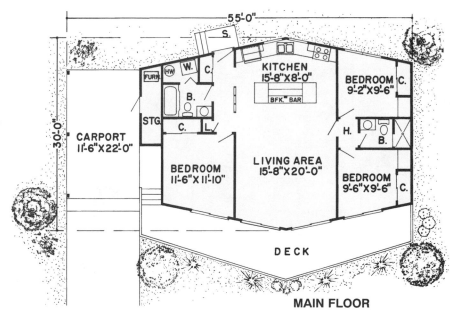

MAIN FLOOR

Distinctive Ranch

■ *Total living area 1,802 sq. ft.* ■ *Price Code C* ■

No. 93143

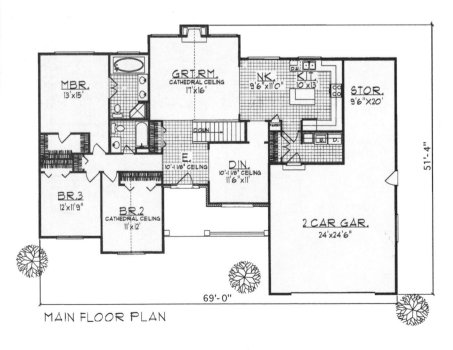

An
EXCLUSIVE DESIGN
By Ahmann Design Inc.

MAIN FLOOR PLAN

■ **This plan features:**

— Three bedrooms

— Two full baths

■ This hipped roofed ranch has an exterior that mixes brick and siding

■ The cozy front porch leads into a recessed entry with sidelights and transoms

■ The Great room has a cathedral ceiling, and a rear wall fireplace

■ The Kitchen has a center island and opens into the Nook

■ The Dining room features a high ceiling and a bright front window

■ The bedroom wing has three large bedrooms and two full baths

■ The two-car garage could easily be expanded to three with a door placed in the rear storage area

■ There is no materials list available for this plan

Main floor — 1,802 sq. ft.
Basement — 1,802 sq. ft.

Attention to Details

No. 93262

This plan features:

— Three bedrooms

— Two full baths

■ Beautiful detailing around the windows and the doors, adding to its curb appeal

■ A large Living Room with a focal point fireplace in the center of the outside wall, and direct access to the rear yard

■ A Master Suite located at the opposite end of the house from the secondary bedrooms, insuring privacy

■ A decorative ceiling in the Master Bedroom and a private Master Bath and walk-in closet

■ An informal Breakfast Room and formal Dining Room both located next to the efficient Kitchen

■ A Laundry Room and a double Garage

■ An optional crawl space or slab foundation — please specify when ordering

■ No materials list is available for this plan

Main floor — 1,708 sq. ft.
Garage — 400 sq. ft.

An EXCLUSIVE DESIGN
By Jannis Vann & Associates, Inc.

Total living area 1,708 sq. ft. ■ Price Code B

MAIN FLOOR

Stately Elevation

No. 99448

This plan features:

— Four bedrooms

— Three full and one half baths

■ The stateliness of this home is evident from the covered stoop with transom and sidelight windows around the front door

■ Once inside the tiled entry turn right into the Dining room which features a decorative ceiling

■ The Great room is the center of the home and has a fireplace with windows beside it

■ The Kitchen is a cook's dream and has plenty of counter space

■ The bright Breakfast bay is a great place to start your day with a cup of coffee

■ The secluded Master bedroom has a tray ceiling, a walk in closet, a private covered porch, and a bath

■ Three additional bedrooms on the other side of the home share two full baths

■ A three-car garage

Main floor — 2,655 sq. ft.
Basement — 2,655 sq. ft.
Garage — 695 sq. ft.

Total living area 2,655 sq. ft. ■ Price Code E

MAIN FLOOR

57

Cozy Traditional with Style

■ Total living area 1,830 sq. ft. ■ Price Code C ■

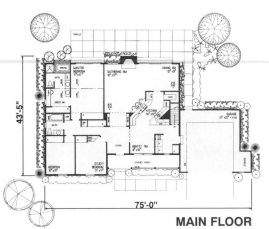

MAIN FLOOR

No. 99208

■ **This plan features:**

— Three bedrooms

— Two full baths

▪ A convenient one-level design

▪ A galley-style Kitchen that shares a snack bar with the spacious Gathering Room

▪ A focal point fireplace making the Gathering Room warm and inviting

▪ An ample Master Suite with a luxury bath which includes a whirlpool tub and separate Dressing Room

▪ Two additional bedrooms, one that could double as a Study, located at the front of the house

Main floor — 1,830 sq. ft.
Basement — 1,830 sq. ft.

Triangular Entrance Extends Into Foyer

■ Total living area 2,396 sq. ft. ■ Price Code D ■

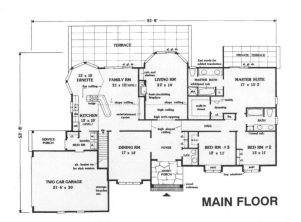

MAIN FLOOR

No. 99614 ✖

■ **This plan features:**

— Three bedrooms

— Two full and one half baths

▪ A triangular ceiling in the entrance porch that extends into the Foyer

▪ A large glazed bay window that extends the full width of the Living Room

▪ A heat-circulating fireplace flanked by shelves and cabinets in the Living Room

▪ A Dinette with a six-sided shape, four sides being windows

▪ A Family Room with a sloped ceiling, sliding glass doors to the terrace and easy access to an angled Kitchen counter acting as a snack bar

▪ A Master Suite with walk-in closet, private terrace, private Master Bath with whirlpool tub, a separate shower and a double vanity

▪ Two additional bedrooms that share a full hall bath

Main floor — 2,396 sq. ft.
Basement — 2,136 sq. ft.
Garage — 509 sq. ft.

Terrific Great Room

■ *Total living area 1,302 sq. ft.* ■ *Price Code A* ■

No. 94041

■ **This plan features:**

— Three bedrooms

— Two full baths

■ A crowning vaulted ceiling and a fireplace in the Great Room

■ Built-in pantry, a breakfast area and a peninsula counter in the Kitchen

■ A private bath in the Master Bedroom

■ Two secondary bedrooms accented by bay windows

■ Front bedroom includes a built-in desk

■ Bay window adding elegance to the formal Dining Room which adjoins with the Great Room

■ No materials list is available for this plan

Main floor — 1,302 sq. ft.
Garage — 440 sq. ft.

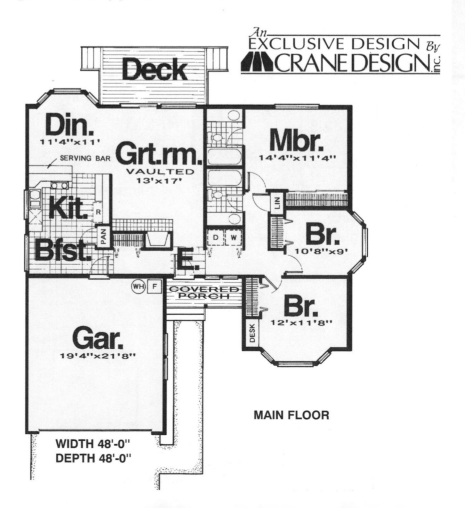

An EXCLUSIVE DESIGN *By* CRANE DESIGN inc.

MAIN FLOOR

WIDTH 48'-0"
DEPTH 48'-0"

Delightful, Compact Home

■ *Total living area 1,146 sq. ft.* ■ *Price Code A* ■

44'-0"

28'-0"

Br 2
10 x 12-8

Br 3
10 x 9-4

Kit
10 x 11

Dining
9 x 11

DN

linen

MBr 1
13-4 x 12

Living Rm
19 x 12-4

slope   slope

Deck

Floor Plan

W

D

slab/crawlspace option

No. 34003

■ This plan features:

— Three bedrooms

— Two full baths

■ A fireplaced Living Room brightened by a wonderful picture window

■ A counter island featuring double sinks separating the Kitchen and Dining areas

■ A Master Bedroom that includes a private Master Bath and double closets

■ Two additional bedrooms with ample closet space that share a full bath

Main floor — 1,146 sq. ft.

Unique Gazebo Shaped Nook

No. 98742

This plan features:

— Three bedrooms

— Two full baths

- Covered porch and rear deck

- A Foyer area with a convenient coat closet

- Vaulted ceiling in the Nook with bay windows and natural illumination

- A uniquely-designed Kitchen with a walk-in pantry, access to formal the Dining area and Nook

- A focal point fireplace with windows on either side in the Living Room

- A large walk-in closet, linen closet and a full private Bath highlight the Master Suite

- Two additional bedrooms that share a full compartmented Bath

- Two-car garage

- Utility/Mud Room located between the Garage and Kitchen

- No materials list is available for this plan

Main area — 1,664 sq. ft.
Width — 70'-0"
Depth — 48'-0"

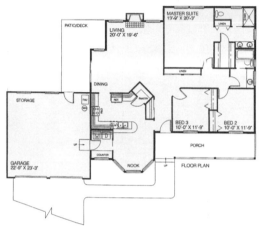

■ *Total living area 1,664 sq. ft.* ■ *Price Code B* ■

Private Master Suite

No. 99835

© 1997 Donald A. Gardner Architects, Inc.

■ *Total living area 1,515 sq. ft.* ■ *Price Code C* ■

This plan features:

— Three bedrooms

— Two full baths

- Working at the Kitchen island focuses your view to the Great Room with a vaulted ceiling and fireplace

- Clerestory dormers emanate light into the Great Room

- Both the Dining Room and Master Bedroom are enhanced by tray ceilings

- Skylights floods natural light into the Bonus space

- The private Master suite has its own Bath and an expansive walk-in closet

Main floor – 1,515 sq. ft.
Bonus – 288 sq. ft.
Garage – 476 sq. ft.

Compact Country Cottage

© 1991 Donald A. Gardner Architects, Inc.

■ *Total living area 1,310 sq. ft.* ■ *Price Code B* ■

No. 99856

■ This plan features:

— Three bedrooms

— Two full baths

■ Foyer opening to a large Great Room with a fireplace and a cathedral ceiling

■ Efficient U-shaped Kitchen with peninsula counter extending work space and separating it from the Dining Room

■ Two front bedrooms, one with a bay window, the other with a walk-in closet, sharing a full bath in the hall

■ Master Suite located to the rear with a walk-in closet and a private bath with a double vanity

■ Partially covered deck with skylights accessible from the Dining Room, Great Room and Master Bedroom

Main floor—1,310 sq. ft.
Garage & storage—455 sq. ft.

FLOOR PLAN

© 1991 Donald A. Gardner Architects, Inc.

Charm and Personality

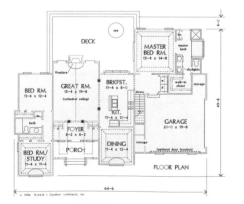

© 1996 Donald A. Gardner Architects, Inc.

■ *Total living area 1,655 sq. ft.* ■ *Price Code C* ■

No. 99871

■ This plan features:

— Three bedrooms

— Two full baths

■ Charm and personality radiate through this country home

■ Interior columns dramatically open the Foyer and Kitchen to the spacious Great Room

■ Drama is heightened by the Great Room cathedral ceiling and fireplace

■ Master Suite with a tray ceiling combines privacy with access to the rear deck with spa, while the skylight bath has all the amenities expected in a quality home

■ Tray ceilings with arched picture windows bring a special elegance to the Dining Room and the front Swing Room

■ An optional basement or crawl space foundation — please specify when ordering

Main floor — 1,655 sq. ft.
Garage — 434 sq. ft.

FLOOR PLAN

© 1996 Donald A. Gardner Architects, Inc.

Attractive Gables and Arches

■ Total living area 1,782 sq. ft. ■ Price Code B ■

No. 94917 ✘

■ This plan features:

— Three bedrooms

— Two full baths

■ Entry opens to formal Dining Room with arched window

■ Angles and transom windows add interest to the Great Room

■ Bright Hearth area expands Breakfast/Kitchen area and shares three-sided fireplace

■ Efficient Kitchen offers an angled snack bar, a large pantry and nearby laundry/Garage entry

■ Secluded Master Bedroom suite crowned by decorative ceiling, a large walk-in closet and a plush bath with a whirlpool tub

■ Two secondary bedrooms in separate wing from master suite for added privacy

Main floor — 1,782 sq. ft.
Basement — 1,782 sq. ft.
Garage — 466 sq. ft.

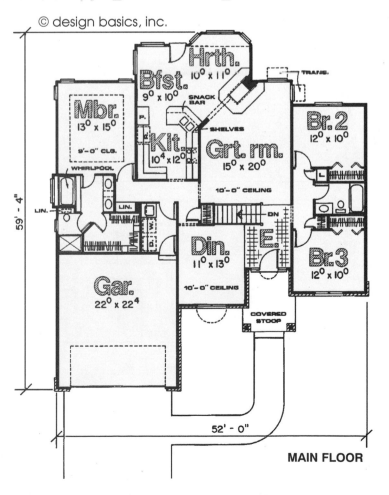

© design basics, inc.

MAIN FLOOR

Your Classic Hideaway

Total living area 1,773 sq ft ■ Price Code B

No. 90423

This plan features:

— Three bedrooms

— Two full baths

■ A lovely fireplace in the Living Room which is both cozy and a source of heat for the core area

■ An efficient country Kitchen, connecting the large Dining and Living Rooms

■ A lavish Master Suite enhanced by a step-up sunken tub, more than ample closet space, and separate shower

■ A screened porch and patio area for outdoor living

■ An optional basement, slab or crawl space foundation — please specify when ordering

Main area — 1,773 sq. ft.
Screened porch — 240 sq. ft.

MAIN AREA

Decorative Ceilings Inside

No. 98468

This plan features:

— Three bedrooms

— Two full baths

- The Family Room has a vaulted ceiling, a corner fireplace, and a French door to the rear yard

- The Breakfast Nook is brightened by window on two walls

- The galley Kitchen has a pantry, and a serving bar into the Family Room

- The Master Suite has a tray ceiling, a walk in closet and a private bath

- Two secondary bedrooms have ample closet space, bright front wall windows, and one has a vaulted ceiling

- This home has a two-car garage with storage space

- No materials list is available for this plan

- An optional basement, slab or crawl space foundation — please specify when ordering

Main floor — 1,104 sq. ft.
Basement — 1,104 sq. ft.
Garage — 400 sq. ft.

Total living area 1,104 sq. ft. ■ Price Code A

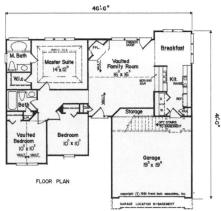

FLOOR PLAN

Dignified French Country Style

No. 92517

This plan features:

— Three bedrooms

— Two full baths

- Sheltered Porch leads into an open Foyer and Great Room enhanced by raised hearth fireplace between book shelves, access to Patio and a vaulted ceiling

- Hub Kitchen with a peninsula counter and Utility Garage entry easily serves Breakfast area and formal Dining Room

- Spacious Master Bedroom offers a sitting area and a plush Master Bath

- Two additional roomy bedrooms with over-sized closets share a double vanity bath

- An optional crawl space or slab foundation — please specify when ordering

Main area — 1,805 sq. ft.
Garage & Storage — 524 sq. ft.

Total living area 1,805 sq. ft. ■ Price Code D

MAIN AREA

Room for a Front Porch Swing

■ *Total living area 1,630 sq. ft.* ■ *Price Code B* ■

MAIN FLOOR

No. 98746

■ **This plan features:**

— Three bedrooms

— One full and one three quarter bath

■ Entry opens to expansive Living/Dining room with vaulted ceiling and loads of windows

■ Convenient Kitchen with walk-in pantry and L-shaped eating bar easily serves Dining area and covered Deck beyond

■ Secluded Master Suite with a vaulted ceiling, walk-in closet, extended vanity and private bath

■ Two additional bedrooms with ample closets share a full bath

Main floor — 1,630 sq. ft.
Width — 50'-0"
Depth — 58'-0"

Arches are Appealing

■ *Total living area 1,642 sq. ft.* ■ *Price Code B* ■

Floor Plan

No. 24717

■ **This plan features:**

— Three bedrooms

— Two full baths

■ Welcoming front Porch enhanced by graceful columns and curved windows

■ Parlor and Dining Room frame entry hall

■ Expansive Great Room accented by a corner fireplace and outdoor access

■ Open and convenient Kitchen with a work island, angled, peninsula counter/eating bar, and nearby laundry and Garage entry

■ Secluded Master Bedroom with a large walk-in closet and luxurious bath with a dressing table

■ Two additional bedrooms with ample closets share a double vanity bath

■ No materials list is available for this plan

Main floor — 1,642 sq. ft.
Garage — 430 sq. ft.

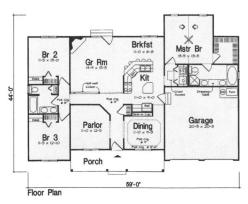

Ultimate Master Suite

■ *Total living area 1,955 sq. ft.* ■ *Price Code C* ■

No. 93030

■ This plan features:

— Three Bedrooms

— Two full baths

■ A columned Dining Room and an expansive Great Room with a large hearth fireplace between sliding glass doors to a covered Porch and a Deck with hot tub

■ Kitchen with a built-in pantry, a peninsula sink and an octagon-shaped Breakfast area

■ A Master Bedroom wing with French doors, a vaulted ceiling, a plush Master Bath with a huge walk-in closet, a double vanity and a window tub

■ Two bedrooms with walk-in closets share a full hall bath

■ No materials list is available for this plan

Main floor — 1,955 sq. ft.
Garage — 561 sq. ft.

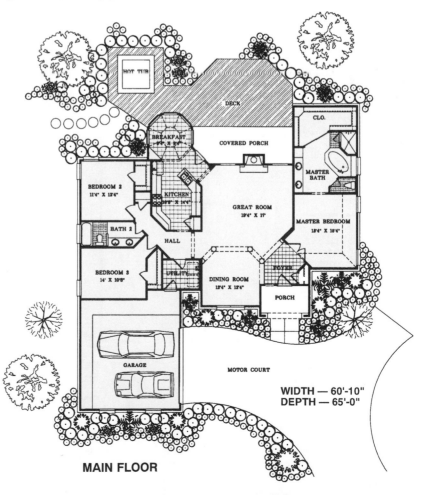

WIDTH — 60'-10"
DEPTH — 65'-0"

MAIN FLOOR

Distinctive Windows Add to Curb Appeal

Total living area 2,735 sq. ft. ■ Price Code F

No. 92550

MAIN FLOOR

WIDTH 68'-10"
DEPTH 67'-4"

■ This plan features:

— Four bedrooms

— Three full baths

■ A private Master Bedroom with a raised ceiling and attached bath with a spa tub

■ A wing of three bedrooms on the right side of the home sharing two full baths

■ An efficient Kitchen is straddled by an eating nook and a dining room

■ A cozy Den with a raised ceiling and a fireplace that is the focal point of the home

■ A two-car garage with a storage area

■ An optional crawl space or slab foundation — please specify when ordering

Main floor – 2,735 sq. ft.
Garage – 561 sq. ft.

Homestead Happiness

No. 90478

This plan features:

— Three bedrooms

— Two full baths

- The brick exterior, columns, and dormers add to the charm of this traditionally styled ranch

- The foyer leads to the Study, Dining room, or the Great room

- The Great room features a fireplace and access to the rear Deck

- The efficient Kitchen is open to the Great room and the breakfast nook

- The Master bedroom is isolated from the other bedrooms and is quite luxurious

- Two secondary bedrooms have ample closet space and share a full bath

- An optional basement, slab or crawl space foundation — please specify when ordering

Main floor — 2,344 sq. ft.
Basement — 2,344 sq. ft.
Garage — 498 sq. ft.

Total living area 2,344 sq. ft. ■ Price Code D

Elegant Dining Room

No. 94922

This plan features:

— Three bedrooms

— Two full baths

- Appealing gables and finish details enhance Covered front Porch

- Formal Dining Room off entry features a double transom window crowned by a decorative ceiling

- Volume Great Room with raised hearth fireplace framed by transom windows

- Well-designed Kitchen with built-in pantry, peninsula snack bar and bright Breakfast area with access to rear yard

- Secluded Master Bedroom suite with a decorative ceiling, triple window, skylit dressing area, twin vanities, corner whirlpool tub and roomy walk-in closet

- Two secondary bedrooms with option of converting to a Sun room with French doors from Breakfast area, and a quiet Den

Main floor — 1,710 sq. ft.
Basement — 1,710 sq. ft.
Garage — 480 sq. ft.

Total living area 1,710 sq. ft. ■ Price Code B

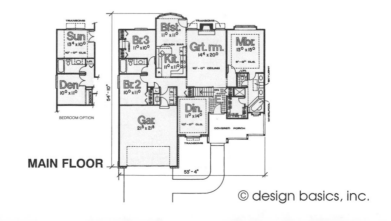

© design basics, inc.

Comfort Zone

■ **This plan features:**

— Three bedrooms

— Two full baths

■ The stunning brick veneer, arched windows, gabled roof lines and herringbone patterns add plenty of character

■ The efficient Master bath includes a double vanity with knee space, a corner whirlpool tub, and a separate shower

■ Bonus area for future expansion is provided over the Garage is accessed by a stairway near the Kitchen

■ Extra features include a Kitchen snackbar, a back Porch, an abundance of closets, and a large Living room

■ There is no materials list available for this plan

Main Level — 1,908 sq. ft.
Bonus — 262 sq. ft.
Garage — 562 sq. ft.

■ Total living area 1,908 sq. ft. ■ Price Code C ■

1st Floor

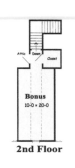

2nd Floor

Cathedral Ceilings Add A Crowning Touch

■ **This plan features:**

— Three bedrooms

— Two full baths

■ The Great Room has a fireplace, a cathedral ceiling and a rear wall of windows

■ The cathedral ceiling continues into the Dining Room that is separated from the Great Room by columns

■ The L-shaped Kitchen opens into the Dining bay

■ Two bedrooms are located in the rear of the home and share a hallway bath

■ The Master bedroom is accented by a cathedral ceiling, a dressing area, a walk-in closet and a private bath

■ Two-car garage

■ No materials list available for this plan

Main floor — 1,724 sq. ft.
Basement — 1,724 sq. ft.
Garage — 448 sq. ft.

■ Total living area 1,724 sq. ft. ■ Price Code C ■

MAIN FLOOR

Hip Roof Ranch

■ *Total living area 1,540 sq. ft.* ■ *Price Code B* ■

No. 93161

■ This plan features:

— Three bedrooms

— Two full baths

■ Cozy front Porch leads into Entry with vaulted ceiling and sidelights

■ Open Living Room enhance by a cathedral ceiling, a wall of windows and corner fireplace

■ Large and efficient Kitchen with an extended counter and a bright Dining area with access to Screen Porch

■ Convenient Utility area with access to Garage and Storage area

■ Spacious Master Bedroom with a walk-in closet and private bath

■ Two additional bedrooms with ample closets, share a full bath

■ No materials list is available for this plan

Main floor — 1,540 sq. ft.
Basement — 1,540 sq. ft.

An
EXCLUSIVE DESIGN
By Ahmann Design Inc.

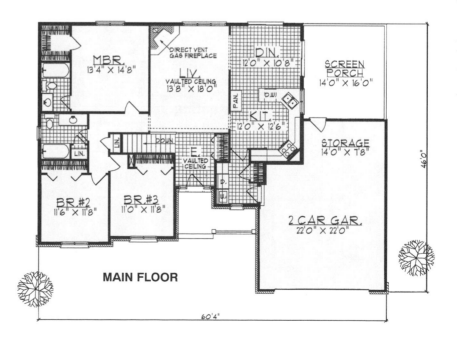

MBR.
13'4" X 14'8"

DIRECT VENT GAS FIREPLACE

LIV.
VAULTED CEILING
13'8" X 18'0"

DIN.
12'0" X 10'8"

SCREEN PORCH
14'0" X 16'0"

PAN.

DW

KIT.
12'0" X 12'6"

STORAGE
14'0" X 7'8"

LIN.

DOWN

E.
VAULTED CEILING

BR.#2
11'6" X 11'8"

BR.#3
11'0" X 11'8"

2 CAR GAR.
22'0" X 22'0"

MAIN FLOOR

46'0"

60'4"

Elegant and Efficient

Total living area 1,959 sq. ft. ▪ Price Code D

No. 92515

This plan features:

— Three bedrooms

— Two full baths

▪ Spacious Den with a decorative ceiling above a hearth fireplace, and French doors

▪ Decorative window and ceiling highlight the formal Dining Room

▪ Large Kitchen with double ovens, a cooktop and a peninsula snackbar

▪ Master Bedroom suite with a decorative ceiling, a walk-in closet and a plush bath with a double vanity and a whirlpool tub

▪ Two additional bedrooms with walk-in closets share a full bath

▪ An optional slab or crawl space foundation — please specify when ordering

Main floor — 1,959 sq. ft.
Garage — 512 sq. ft.

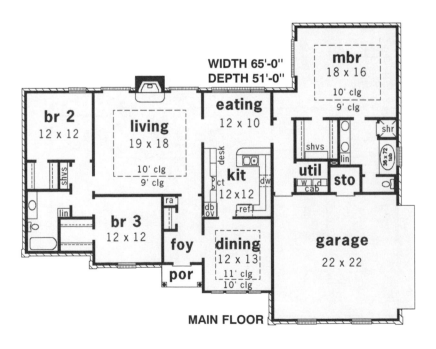

WIDTH 65'-0"
DEPTH 51'-0"

mbr 18 x 16
10' clg
9' clg

br 2 12 x 12

living 19 x 18
10' clg
9' clg

eating 12 x 10

shvs

shr

36 x 72 tub

util
w d
cab

sto

kit 12 x 12
desk
db
ov
ref
dw
ct

br 3 12 x 12
ra
lin

foy

dining 12 x 13
11' clg
10' clg

garage 22 x 22

por

MAIN FLOOR

Angles Add Interest

No. 84426

This plan features:

— Three bedrooms

— One full and one three quarter baths

■ Covered entry that leads into the Foyer with a vaulted ceiling and a coat closet

■ Great Room with a rear wall fireplace and access to the rear deck

■ Kitchen arranged in a U-shape and shares a serving bar with the nook

■ Master bedroom complete with walk in closet and three quarter bath

■ Two uniquely shaped bedrooms combining to form a bay window in the front

■ A full bath in the bedroom hallway

■ Two-car garage

■ No materials list is available for this plan

Main floor — 1,660 sq. ft.
Garage — 612 sq. ft.

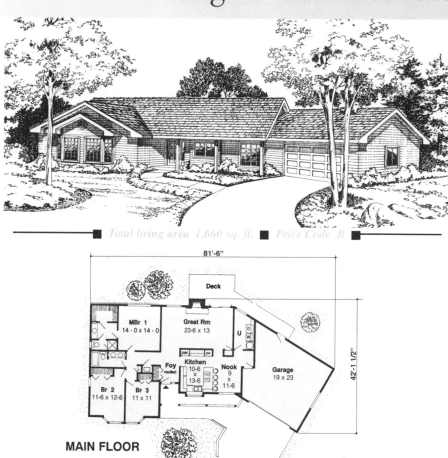

Total living area 1,660 sq. ft. ■ Price Code B

MAIN FLOOR

Comfortable Design Encourages Relaxation

No. 96413

This plan features:

— Four bedrooms

— Three full baths

■ A wide front porch providing a warm welcome

■ Center dormer lighting foyer, as columns punctuate the entry to the Dining Room and Great Room

■ Spacious Kitchen with angled countertop and open to the Breakfast Bay

■ Tray ceilings adding elegance to the Dining Room and the Master Bedroom

■ Master Suite located on the opposite end of the home and features an arrangement for physically challenged

■ Two bedrooms share a third full bath with a linen closet

■ Skylight Bonus room is located over the garage

Main floor — 2,349 sq. ft.
Bonus — 435 sq. ft.
Garage — 615 sq. ft.

© 1997 Donald A. Gardner Architects, Inc.

Total living area 2,349 sq. ft. ■ Price Code D

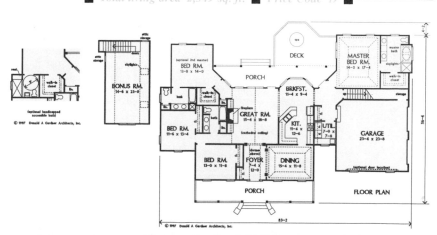

FLOOR PLAN

Simply Put

■ Total living area 1,454 sq. ft. ■ Price Code A ■

Gar.
20'8"x21'4"

Br.
11'x11'

Br.
10'8"x11'

Mbr.
13'x14'8"

D W LIN

WH STOR PANT

SHELVES

MAIN FLOOR

COVERED PORCH

Liv. rm. Din.
27'x15'6"

SERVING BAR

Kit.
13'6"x
15'6"

R

Deck

No. 94066

■ **This plan features:**

— Three bedrooms

— Two full baths

■ Combination Living Room/Dining Room accented by a cozy fireplace

■ Kitchen enhanced by a serving bar to the Dining Room and access to the Deck

■ Master Bedroom including a walk-in closet and a private bath

■ Two additional bedrooms sharing a family bath in the hall

■ Garage enters through the Laundry Room keeping down tracked in dirt

■ No materials list is available for this plan

Main floor — 1,454 sq. ft.
Garage — 462 sq. ft.
Width 38'-0"
Depth 60'-0"

An EXCLUSIVE DESIGN *By* CRANE DESIGN inc.

Lots of Natural Light

■ Total living area 1,506 sq. ft. ■ Price Code B ■

61'-4"

TERR.

f.p.

high ceiling

MASTER B.R. DR'S'G W.I.C.
15'-7"x 16' AV.

B.R.
11' x 10'

D. R.
10'x 11'-4"

skylight

40'-2"

GREAT RM
15 x 27

d. w

KIT.

ref

B.R.
11' x 10'

10'x15'-4"
D'N'TTE

2-CAR GAR.
20' x 20'

cl lin

WORK AREA

FLOOR PLAN

No. 99651 ✖

■ **This plan features:**

— Three bedrooms

— Two full baths

■ Welcoming elevation with softly arched windows and front porch entrance

■ Spacious Great Room with a cozy fireplace and skylight opens to Dining Room

■ Convenient Kitchen with Dinette, formal Dining Room and Terrace beyond

■ Private Master Bedroom offers a dressing area with walk-in closet and a double vanity bath

■ Two additional bedrooms with large closets share a full bath and laundry

Main floor — 1,506 sq. ft.
Garage — 455 sq. ft.
Basement — 1,506 sq. ft.

Windows Add Warmth To All Living Areas

■ *Total living area 1,672 sq. ft.* ■ *Price Code B* ■

No. 34011

■ This plan features:

- Three bedrooms
- Two full baths
- ■ A Master Suite with huge his-n-her walk-in closets and private bath
- ■ A second and third bedroom with ample closet space
- ■ A Kitchen equipped with an island counter, and flowing easily into the Dining and Family Rooms
- ■ A Laundry Room conveniently located near all three bedrooms
- ■ An optional garage

Main area— 1,672 sq. ft.
Optional garage — 566 sq. ft.

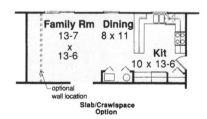

Family Rm
13-7 x 13-6

Dining
8 x 11

Kit
10 x 13-6

optional wall location

Slab/Crawlspace Option

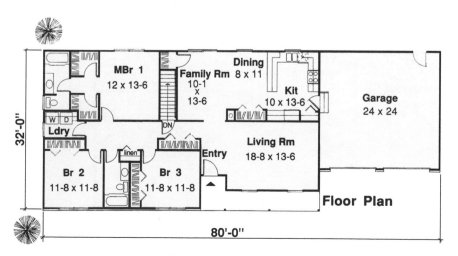

MBr 1
12 x 13-6

Family Rm
10-1 x 13-6

Dining
8 x 11

Kit
10 x 13-6

Garage
24 x 24

Ldry

W D

linen

Br 2
11-8 x 11-8

Br 3
11-8 x 11-8

Entry

Living Rm
18-8 x 13-6

DN

32'-0"

80'-0"

Floor Plan

Turret Adds Appeal

■ Total living area 2,214 sq. ft. ■ Price Code D ■

No. 94206

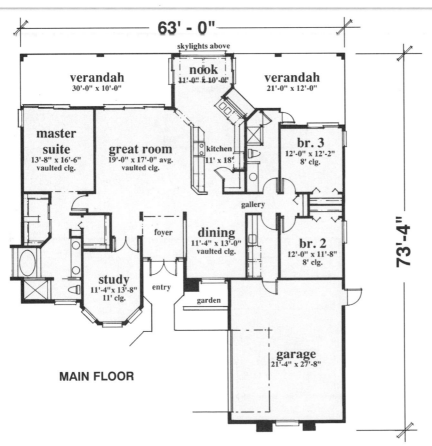

MAIN FLOOR

63' - 0"

73' - 4"

skylights above

verandah
30'-0" x 10'-0"

nook
11'-0" x 10'-0"

verandah
21'-0" x 12'-0"

master suite
13'-8" x 16'-6"
vaulted clg.

great room
19'-0" x 17'-0" avg.
vaulted clg.

kitchen
11' x 18'

br. 3
12'-0" x 12'-2"
8' clg.

gallery

foyer

dining
11'-4" x 13'-0"
vaulted clg.

br. 2
12'-0" x 11'-8"
8' clg.

study
11'-4" x 13'-8"
11' clg.

entry

garden

garage
21'-4" x 27'-8"

This plan features:

— Three bedrooms

— Two full baths

■ A double door garden Entry leads to the Foyer and Great Room

■ Vaulted ceilings above a decorative window in the Dining area and sliding glass doors to the Veranda in the Great Room

■ A private Study with double door and turret windows

■ Kitchen featuring a walk-in pantry and a glassed Nook with skylights

■ A Master Suite with a vaulted ceiling, walk-in closets, a private bath and sliding glass doors to the Veranda

■ Two bedrooms with over-sized closets sharing a full bath

■ No materials list is available for this plan

Main floor — 2,214 sq. ft.
Garage — 652 sq. ft.

Fieldstone and Wood Siding Accent Ranch

No. 99031 ✖

This plan features:

- Three bedrooms
- Two full baths
- Covered Entry Porch leads into fieldstone Foyer and sunken Living Room
- Beautiful bow window and raised, hearth fireplace and built-in bookshelves compliment Living Room
- Window seat in bay window and French doors to Breezeway accent room
- Efficient U-shaped Kitchen with built-in pantry, eating area and laundry closet
- Private Master Bedroom with two closets, French door and private bath
- Two additional bedrooms with ample closets share double vanity bath
- Oversized two-car Garage with workbench and storage space

Main floor — 1,598 sq. ft.

Total living area 1,598 sq. ft. ■ Price Code B

floor plan

Grand Front Porch

No. 99469 ✖

This plan features:

- Three bedrooms
- Two full and one half baths
- The covered porch is overlooked by four windows with transoms above them
- The tiled entry leads to the Dining Room that is distinguished by columns in the front and a bow transom windowed wall in the rear
- The L-shaped Kitchen has a center island, and a snack bar
- The Breakfast Nook has a unique ceiling treatment and a door to the rear yard
- The Family Room has a cathedral ceiling and a fireplace
- The Master Bedroom is uniquely shaped and has a walk-in closet, plus a luxurious bath
- Two additional bedrooms sport bright windows and large closets

Main floor — 2,538 sq. ft.
Garage — 755 sq. ft.

Total living area 2,538 sq. ft. ■ Price Code D

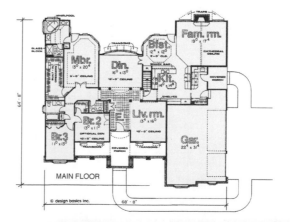

MAIN FLOOR

© design basics inc.

Visually Open Plan

Total living area 2,133 sq. ft. ■ Price Code C

MAIN FLOOR

© design basics, inc.

No. 94959

This plan features:

— Three bedrooms

— Two full and one half baths

■ Diagonal views of this open plan giving it an expansive look

■ The covered stoop opens into a Y-shaped tiled Foyer with the Great Room beyond it

■ The Great Room has a high ceiling, a fireplace and louvered openings in the roof

■ The Kitchen/Breakfast area is open and boasts an island with a snack bar and bay window

■ Attention grabbing diamond shaped Dining room

■ The Bedroom wing contains three large bedrooms and two full baths

■ A three-car garage with storage rounds out this plan

Main floor — 2,133 sq. ft.
Garage — 656 sq. ft.

European Sophistication

© 1996 Donald A Gardner Architects, Inc.

Total living area 1,699 sq. ft. ■ Price Code C

FLOOR PLAN

© 1996 Donald A Gardner Architects, Inc.

No. 99831

This plan features:

— Three bedrooms

— Two full baths

■ Keystone arches, gables, and stucco give the exterior European sophistication

■ Large Great Room with fireplace, and U-shaped Kitchen and a large utility room nearby

■ Octagonal tray ceiling dresses up the Dining Room

■ Special ceiling treatments include a cathedral ceiling in the Great Room and tray ceilings in both the Master and front bedrooms

■ Indulgent Master Bath with a separate toilet area, a garden tub, shower and twin vanities

■ Bonus room over the garage adds flexibility

Main floor — 1,699 sq. ft.
Bonus — 386 sq. ft.
Garage — 637 sq. ft.

Beautiful Arched Window

■ *Total living area 1,911 sq. ft.* ■ *Price Code C* ■

No. 94966

This plan features:

—Three bedrooms

—Two full baths

■ 10' ceilings topping the Entry and the Great Room

■ A see-through fireplace is shared between the Great Room and the Hearth Room

■ Built-in entertainment center and bayed window in the Hearth Room

■ Built-in pantry and corner sinks enhancing efficiency in the Kitchen

■ Split bedroom plan assures privacy in the Master Suite, which includes a decorative ceiling, private bath and a large walk-in closet

■ Two additional bedrooms at the opposite side of the home share a full, skylit bath in the hall

Main floor — 1,911 sq. ft.
Garage — 481 sq. ft.

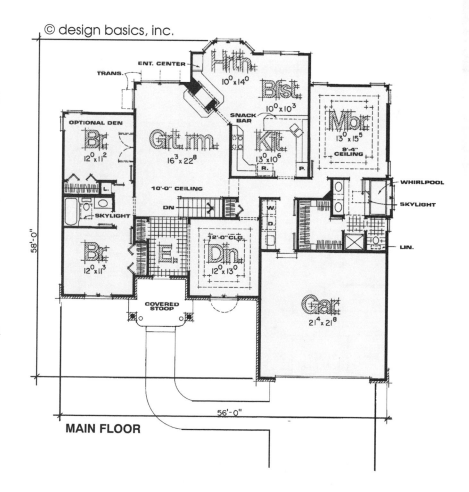

© design basics, inc.

MAIN FLOOR

Dream Home for Contemporary Buyers

©1995 Donald A. Gardner Architects, Inc.

Total living area 2,050 sq. ft. ▪ Price Code D

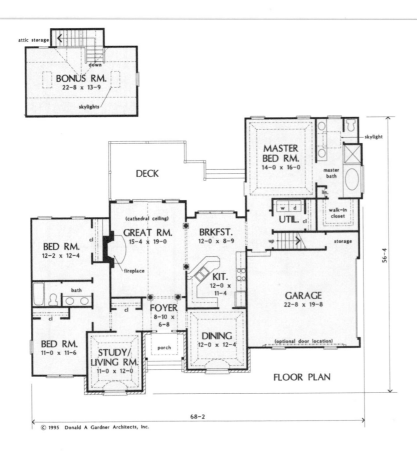

© 1995 Donald A Gardner Architects, Inc.

No. 96465

This plan features:

— Three bedrooms

— Two full baths

▪ Gables, a center front dormer, and a touch of brick combine for an efficient floor plan

▪ Dormer floods the Foyer with sunlight while a cathedral ceiling enlarges the Great room

▪ The Kitchen and Breakfast area punctuated by interior columns

▪ Tray ceilings and arched picture windows in the Dining room and the Living room

▪ Two family Bedrooms share a large full Bath with a double vanity in one wing, while the luxurious Master suite enjoys privacy in the rear

Main floor — 2,050 sq. ft.
Bonus — 377 sq. ft.
Garage — 503 sq. ft.

Four-Bedroom Beauty

No. 98510

■ **This plan features:**

— Four bedrooms

— Two full baths

■ Formal Dining Room with a 9' ceiling, a bay window and direct access to the Kitchen

■ A 10' ceiling continues from the entry into the Living Room, which is accented by a fireplace and book shelves

■ The Kitchen has an angled serving bar, a pantry, and is open to the Breakfast Nook

■ Three bedrooms have 8' ceilings and large closets; they share a bath in the hall

■ The Master Bedroom has a 9' ceiling, a private bath and a walk in closet

■ A patio in the rear of the home

■ A three-car garage in the front of the home

■ No materials list is available for this plan

Main floor — 1,840 sq. ft.
Garage — 612 sq. ft.

Total living area 1,840 sq. ft. ■ Price Code C

MAIN FLOOR

Spread Out Ranch

No. 91720 ✗

■ **This plan features:**

— Three bedrooms

— Two full baths

■ The covered front Porch protects from the elements

■ The Living Room has a vaulted ceiling, bright windows, and a corner fireplace

■ The Dining Room features a bay with windows

■ The Kitchen has an island with a range, and adjoins the unique angled Nook

■ The Master Suite has a closet that spans the entire rear wall, plus a private bath

■ Two additional bedrooms share a full bath with dual vanity

Main floor — 1,870 sq. ft.
Garage — 588 sq. ft.
Width — 84'-7"
Depth — 46'-8"

Total living area 1,870 sq. ft. ■ Price Code C

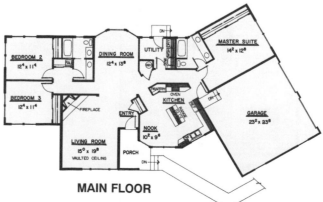

MAIN FLOOR

Appealing Arches

Total living area 1,756 sq. ft. ■ Price Code B

■ **This plan features:**

— Three bedrooms

— Two full baths

■ Brick exterior accented by quoins and arched windows

■ Foyer opens to formal Dining Room and spacious Great Room

■ Sloped ceiling above corner fireplace and atrium door to Deck enhance Great Room

■ Efficient Kitchen with serving counter, bright Breakfast area, pantry and nearby Laundry/Garage entry

■ Secluded Master Bedroom offers a sloped ceiling above arched window, a large walk-in closet and lavish bath with a garden window tub

■ Two additional bedrooms with ample closets, share a full bath

■ No materials list is available for this plan

Main floor — 1,756 sq. ft.
Basement — 1,669 sq. ft.
Garage — 485 sq. ft.

Compact And Open Cabin

Total living area 768 sq. ft. ■ Price Code A

■ **This plan features:**

— Three bedrooms

— One full bath

■ An open Living Room leading into an efficient Kitchen

■ Three bedrooms, with ample closets, sharing a full hall bath

■ A full basement option or a separate washer and dryer area

■ No materials list is available for this plan

Main floor — 768 sq. ft.

Slab/Crawlspace Option

Floor Plan

Four Bedroom with One Floor Convenience

■ Total living area 2,675 sq. ft. ■ Price Code E ■

No. 92275

■ **This plan features:**

— Four bedrooms

— Three full baths

■ A distinguished brick exterior adds curb appeal

■ Formal Entry/Gallery opens to large Living Room with hearth fireplace set between windows overlooking Patio and rear yard

■ Efficient Kitchen with angled counters and serving bar easily serves Breakfast Room, Patio and formal Dining Room

■ Corner Master Bedroom enhanced by a vaulted ceiling and pampering bath with a large walk-in closet

■ Three additional bedrooms with walk-in closets have access to full baths

■ No materials list is available for this plan

Main floor —2,675 sq. ft.
Garage — 638 sq. ft.

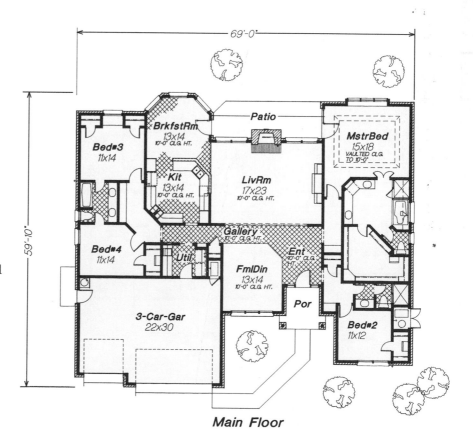

Main Floor

Clever Design Packs in Plenty of Living Space

No! (Entrance from garage— No util. Rm.)

■ Total living area 1,700 sq. ft. ■ Price Code B ■

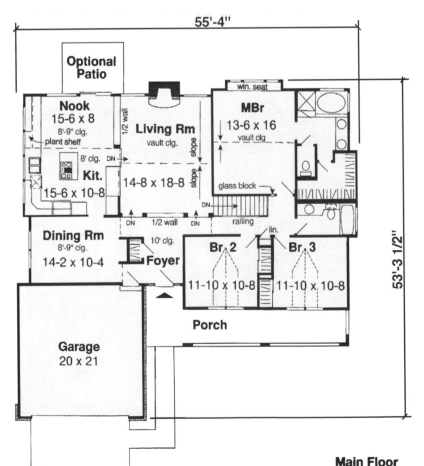

Main Floor

No. 24250

■ This plan features:

— Three bedrooms

— Two full baths

■ Custom, volume ceilings

■ A sunken Living Room with a vaulted ceiling, and a fireplace with oversized windows framing it

■ A center island and an eating nook in the Kitchen

■ A formal Dining Room that adjoins the Kitchen, allowing for easy entertaining

■ A spacious Master Suite including a vaulted ceiling and lavish bath

■ Secondary bedrooms with custom ceiling treatments and use of full hall bath

Main area — 1,700 sq. ft.

An
EXCLUSIVE DESIGN
By Energetic Enterprises

Family Room Boasts Vaulted Ceiling

No. 93425

This plan features:

- Three bedrooms

- Two full baths

■ The covered front Porch opens into the Foyer, and the Dining Room beyond that sports a 10' ceiling

■ The Kitchen has a bright skylight, a center island and an abundance of counter space

■ The Breakfast Nook is open to the Kitchen and features a 9' ceiling

■ The Family Room is located in the rear and offers a fireplace, a bookcase, a vaulted ceiling and access to the rear Porch

■ Two secondary bedrooms have 9' ceilings, and walk in closets

■ The Master Bedroom also has a 9' ceiling, plus a walk in closet and a private bath

■ There is a two-car garage in the front of the home

■ There is no materials list available for this plan

Main floor — 1,842 sq. ft.
Garage — 507 sq. ft.

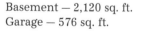

An
EXCLUSIVE DESIGN
By Greg Marquis

■ Total living area 1,842 sq. ft. ■ Price Code C ■

MAIN FLOOR

Windows Add Light and Space

No. 20108

This plan features:

- Three bedrooms

- Two full and one half baths

■ Shutters, round-cut shingles, and an attractive railed porch adding classic charm to the Traditional exterior of this home

■ A central Entry leading to the formal Living Room and also to the informal Family Room

■ Elegant ceiling treatment and a room-sized, walk-in closet in the Master Suite

■ A Kitchen with a range-top island, bump-out window and a strategic location between the Family and Dining Rooms

Main floor — 2,120 sq. ft.
Basement — 2,120 sq. ft.
Garage — 576 sq. ft.

An
EXCLUSIVE DESIGN
By Karl Kreeger

■ Total living area 2,120 sq. ft. ■ Price Code C ■

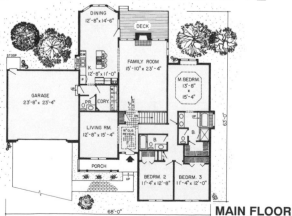

MAIN FLOOR

Deck Doubles Outdoor Living Space

Total living area 2,352 sq. ft. ■ Price Code D

No. 10619

This plan features:

— Three bedrooms

— Two full and one three quarter baths

■ A design made for the sun lover with a front deck and patio

■ A sunken Living Room with three window walls and a massive fireplace

■ A hot tub with skylight, a vaulted Master Suite and a utility area

Main floor — 2,352 sq. ft.
Basement — 2,352 sq. ft.
Garage — 696 sq. ft.

MAIN FLOOR

An EXCLUSIVE DESIGN
By Karl Kreeger

Cozy Three Bedroom

Total living area 1,515 sq. ft. ■ Price Code B

No. 96522

This plan features:

— Three bedrooms

— Two full baths

■ The expansive Great Room is accented by a cozy gas fireplace

■ The efficient Kitchen includes an eating bar that separates it from the Great Room

■ The Master bedroom is highlighted by a walk-in closet and a whirlpool bath

■ Two secondary bedrooms share use of the full bath in the hall

■ The triple arched front porch adds to the curb appeal of the home

■ The rear porch extends dining to the outdoors

Main floor — 1,515 sq. ft.
Garage — 528 sq. ft.

MAIN FLOOR

Inviting Porch Has Dual Function

■ *Total living area 1,295 sq. ft.* ■ *Price Code A* ■

No. 91021 ✖

■ This plan features:

— Three bedrooms

— One full and one three quarter baths

■ An inviting, wrap-around porch Entry with sliding glass doors leading right into a bayed Dining Room

■ A Living Room with a cozy feeling, enhanced by the fireplace

■ An efficient Kitchen opening to both Dining and Living Rooms

■ A Master Suite with a walk-in closet and private Master Bath

■ An optional basement, slab or crawl space foundation — please specify when ordering

Main floor — 1,295 sq. ft.

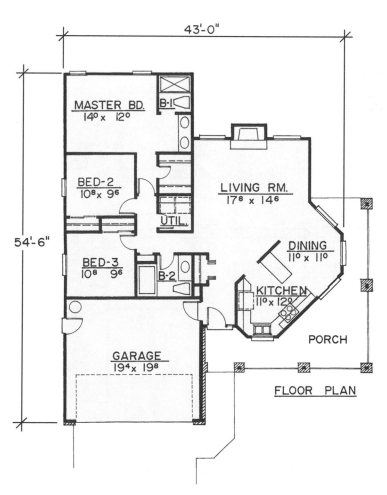

43'-0"

54'-6"

MASTER BD.
14⁰ x 12⁰

B-1

BED-2
10⁸ x 9⁶

UTIL.

LIVING RM.
17⁸ x 14⁶

BED-3
10⁸ 9⁶

B-2

DINING
11⁰ x 11⁰

KITCHEN
11⁰ x 12⁸

PORCH

GARAGE
19⁴ x 19⁸

FLOOR PLAN

Relax on the Veranda

Total living area 3,051 sq. ft. ■ Price Code E

No. 91749

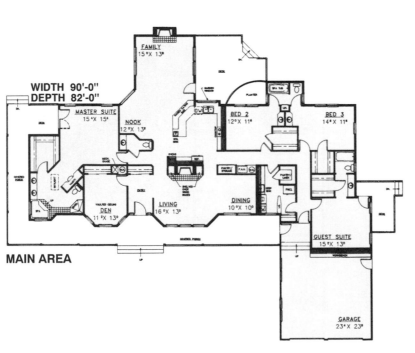

WIDTH 90'-0"
DEPTH 82'-0"

MAIN AREA

FAMILY
15⁸X 13⁰

MASTER SUITE
15⁴X 15⁴

NOOK
12⁰X 13⁰

BED 2
12⁰X 11⁰

BED 3
14⁶X 11⁰

DEN
11⁸X 13⁰

LIVING
16⁶X 13⁰

DINING
10⁰X 10⁰

GUEST SUITE
15⁴X 13⁰

GARAGE
23⁴X 23⁰

This plan features:

— Four bedrooms

— Three full and one half baths

■ A wrap-around veranda

■ A sky-lit Master Suite with elevated custom spa, twin basins, a walk-in closet, and an additional vanity outside the bathroom

■ A vaulted ceiling in the Den

■ A fireplace in both the Family Room and the formal Living Room

■ An efficient Kitchen with a peninsula counter and a double sink

■ Two additional bedrooms with walk-in closets, served by a compartmentalized bath

■ A Guest Suite with a private bath

Main Area — 3,051 sq. ft.
Garage — 646 sq. ft.

Affordable Ranch

No. 99318

This plan features:

— Three bedrooms

— Two full baths

■ A sheltered entrance leading to a small Foyer with a convenient coat closet and access to the garage

■ A vaulted ceiling and corner fireplace gracing the Living Room and the Dining Room

■ Sliding glass doors in the Living Room and the Dining Room adding natural light and extending entertainment space

■ A Master Bedroom with a full bath and a walk-in closet

■ Two additional bedrooms that share a full hall bath, one with a double door providing a Den option if desired

Main area — 1,159 sq. ft.

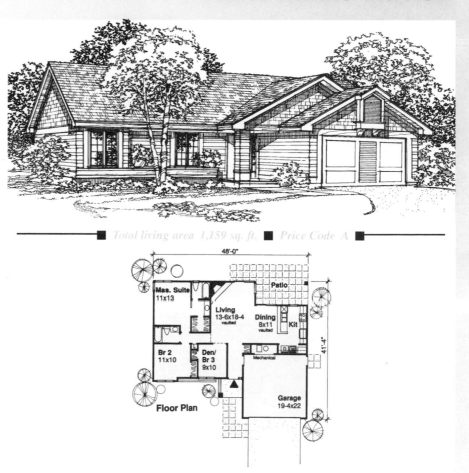

■ *Total living area 1,159 sq. ft.* ■ *Price Code A* ■

48'-0"

41'-4"

Mas. Suite 11x13

Living 13-6x18-4 vaulted

Patio

Dining 8x11 vaulted

Kit

Br 2 11x10

Den/ Br 3 9x10

Mechanical

Garage 19-4x22

Floor Plan

Casual Country Charmer

No. 96493

This plan features:

— Three bedrooms

— Two full baths

■ Columns and arches frame the front Porch

■ The open floor plan combines the Great Room, Kitchen, and the Dining Room

■ The Kitchen offers a convenient breakfast bar for meals on the run

■ The Master Suite features a private bath oasis

■ Secondary Bedrooms share a full bath with a dual vanity

Main floor — 1,770 sq. ft.
Bonus — 401 sq. ft.
Garage — 630 sq. ft.

© 1997 Donald A. Gardner Architects, Inc.

■ *Total living area 1,770 sq. ft.* ■ *Price Code C* ■

PORCH

DINING 11-4 x 12-0

(dormers above)

PORCH

master bath

walk-in closet

walk-in closet

UTIL. 7-0 x 10-0

KIT. 13-0 x 12-0

fireplace

MASTER BED RM. 13-0 x 14-6

storage

GREAT RM. 17-8 x 20-4

shelves

(cathedral ceiling)

GARAGE 22-0 x 24-0

FOYER 8-0 x 9-3

BED RM. 11-4 x 11-8

BED RM. 11-0 x 11-0

PORCH

attic storage

down

BONUS RM. 13-6 x 24-0

57'-4"

FLOOR PLAN

54'-0

© 1997 Donald A. Gardner Architects, Inc.

Bedrooms Sliders Open Onto Wooden Deck

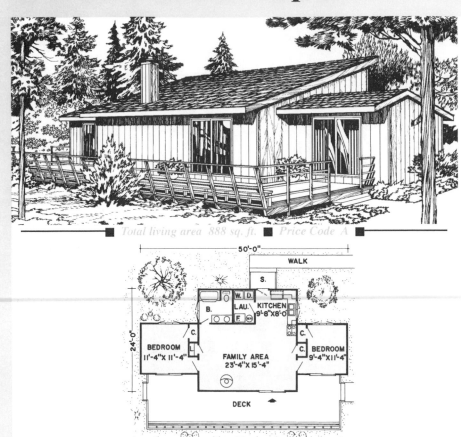

Total living area 888 sq. ft. ■ Price Code A

MAIN AREA

No. 10220

■ This plan features:

— Two bedrooms

— One full bath

■ A 50' deck setting the stage for a relaxing lifestyle encouraged by this home

■ A simple, yet complete floor plan centering around the large Family Area, warmed by a prefab fireplace sliders to the deck

■ An efficient L-shaped Kitchen that includes a double sink with a window above, and direct access to the rear yard and the Laundry Room

■ Two bedrooms privately located, each outfitted with sliding doors to the deck and a large window for plenty of light

Main area — 888 sq. ft.

European Flavor

Total living area 1,779 sq. ft. ■ Price Code B

FIRST FLOOR

SECOND FLOOR

No. 98464

■ This plan features:

— Three bedrooms

— Two full baths

■ A covered entry reveals a foyer inside with a 14' ceiling

■ The Family Room has a vaulted ceiling, a fireplace, and a French door to the rear yard

■ The Breakfast area has a tray ceiling and a bay of windows that overlooks the backyard

■ The Kitchen has every imaginable convenience including a walk-in pantry

■ The Dining Room is delineated by columns and has a plant shelf above it

■ The privately located Master Suite has a tray ceiling, a walk in closet and a private bath

■ Two other bedrooms share a full bath on the opposite side of the home

■ No materials list available for this plan

■ An optional basement or crawl space foundation — please specify when ordering

Main floor — 1,779 sq. ft.
Basement — 1,818 sq. ft.
Garage — 499 sq. ft.

Home Recalls the South

Total living area 2,466 sq. ft. ■ Price Code D

No. 9850

This plan features:

— Three bedrooms

— Two full and one half baths

A Master Bedroom Suite with a private Study

Fireplaces enhancing the formal Living Room and spacious Family Room

A lovely, screened porch/patio skirting the Family Room and the Kitchen

A Utility Room with access into the storage and garage areas

Main area — 2,466 sq. ft.
Basement — 1,477 sq. ft.
Garage — 664 sq. ft.

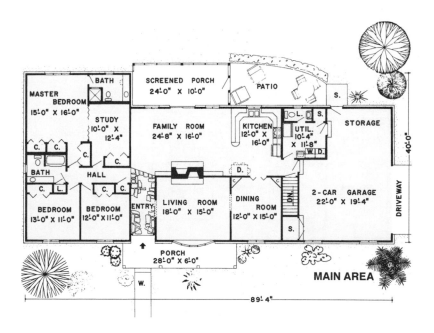

Inviting Porch Adorns Affordable Home

■ *Total living area — 1,243 sq. ft.* ■ *Price Code A* ■

No. 90682

■ **This plan features:**

— Three bedrooms

— Two full baths

■ A large and spacious Living Room that adjoins the Dining Room for ease in entertaining

■ A private bedroom wing offering a quiet atmosphere

■ A Master Bedroom with his-n-her closets and a private bath

■ An efficient Kitchen with a walk-in pantry

Main area — 1,160 sq. ft.
Laundry/mudroom — 83 sq. ft.

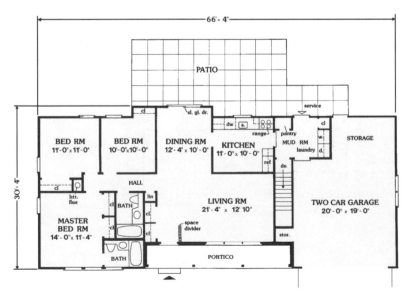

MAIN AREA

Victorian Accents the Exterior

No. 99857

This plan features:

- Three bedrooms
- Two full baths
- The covered wrap-around porch connects to the rear Deck
- The foyer opens into the octagonal Great Room that is warmed by a fireplace
- The Dining Room has a tray ceiling and convenient access to the Kitchen
- The galley Kitchen opens into the Breakfast bay
- The Master Bedroom has a bay area in the rear, a walk in closet, and a fully appointed bath
- Two more bedrooms complete this plan as does another full bath

Main floor — 1,865 sq. ft.
Garage — 505 sq. ft.

Total living area 1,865 sq. ft. ■ Price Code C

© 1991 Donald A. Gardner Architects, Inc.

Unique Brick and Shake Siding

No. 93104

This plan features:

- Three bedrooms
- Two full baths
- Sheltered entrance surrounded by glass leads into the Foyer and the expansive Great Room
- Windows surround a cozy fireplace in the Great Room topped by a vaulted ceiling
- Well-appointed Kitchen with loads of counter and storage space, and a snackbar serving the bright Dining area with access to the rear yard
- French doors lead into the Master Bedroom Suite with a huge walk-in closet and a double vanity bath
- Two additional bedrooms with ample closets, share a full bath
- No materials list is available for this plan

Main floor — 1,756 sq. ft.
Basement — 1,756 sq. ft.
Garage — 536 sq. ft.

Total living area 1,756 sq. ft. ■ Price Code B

An EXCLUSIVE DESIGN *By Ahmann Design Inc.*

Elegant Exterior Attracts Attention

Total living area 2,289 sq. ft. ■ Price Code D

MAIN FLOOR

No. 96530

This plan features:

— Three bedrooms

— Three full baths

■ The exterior is highlighted by a high columned porch and many windows

■ The Receiving Room is graced by a see-through fireplace that is shared with the Great Room

■ The Great Room is spacious and opens onto the verandah

■ The Kitchen/Dining area adjoins the Great Room adding a spacious feeling to the home

■ A vaulted ceiling, a private whirlpool bath and a Lounging Room are in the Master Suite

■ Two additional bedrooms have access to a full bath

Main floor — 2,289 sq. ft.
Garage — 758 sq. ft.

A Little Extra, Economical Space

Total living area 1,592 sq. ft. ■ Price Code B

MAIN FLOOR

No. 99900

This plan features:

— Three bedrooms

— Two full baths

■ Covered walk leads into the Living Room with a bay window and a gas fireplace, and a formal Dining Room adjoining the Kitchen

■ Open Kitchen with an island snack bar efficiently serves the Nook, the Family Room and the Patio beyond

■ Master Bedroom is highlighted by a walk-in closet, private bath and a decorative window overlooking the rear yard

■ Two additional bedrooms with ample closets share a full bath

■ Bonus area over the double Garage offers many options

Main Floor — 1,592 sq. ft.
Bonus area — 275 sq. ft.
Garage — 462 sq. ft.

An EXCLUSIVE DESIGN
By Westhome Planners, Ltd.

94

■ *Total living area 1,849 sq. ft.* ■ *Price Code C* ■

No. 92705

■ **This plan features:**

— Three bedrooms

— Two full baths

■ A raised, tile Foyer with a decorative window leading into an expansive Living Room, accented by a tiled fireplace and framed by French doors

■ An efficient Kitchen with a walk-in pantry and serving bar adjoining the Breakfast and Utility areas

■ A private Master Bedroom, crowned by a stepped ceiling, offering an atrium door to outside, a huge, walk-in closet and a luxurious bath

■ Two additional bedrooms with walk-in closets, share a full hall bath

■ No materials list is available for this plan

Main floor — 1,849 sq. ft.
Garage — 437 sq. ft.

MAIN FLOOR

Gabled Roofline and Arched Windows

■ Total living area—1,207 sq. ft. ■ Price Code A ■

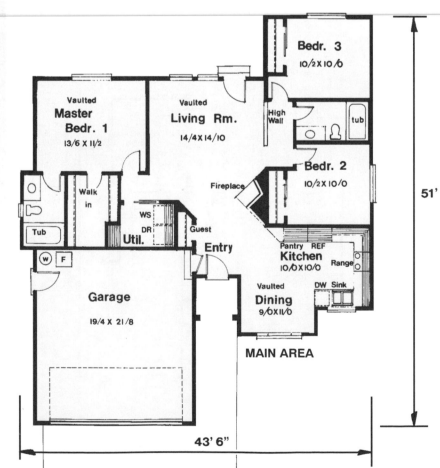

MAIN AREA

No. 91063

■ **This plan features:**

— Three bedrooms

— Two full baths

■ Vaulted ceilings and an open interior creating a spacious feeling

■ A private Master Bedroom with a generous closet and Master Bath

■ Two additional bedrooms sharing the second full bath

■ A Kitchen with ample storage, countertops, and a built-in pantry

■ No materials list is available for this plan

Main area — 1,207 sq. ft.
Garage — 440 sq. ft.

Elegant European Styling

No. 92554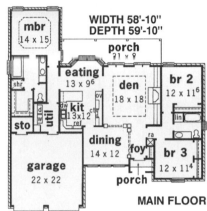

This plan features:

— Three bedrooms

— Two full baths

- Quoins and dentil molding give this home a European flair

- The split bedroom plans affords privacy to the Master bedroom

- The Dining room is separated from the Foyer and the Den by columns

- The Den has a decorative ceiling, a fireplace, built-in shelves, and access to the rear Porch

- Two bedrooms share a full hall bath and linen closet

- The U-shaped Kitchen is open to the Eating bay that overlook the rear Porch

- An optional slab or a crawl space foundation — please specify when ordering

Main floor — 1,871 sq. ft.
Garage — 519 sq. ft.

Total living area 1,871 sq. ft. ■ Price Code D

WIDTH 58'-10"
DEPTH 59'-10"

MAIN FLOOR

French Country Styling

No. 98513

This plan features:

— Three bedrooms

— Three full and one half baths

- Brick and stone blend masterfully for an impressive French country exterior

- Separate Master Suite with expansive bath and closet

- Study containing a built-in desk and bookcase

- Angled island Kitchen highlighted by walk-in pantry and open to the Breakfast Bay

- Fantastic Family Room including a brick fireplace and a built-in entertainment center

- Three additional bedrooms with private access to a full bath

- No materials list is available for this plan

Main floor — 3,352 sq. ft.
Garage — 672 sq. ft.

Total living area 3,352 sq. ft. ■ Price Code F

MAIN FLOOR

Bonus Loft with Balcony

■ *Total living area 1,941 sq. ft.* ■ *Price Code C* ■

MAIN FLOOR

No. 92132

■ **This plan features:**

— Three bedrooms

— Two full and one half baths

■ Exterior details and decorative windows surround sheltered Entry

■ Central Great Room with an inviting fireplace, vaulted, two-story ceiling, entertainment wall and Deck access

■ Open Kitchen efficiently serves bright Eating area and Deck with cooktop work island and peninsula counter

■ Utility/Mud Room with Loft stairs and Garage entry

■ Corner Master Bedroom offers back yard view, large walk-in closet and double vanity bath with window tub

■ Two additional bedrooms with decorative windows and ample closets share a full bath

■ Loft/Bonus opens to Balcony and Great Room below

■ An optional basement or crawl space foundation — please specify when ordering

■ No materials list is available for this plan

Main floor — 1,941 sq. ft.
Basement — 1,592 sq. ft.
Bonus room — 200 sq. ft.
Garage — 720 sq. ft.

Rambling Ranch

■ *Total living area 1,042 sq. ft.* ■ *Price Code A* ■

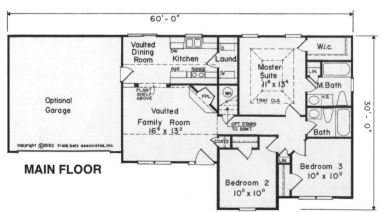

MAIN FLOOR

No. 98469

This plan features:

— Three bedrooms

— Two full baths

■ The Living room is complemented by a vaulted ceiling, a corner fireplace, and a plant shelf

■ The Dining room also has a vaulted ceiling, and is open to the Kitchen

■ The galley Kitchen is fully equipped and the entry to the Laundry room is at it's far end

■ The Master suite has a tray ceiling, a walk in closet, and a private bath

■ There are two secondary bedrooms located in the front of the home, they share a full bath

■ This plan has an optional two-car garage

■ No materials list is available for this plan

■ An optional basement or crawl space foundation — please specify when ordering

Main floor — 1,042 sq. ft.
Basement — 1,042 sq. ft.
Garage — 400 sq. ft.

■ *Total living area 1,600 sq. ft.* ■ *Price Code B* ■

No. 92803

■ **This plan features:**

— Four bedrooms

— Two full baths

■ A long wooden Deck and a Screened Porch providing outdoor living space

■ An expansive Great Room/Dining Area with a fireplace and glass on three sides

■ An efficient Kitchen with ample storage space and an open counter separating it from the Dining area

■ A Master Bedroom with windows on two sides and a walk-in closet adjacent to a full hall bath

■ An optional post, crawl space, or slab foundation — please specify when ordering

Main floor — 1,600 sq. ft.

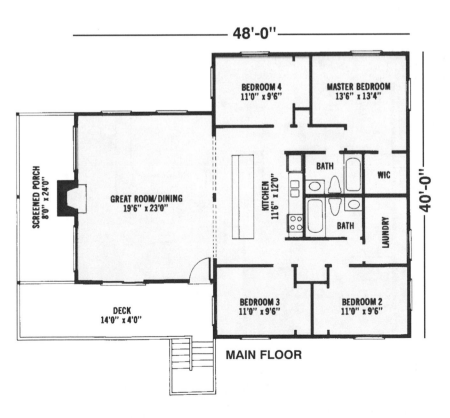

48'-0"

40'-0"

BEDROOM 4
11'0" x 9'6"

MASTER BEDROOM
13'6" x 13'4"

SCREENED PORCH
8'0" x 24'0"

GREAT ROOM/DINING
19'6" x 23'0"

KITCHEN
11'6" x 12'0"

BATH

WIC

BATH

LAUNDRY

DECK
14'0" x 4'0"

BEDROOM 3
11'0" x 9'6"

BEDROOM 2
11'0" x 9'6"

MAIN FLOOR

Roomy and Rustic Fieldstone

■ Total living area 3,079 sq. ft. ■ Price Code E ■

No. 92279

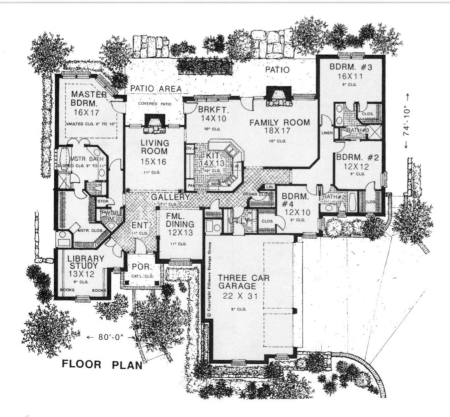

FLOOR PLAN

■ **This plan features:**

— Four bedrooms

— Three full and one half baths

■ Cathedral Porch leads into easy-care Entry and formal Living Room with fieldstone fireplace

■ Hub Kitchen with curved peninsula serving counter convenient to Breakfast area, Covered Patio, Family Room, Utility/Garage entry and Dining Room

■ Corner Master Bedroom enhanced by vaulted ceiling, plush bath and a huge walk-in closet

■ Three additional bedrooms with walk-in closets and private access to a full bath

■ No materials list is available for this plan

MAIN FLOOR — 3,079 SQ. FT.
GARAGE — 630 SQ. FT.

Convenient Single Level

This plan features:

— Three bedrooms

— Two full baths

■ A well-appointed U-shaped Kitchen that includes a view of the front yard and a built-in pantry

■ An expansive Great Room with direct access to the rear yard, expanding the living space

■ A Master Bedroom equipped with two closets—one is a walk-in—and a private bath

■ Two additional bedrooms that share a full hall Bath

■ A step-saving, centrally located laundry center

■ No materials list is available for this plan

Main floor — 1,644 sq. ft.

Garage — 576 sq. ft.

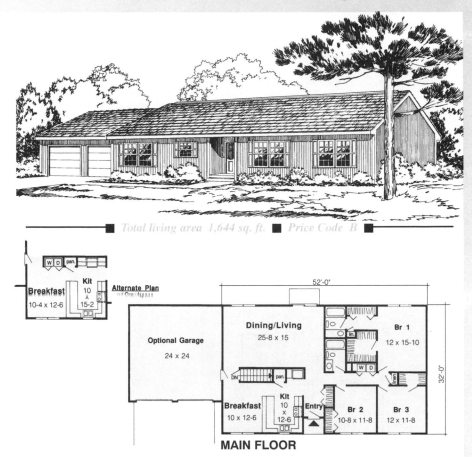

Total living area 1,644 sq. ft. ■ Price Code B

MAIN FLOOR

Cozy See-Through Fireplace

This plan features:

— Three bedrooms

— Two full baths

■ Spacious Family Room enhanced by a see-through fireplace and a pass-through from the Kitchen

■ Dining area has access to the outside

■ Kitchen including a work island, a double sink and direct access to the laundry room

■ Master suite, located to the rear of the home accessed from the Dining area

■ Compartmental bath and walk-in closet highlighting the Master Suite

■ Two additional bedrooms with walk-in closets and easy access to the full bath in the hall

■ No material list is available for this plan

Main floor — 1,655 sq. ft.

Garage — 484 sq. ft.

Total living area 1,655 sq. ft. ■ Price Code B

An EXCLUSIVE DESIGN *By Greg Marquis*

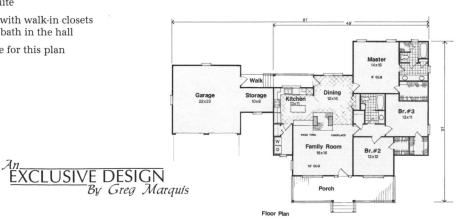

Floor Plan

101

Privacy is Assured with Separate Bedroom Wing

■ *Total living area 1,652 sq. ft.* ■ *Price Code B* ■

MAIN FLOOR

No. 20114

■ **This plan features:**

— Three bedrooms

— Two full baths

■ Sturdy brick construction and arched window treatment distinguishing the facade of this efficient one-level home

■ A central foyer with access to every area of the home

■ A wide-open Kitchen with an adjoining Breakfast area

■ A spacious L-shaped Living and Dining Room arrangement

■ A step-saving Laundry located near the bedrooms

Main floor — 1,652 sq. ft.
Basement — 1,652 sq. ft.
Garage — 484 sq. ft.

An
EXCLUSIVE DESIGN
By Karl Kreeger

Details Add Luxury

■ *Total living area 2,041 sq. ft.* ■ *Price Code D* ■

FIRST FLOOR

LOWER LEVEL

No. 92688

■ **This plan features:**

— Three bedrooms

— Two full baths

■ The covered Front Porch leads into a raised foyer

■ The Great room has a high ceiling, a fireplace, and views of the rear deck

■ The large Kitchen offers plenty of counter space, and opens into the Dining area

■ The Master bedrooms has an octagonal sitting area, a dressing area, a walk in closet, and a bath

■ On the opposite side of the house is a second bedroom, a bath, and a bedroom/library

■ The lower level can be finished at your convenience and includes a Rec room, a Kitchen, storage, and much more

■ No materials list is available for this plan

First Floor — 2,041 sq. ft.
Unfinished Lower level —
1,942 sq. ft.
Garage — 547 sq. ft.

European Styling with a Georgian Flair

■ *Total living area 1,873 sq. ft.* ■ *Price Code D* ■

No. 92552

■ This plan features:

— Four bedrooms

— Two full baths

■ Elegant European styling of this home has been spiced with Georgian Styling

■ Arch top windows, quoins and shutters on the exterior, a columned covered front and a rear porch

■ Formal foyer gives access to the dining room to the left and spacious Den straight ahead

■ Kitchen flows into the informal eating area and is separated from the den by an angled extended counter eating bar

■ An optional crawl space or slab foundation — please specify when ordering

Main floor — 1,873 sq. ft.
Bonus area — 145 sq. ft.
Garage — 613 sq. ft.

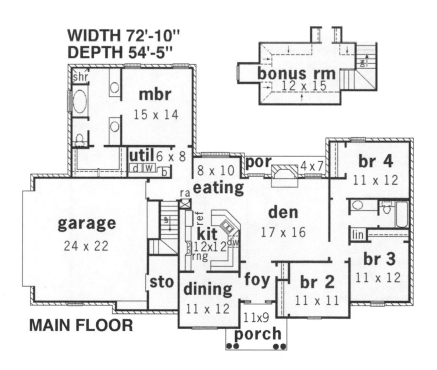

WIDTH 72'-10"
DEPTH 54'-5"

bonus rm
12 x 15

shr

mbr
15 x 14

util 6 x 8
d w

eating 8 x 10

por 4 x 7

br 4
11 x 12

garage
24 x 22

kit
12x12
ref
rng
dw
ra

den
17 x 16

lin

br 3
11 x 12

sto

dining
11 x 12

foy

porch
11x9

br 2
11 x 11

MAIN FLOOR

Ten Foot Entry

━━━━ ■ *Total living area 1,604 sq. ft.* ■ *Price Code B* ■ ━━━━

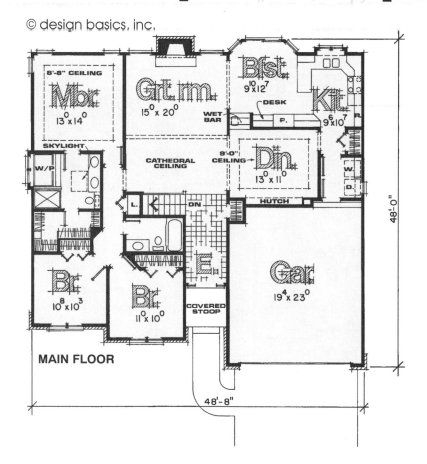

© design basics, inc.

MAIN FLOOR

48'-8"

No. 94986

■ **This plan features:**

— Three bedrooms

— Two full baths

■ Large volume Great Room highlighted by a fireplace flanked by windows

■ See-through wetbar enhancing the Breakfast area and the Dining Room

■ Decorative ceiling treatment giving elegance to the Dining Room

■ Fully equipped Kitchen with a planning desk and a pantry

■ Roomy Master Bedroom Suite has a skylighted dressing — bath area, plant shelf, a double vanity and a whirlpool tub

■ Secondary bedrooms share a convenient hall Bath

Main floor — 1,604 sq. ft.
Garage — 466 sq. ft.

Under A Spanish Influence

No. 10742

This plan features:

— Three bedrooms

— Two full baths

A trio of arches grace the Front Porch of this home

A fireplace, a half wall, and a cathedral ceiling add excitement to the Living room

The Dining room is conveniently located and features sliding doors to the rear Patio

The L-shaped Kitchen features a center island with a cooktop, while the skylight above lets in light

The Master bedroom has rear patio access, and a private bath

Two secondary bedrooms share a full bath in the hall

This plan has a two-car garage and a laundry room

Main floor — 1,617 sq. ft.
Garage — 528 sq. ft.

■ *Total living area 1,617 sq. ft.* ■ *Price Code B* ■

MAIN FLOOR

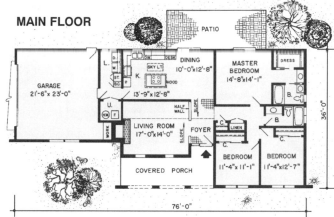

Outstanding Family Home

No. 96504

This plan features:

— Three bedrooms

— Two full baths

Split bedroom layout, perfect floor plan for a family with older children

Great Room including a cozy fireplace, access to the rear Porch and an open layout with the nook and kitchen

Extended counter in the kitchen providing a snack bar for meals or snacks

Formal dining room directly accessing the Kitchen

Bright Nook with a built-in pantry

Master suite includes access to rear Porch and a pampering bath and walk-in closet

Main floor — 2,162 sq. ft.
Garage — 498 sq. ft.

■ *Total living area 2,162 sq. ft.* ■ *Price Code C* ■

Main floor

Lakeside or Mountain Retreat

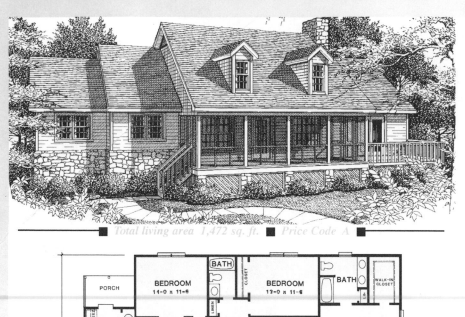

Total living area 1,472 sq. ft. ■ Price Code A

MAIN FLOOR

BEDROOM 14-0 x 11-6
BEDROOM 13-0 x 11-6
BATH
WALK-IN CLOSET
PORCH
CLOSET
LINEN
FREEZ CAB
WH
PANT
CLOSET
UTILITY 9-8 x 11-4
KITCHEN 11-0 x 11-2
W D
LIVING / DINING 24-2 x 13-6 CATHEDRAL CEILING
BEDROOM 15-8 x 16-0
CAB
SCREENED PORCH 26-0 x 10-0
WOOD DECK 16-0 x 8-0
36'-0"
62'-0"

■ **This plan features:**

— Three bedrooms

— Two full baths

■ The large Screened Porch allows for peaceful evening entertaining or relaxation

■ The Living/Dining room has a cathedral ceiling and a fireplace

■ The U-shaped see through Kitchen has a breakfast counter

■ The Master Bedroom has a walk-in closet and a private Bath

■ Two additional bedrooms share a full Bath

■ There is a Porch located in the rear of the home off of the utility room

■ An optional crawl space or a slab foundation — please specify when ordering

Main floor — 1,472 sq. ft.

Spacious Living Room

Total living area 2,483 sq. ft. ■ Price Code D

MAIN FLOOR

75'
BATH
CLOSET
MASTER SUITE 13×19
CLOSET
GARAGE 21×23
NOOK 9×9
PORCH
UTIL
KIT'N 12×14
DINING 12×12
STUDY 9×9
FOYER
PORCH
LIVING RM 18×25
BEDRM 11×15
CLOS.
BATH
HALL
BEDRM 12×12
BEDRM 11×13
BATH
8'-0" CEILINGS (TYPICAL)
61'-9"

■ **This plan features:**

— Four bedrooms

— Three full and one half baths

■ The spacious Living Room is topped by a decorative ceiling treatment and is enhanced by a corner fireplace

■ The Kitchen boasts a built in desk and an angled counter/snack bar

■ There is direct access to the formal Dining Room and the Breakfast Nook from the Kitchen

■ The secluded Master Suite has two walk-in closets and a five-piece Bath

■ Three additional bedrooms, located at the opposite side of the home, each have private access to the full Bath

■ An optional basement or a crawl space foundation — please specify when ordering

Main floor — 2,483 sq. ft.
Garage — 504 sq. ft.

■ *Total living area 3,477 sq. ft.* ■ *Price Code F* ■

No. 94220

■ This plan features:

— Three bedrooms

— Two full, one three quarter, and one half baths

■ Entry doors opening into the formal Living Room focusing to the Lanai

■ Double sided fireplace in the Living Room shared by the Master Suite

■ Island Kitchen easily serves all informal family areas

■ Octagon Nook with windows spanning to all views

■ Spacious Master suite including a fireplace, morning kitchen bar, and Lanai access

■ No materials list is available for this plan

Main floor – 3,477 sq. ft.
Garage – 771 sq. ft.

Classic Stucco with a High Hip Roof

■ *Total living area 2,598 sq. ft.* ■ *Price Code D* ■

No. 92127

Floor Plan
No. 92127

- Patio
- M. Br 18 x 17
- Living 13-8 x 17
- Patio
- Nook
- Kit.
- Family 16 x 18
- M.Bath
- Foyer
- DN.
- DN.
- PANTRY
- Br #3 10-3 x 11-6
- DESK
- Den 12-6 x 11
- BOOKS
- Dining 11-4 x 13
- Br #2 10-8 x 11
- Porch
- DESK
- Util.
- Garage 34-8 x 23-4
- 104'
- 78'

■ **This plan features:**

— Three bedrooms

— Two full and one half baths

■ An open layout between the Kitchen, Nook and Family Room allowing for spacious entertaining

■ An island Kitchen including a double sink, walk-in pantry and an abundance of counter and storage space

■ A fireplace in the sunken Family Room, adding a coziness to the entire family living area

■ A Master Suite that includes a private, compartmented Master Bath, walk-in closet and private Patio

■ A Den that includes built-in bookshelves and is located close to the Master Suite, making it convenient for late night work

Main floor — 2,598 sq. ft.
Garage — 828 sq. ft.

Cozy Front and Back Porches

No. 96523

This plan features:

— Three bedrooms

— Two full baths

A spacious Great Room is highlighted by a corner fireplace and access to the rear Porch

The Dining area with views of the front yard is separated from the Kitchen by an eating bar

The private Master Suite is tucked into the rear left corner of the home

A tray ceiling, a whirlpool tub and a walk-in closet highlight the Master Suite

Two additional bedrooms are located on the opposite side of the home, a full bath is between the bedrooms

Main floor — 1,652 sq. ft.
Garage — 497 sq. ft.

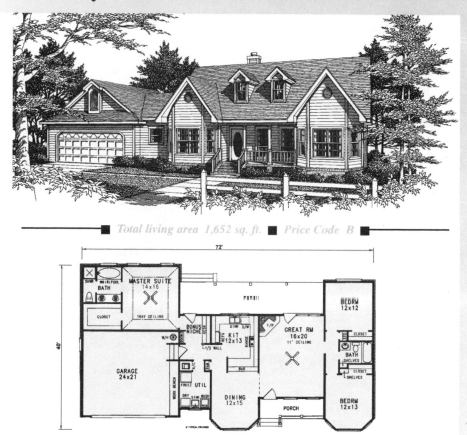

■ *Total living area 1,652 sq. ft.* ■ *Price Code B* ■

MAIN FLOOR

Larger Feeling Than Square Footage Indicates

No. 96419

This plan features:

— Three bedrooms

— Two full baths

Arched windows, dormers, front and side porches, rear deck, and an open interior give this home a larger feeling

Elegant columns define the Dining Room, while the Great Room gains an open and airy feeling from the cathedral ceiling and arched window above the sliding door

Master Suite pampers the owner with a private bath which includes a whirlpool tub, separate shower, double vanity, linen closet, and walk-in closet

An optional crawl space or basement foundation — please specify when ordering

First floor — 1,514 sq. ft.
Garage & Storage — 446 sq. ft.

© 1991 Donald A. Gardner Architects, Inc.

■ *Total living area 1,514 sq. ft.* ■ *Price Code C* ■

ALTERNATE PLAN
FOR BASEMENT

FLOOR PLAN

Morning Room Accents

■ *Total living area 2,466 sq. ft.* ■ *Price Code D* ■

No. 10445

■ **This plan features:**

— Three bedrooms

— Two full and one half baths

■ Tiled floors unifying the Dining and food preparation areas

■ A Morning Room located off the well-organized Kitchen

■ A Family Room employing more tile accents which opens to the patio

■ A secluded Master Bedroom which includes a sunken tub, small greenhouses, and ample closet space

Main floor — 2,466 sq. ft.
Garage — 482 sq. ft.

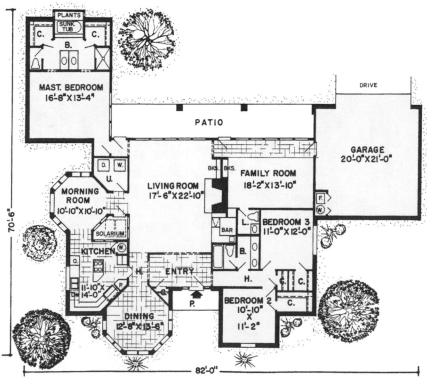

MAIN FLOOR

©1996 Donald A. Gardner Architects, Inc.

B. NATHAN

■ *Total living area 1,864 sq. ft.* ■ *Price Code C* ■

No. 96468

■ **This plan features:**

— Three bedrooms

— Two full baths

■ Sunlit Foyer flows easily into the generous Great Room

■ Great Room crowned in a cathedral ceiling and accented by a fireplace

■ Accent columns define the open Kitchen and Breakfast Bay

■ Master Bedroom topped by a tray ceiling and highlighted by a well-appointed Master Bath

■ Two additional bedrooms, sharing a skylit bath in the hall, create the children's wing

First floor—1,864 sq. ft.
Bonus room—319 sq. ft.
Garage—503 sq. ft.

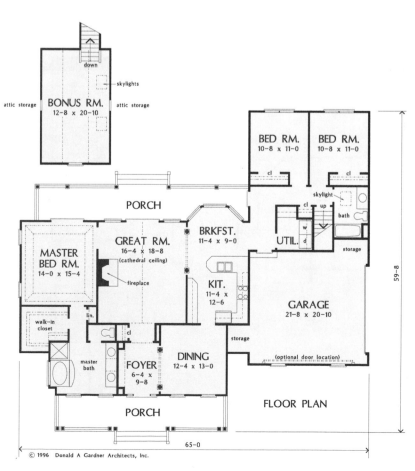

Small, Yet Lavishly Appointed

■ Total living area 1,845 sq. ft. ■ Price Code C ■

No. 98425

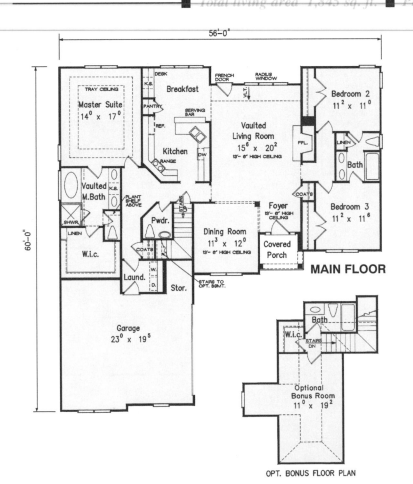

MAIN FLOOR

Master Suite 14⁰ x 17⁰
Breakfast
Vaulted Living Room 15⁶ x 20²
13'- 6" High Ceiling
Bedroom 2 11² x 11⁰
Kitchen
Vaulted M.Bath
Bath
Bedroom 3 11² x 11⁶
Pwdr.
Dining Room 11³ x 12⁰
13'- 6" High Ceiling
Foyer 13'- 6" High Ceiling
Covered Porch
W.i.c.
Laund.
Stor.
Garage 23⁰ x 19⁵

56'-0"
60'-0"

STAIRS TO OPT. BSMT.

Bath
W.i.c.
STAIRS DN
Optional Bonus Room 11⁰ x 19²

OPT. BONUS FLOOR PLAN

This plan features:

— Three bedrooms

— Two full and one half baths

■ The Dining Room, Living Room, Foyer and Master Bath all topped by high ceilings

■ Master Bedroom includes a decorative tray ceiling and a walk-in closet

■ Kitchen open to the Breakfast Room enhanced by a serving bar and a pantry

■ Living Room with a large fireplace and a French door to the rear yard

■ Master Suite located on opposite side from secondary bedrooms, allowing for privacy

■ An optional basement or crawl space foundation — please when ordering

Main floor — 1,845 sq. ft.
Bonus — 409 sq. ft.

Split Bedroom Plan

No. 98415

This plan features:

— Three bedrooms

— Two full baths

■ A tray ceiling giving a decorative touch the Master Bedroom and a vaulted ceiling topping the five-piece Master Bath

■ A full bath located between the secondary bedrooms

■ A corner fireplace and a vaulted ceiling highlighting the heart of the home, the Family Room

■ A wetbar, serving bar to the Family Room and a built-in pantry adding to the convenience of the Kitchen

■ A formal Dining Room crowned in an elegant high ceiling

■ An optional basement, crawl space or slab foundation — please specify when ordering

Main floor — 1,429 sq. ft.
Basement — 1,472 sq. ft.
Garage — 438 sq. ft.

Total living area 1,429 sq. ft. ■ Price Code A

MAIN FLOOR
WIDTH 49'-0"
DEPTH 53'-0"

One Level Beauty

No. 94967

This plan features:

— Three bedrooms

— Two full and one half baths

■ From the tiled entry one can view the terrific Great Room

■ A built-in wetbar and a three-sided fireplace, shared with the hearth room highlight the Great Room

■ A built-in entertainment center in the Hearth Room, which is open to the Kitchen and Breakfast Room

■ A sloped gazebo ceiling and a built-in hutch highlighting the Breakfast Room

■ Master Bedroom with an impressive and luxurious bath and a walk-in closet

■ Secondary bedrooms having private access to a full bath

Main floor — 2,355 sq. ft.
Garage — 673 sq. ft.

Total living area 2,355 sq. ft. ■ Price Code D

© design basics, inc.

WIDTH 70'-0"
DEPTH 62'-0"

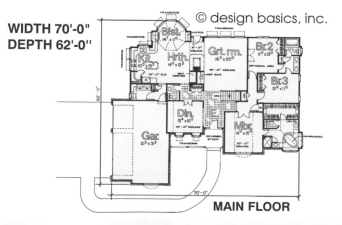

MAIN FLOOR

Cabin in the Country

Total living area 928 sq. ft. ■ *Price Code A* ■

No. 90433

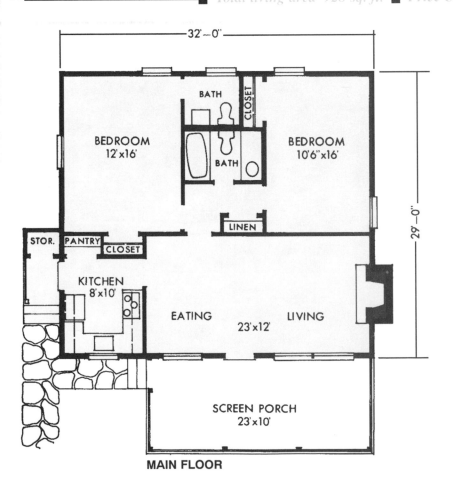

MAIN FLOOR

This plan features:

— Two bedrooms

— One full and one half baths

■ A Screened Porch for enjoyment of your outdoor surroundings

■ A combination Living and Dining area with cozy fireplace for added warmth

■ An efficiently laid out Kitchen with a built-in pantry

■ Two large bedrooms located at the rear of the home

■ An optional slab or crawl space foundation — please specify when ordering

Main floor — 928 sq. ft.
Screened porch — 230 sq. ft.
Storage — 14 sq. ft.

Vaulted Ceilings and Skylights

■ *Total living area 2,496 sq. ft.* ■ *Price Code D* ■

No. 98733 ⚒

■ **This plan features:**

— Three bedrooms

— Two full baths

■ A sheltered entrance leading to a large Living Room topped by a vaulted ceiling and enhanced by a large bay window and a fireplace

■ A formal Dining Room with arched openings and a vaulted ceiling

■ A large fireplace in the Family Room is equipped with a built-in entertainment center

■ A cooktop island/eating bar and a walk-in pantry add to the Kitchen that is open to the Nook

■ A privately situated Master Suite including an ultra bath and direct access to the side Porch that is equipped with a hot tub

Main floor — 2,496 sq. ft.
Garage — 827 sq. ft.

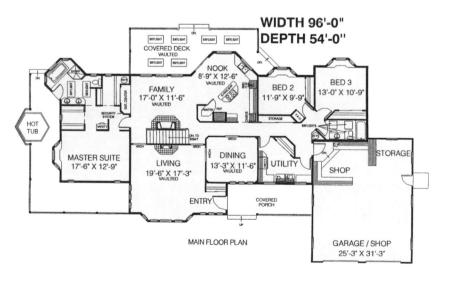

WIDTH 96'-0"
DEPTH 54'-0"

COVERED DECK
VAULTED

NOOK
8'-9" X 12'-6"
VAULTED

FAMILY
17'-0" X 11'-6"
VAULTED

BED 2
11'-9" X 9'-9"

BED 3
13'-0" X 10'-9"

SECURITY
SYSTEM

PANTRY REF

STORAGE

SKYLIGHTS

HOT
TUB

VANITY

STORAGE

MASTER SUITE
17'-6" X 12'-9"

LIVING
19'-6" X 17'-3"
VAULTED

ARCH

DINING
13'-3" X 11'-6"
VAULTED

UTILITY

SHOP

ENTRY

COVERED
PORCH

MAIN FLOOR PLAN

GARAGE / SHOP
25'-3" X 31'-3"

Fireplace Center of Circular Living Area

■ **This plan features:**

— Three bedrooms

— One full and one three quarter baths

■ A dramatically positioned fireplace as a focal point for the main living area

■ The Kitchen, Dining and Living Rooms form a circle that allows work areas to flow into living areas

■ Sliding glass doors accessible to wood a Deck

■ A convenient Laundry Room located off the Kitchen

■ A double Garage providing excellent storage

Main area— 1,783 sq. ft.
Garage — 576 sq. ft.

■ Total living area 1,783 sq. ft. ■ Price Code B ■

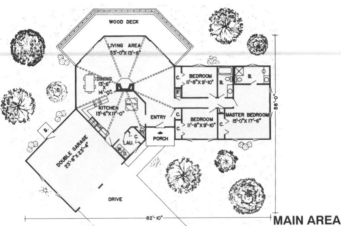

MAIN AREA

Small, But Not Lacking

No. 94116

■ **This plan features:**

— Three bedrooms

— One full and one three quarter baths

■ Great Room adjoining the Dining Room for ease in entertaining

■ Kitchen highlighted by a peninsula counter/snack bar extending work space and offering convenience in serving informal meals or snacks

■ Split bedroom plan allowing for privacy for the Master Bedroom suite with a private bath and a walk-in closet

■ Two additional bedrooms sharing the full family bath in the hall

■ Garage entry convenient to the kitchen

Main floor — 1,546 sq. ft.
Basement — 1,530 sq. ft.
Garage — 440 sq. ft.

■ Total living area 1,546 sq. ft. ■ Price Code C ■

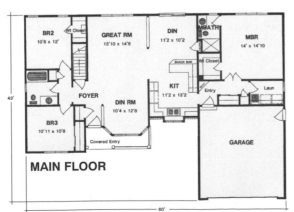

MAIN FLOOR

Spacious and Convenient Ranch

■ *Total living area 1,720 sq. ft.* ■ *Price Code B*

No. 99057

This plan features:

— Three bedrooms

— One full and one three-quarter baths

■ Portico offers a sheltered entrance into Foyer and formal Living Room

■ Convenient Family Room with inviting fireplace, Patio access and nearby Laundry/Garage entry

■ Formal Dining Room highlighted by back yard view

■ U-shaped, efficient Kitchen with pantry and peninsula serving counter

■ Corner Master Bedroom offers three closets and a private bath

■ Two additional bedrooms share a full bath

Main floor — 1,720 sq. ft.
Basement — 1,630 sq. ft.

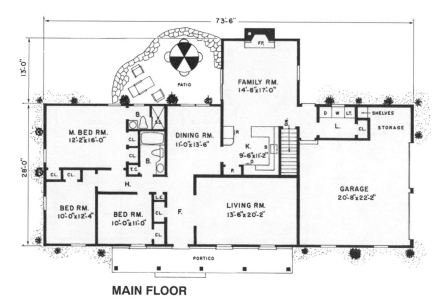

MAIN FLOOR

Formal Balance

Total living area 1,476 sq. ft. ■ Price Code A

No. 90689

This plan features:

— Three bedrooms

— Two full baths

■ A cathedral ceiling in the Living Room with a heat-circulating fireplace as the focal point

■ A bow window in the Dining Room that adds elegance as well as natural light

■ A well-equipped Kitchen that serves both the Dinette and the formal Dining Room efficiently

■ A Master Bedroom with three closets and a private Master Bath with sliding glass doors to the Master Deck with a hot tub

Main floor — 1,476 sq. ft.
Basement — 1,361 sq. ft.
Garage — 548 sq. ft.

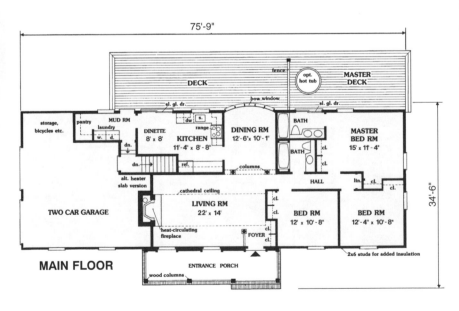

Elegant Entry Adorned With Columns

■ *Total living area 1,955 sq. ft.* ■ *Price Code C* ■

No. 93031

■ This plan features:

— Three bedrooms

— Two full baths

■ An angled Foyer opens to a large Great Room with a fireplace

■ A formal Dining Room is defined with a series of columns

■ A Master Bath with an angled whirlpool tub, separate shower and double vanity

■ A coffered ceiling treatment in the Breakfast Room which adds character

■ No materials list is available for this plan

Main floor — 1,955 sq. ft.
Bonus area — 240 sq. ft.
Garage — 561 sq. ft.

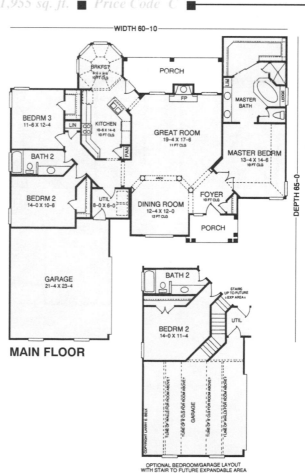

Luxury on One Level

Total living area 2,196 sq. ft. ■ Price Code C

✩ Good!

No. 93190

This plan features:

— Three bedrooms

— Two full and one half bath

■ Covered Front Porch leads into Entry and Great Room with vaulted ceilings

■ Huge Great Room perfect for entertaining or family gatherings with cozy fireplace

■ Arched soffits and columns surround the formal Dining Room

■ Country-size Kitchen with a pantry, work island, bright, eating Nook with Screen Porch beyond, and nearby Laundry/Garage entry

■ Corner Master Bedroom offers a large walk-in closet and a luxurious bath with a double vanity and spa tub

Main floor — 2,196 sq. ft.

Basement — 2,196 sq. ft.

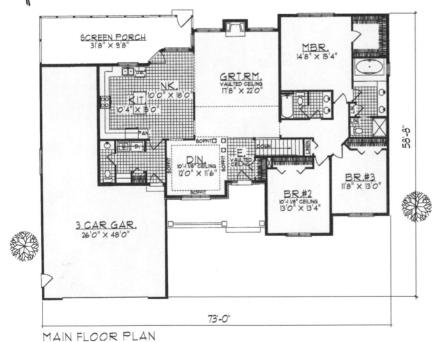

MAIN FLOOR PLAN

An
EXCLUSIVE DESIGN
By Ahmann Design Inc.

Gazebo Porch Creates Old-Fashioned Feel

No. 24718

This plan features:

— Three bedrooms

— Two full baths

■ An old-fashioned welcome is created by the covered Porch

■ The Breakfast area overlooks the Porch and is separated from the Kitchen by an extended counter

■ The Dining room and the Great room are highlighted by a two sided fireplace, enhancing the temperature as well as the atmosphere

■ The roomy Master suite is enhanced by a whirlpool bath with double vanity and a walk in closet

■ Each of the two secondary Bedrooms feature a walk-in closet

■ No materials list is available for this plan

Main floor — 1,452 sq. ft.
Garage — 584 sq. ft.

Total living area 1,452 sq. ft. ■ Price Code A

MAIN FLOOR

Ideal Ranch

No. 93130

This plan features:

— Three bedrooms

— Two full baths

■ A spacious Living Room with a vaulted ceiling that catches your eye as you enter

■ An open floor plan, making the rooms seem more spacious

■ A private Master Suite with a walk-in closet and terrific Master Bath

■ Two additional bedrooms with ample closet space that share a full bath

■ Stairs off the Foyer that lead to a lower level, where there is plenty of room for future expansion

■ No materials list is available for this plan

Main floor — 1,508 sq. ft.
Basement — 1,508 sq. ft.
Garage — 400 sq. ft.

Total living area 1,508 sq. ft. ■ Price Code B ■

An EXCLUSIVE DESIGN *By Ahmann Design Inc.*

WIDTH — 52'-0"
DEPTH — 44'-0"

MAIN FLOOR PLAN

Attractive Combination of Brick and Siding

Total living area 2,010 sq. ft. ■ Price Code C

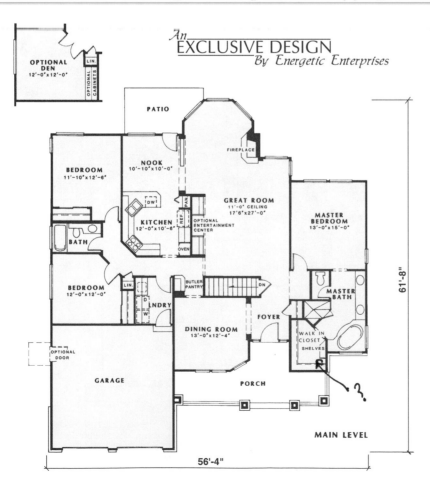

OPTIONAL DEN
12'-0"x12'-0"

OPTIONAL CABINETS

LIN.

An EXCLUSIVE DESIGN
By Energetic Enterprises

PATIO

BEDROOM
11'-10"x12'-6"

NOOK
10'-10"x10'-0"

FIREPLACE

KITCHEN
12'-0"x10'-6"

OPTIONAL ENTERTAINMENT CENTER

OVEN

GREAT ROOM
11'-0" CEILING
17'6"x27'-0"

MASTER BEDROOM
13'-0"x15'-0"

BEDROOM
12'-0"x12'-0"

LIN.

BUTLER PANTRY

LNDRY

D W

DN

MASTER BATH

BATH

DINING ROOM
13'-0"x12'-4"

FOYER

WALK IN CLOSET
SHELVES

OPTIONAL DOOR

GARAGE

PORCH

MAIN LEVEL

56'-4"

61'-8"

No. 24259

■ **This plan features:**

— Three Bedrooms

— Two full Baths

■ A Great Room sunny bayed area, fireplace and built-in entertainment center

■ A private Master Bedroom with luxurious Master Bath and walk-in closet

■ Dining Room has a Butler Pantry

■ Two additional Bedrooms have use of hall full Bath

Main level — 2,010 sq. ft.
Basement — 2,010 sq. ft.

Traditional Beauty

© 1993 Donald A Gardner Architects, Inc.

■ Total living area 1,576 sq. ft. ■ Price Code C ■

No. 99802

■ **This plan features:**

— Three bedrooms

— Two full baths

■ Traditional beauty with large arched windows, round columns, covered porch, brick veneer, and an open floor plan

■ Clerestory dormers above covered porch lighting the Foyer

■ Cathedral ceiling enhancing the Great Room along with a cozy fireplace

■ Island Kitchen with Breakfast area accessing the large Deck with an optional spa

■ Tray ceiling over the Master Bedroom, Dining Room and Bedroom/Study

■ Dual vanity, separate shower, and whirlpool tub in the Master Bath

Main floor — 1,576 sq. ft.
Garage — 465 sq. ft.

123

Plenty of Room

Total living area 1,199 sq. ft. ■ *Price Code C*

MAIN FLOOR

No. 91107

■ **This plan features:**

— Three bedrooms

— Two full baths

■ The entry to this home has a covered Porch and an 11' ceiling in the Foyer

■ The 11' ceiling continues into the Living room which is highlighted by a corner fireplace

■ A plant shelf is located above the Dining room

■ The galley Kitchen has a pantry, a double sink, and a snack bar

■ The large Master bedroom, has a built in book shelf, a walk-in closet, and a private bath

■ Just down the hall is a laundry closet, a full bath, and two secondary bedrooms

■ No materials list is available for this plan

Main floor — 1,199 sq. ft.
Garage — 484 sq. ft.

Convenient and Efficient Ranch

Total living area 1,810 sq. ft. ■ *Price Code C*

No. 93311

■ **This plan features:**

— Three bedrooms

— Two full and one half baths

■ A barrel vault ceiling in the Foyer

■ A stepped ceiling in both the Dinette and the formal Dining Room

■ An expansive Gathering Room with a large focal point fireplace and access to the wood deck

■ An efficient Kitchen that includes a work island and a built-in pantry

■ A luxurious Master Suite with a private bath that includes a separate tub and step-in shower

■ Two additional bedrooms that share a full hall bath

■ No materials list is available for this plan

Main floor — 1,810 sq. ft.
Garage — 528 sq. ft.

An EXCLUSIVE DESIGN
By Patrick Morabito, A.I.A. Architect

■ *Total living area 1,293 sq. ft.* ■ *Price Code B* ■

No. 92523

■ This plan features:

— Three bedrooms

— Two full baths

■ A spacious Great Room enhanced by a vaulted ceiling and fireplace

■ A well-equipped Kitchen with windowed double sink

■ A secluded Master Suite with decorative ceiling, private Master Bath, and walk-in closet

■ Two additional bedrooms sharing hall bath

■ Optional crawl space or slab foundation — please specify when ordering

Main floor — 1,293 sq. ft.
Garage — 433 sq. ft.

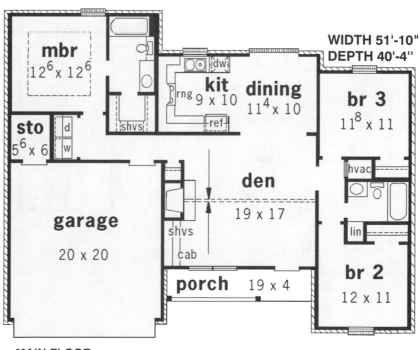

WIDTH 51'-10"
DEPTH 40'-4''

mbr
12^6 x 12^6

sto
5^6 x 6

garage
20 x 20

kit
9 x 10

dining
11^4 x 10

den
19 x 17

br 3
11^8 x 11

br 2
12 x 11

porch 19 x 4

shvs

rng

ref

shvs

cab

hvac

lin

d w

MAIN FLOOR

Affordable Style

Total living area 1,490 sq. ft. ■ Price Code A

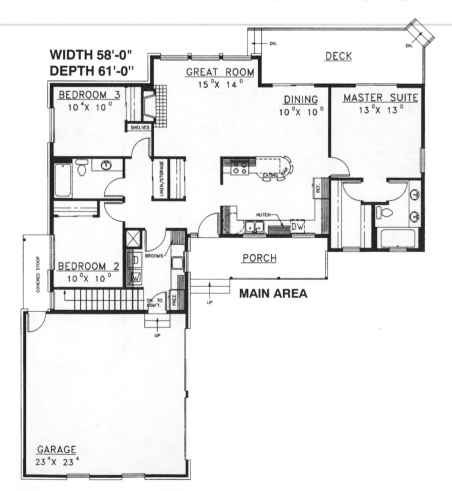

WIDTH 58'-0"
DEPTH 61'-0"

GREAT ROOM
15⁰ X 14⁰

DECK

BEDROOM 3
10⁴ X 10⁰

SHELVES

DINING
10⁰ X 10⁰

MASTER SUITE
13⁰ X 13⁰

LINEN/STORAGE

EATING BAR

REF.

DW

HUTCH

BROOMS

BEDROOM 2
10⁰ X 10⁰

COVERED STOOP

PORCH

W

DN. TO BSM'T.

FREZ.

UP

MAIN AREA

UP

GARAGE
23⁴ X 23⁴

No. 91753

■ This plan features:

— Three bedrooms

— Two full baths

■ A well-appointed Kitchen boasts a double sink, ample counter and storage space, a peninsula eating bar and a built-in hutch

■ A terrific Master Suite including a private bath and a walk-in closet

■ A Dining Room that flows from the Great Room and into the Kitchen that includes sliding glass doors to the deck

■ A Great Room with a cozy fireplace that can also be enjoyed from the Dining area

■ No materials list is available for this plan

Main area— 1,490 sq. ft.
Covered porch — 120 sq. ft.
Basement — 1,490 sq. ft.
Garage — 579 sq. ft.

■ *Total living area 1,484 sq. ft.* ■ *Price Code A* ■

No. 35005

■ This plan features:

— Three bedrooms

— One full and one three quarter baths

■ A sheltered front entrance

■ A formal Living Room, located at the front of this home, flows to the rear into the formal Dining Room

■ An efficient U-shaped Kitchen situated between the formal Dining Room and the Family Room

■ A double sink, built-in pantry, and a peninsula counter/eating bar highlighting the Kitchen

■ A large fireplace in the Family Room that can also be enjoyed from the Kitchen

■ A Master Suite equipped with a full Bath and a double closet

Main floor — 1,484 sq. ft.
Garage — 480 sq. ft.

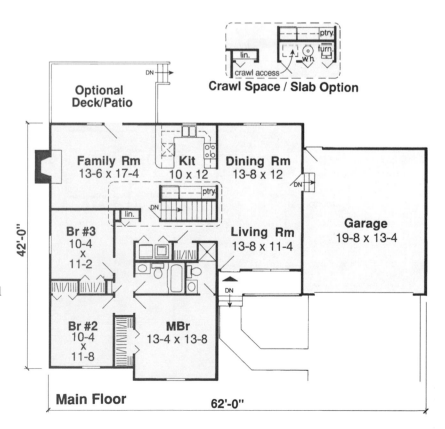

Crawl Space / Slab Option

Main Floor

Optional Deck/Patio

Family Rm
13-6 x 17-4

Kit
10 x 12

Dining Rm
13-8 x 12

Br #3
10-4 x 11-2

Living Rm
13-8 x 11-4

Garage
19-8 x 13-4

Br #2
10-4 x 11-8

MBr
13-4 x 13-8

42'-0"

62'-0"

Covered Porch with Columns

Total living area 1,856 sq. ft. ■ *Price Code C*

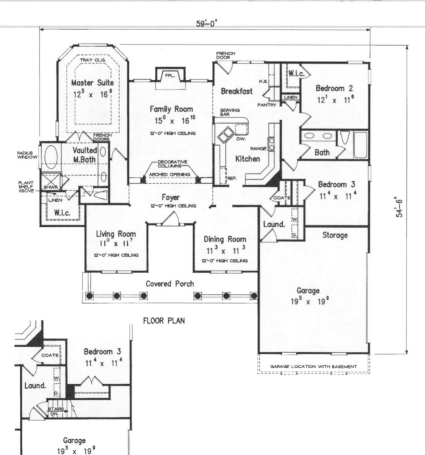

FLOOR PLAN

OPT. BASEMENT STAIR LOCATION

No. 98408

This plan features:

— Three bedrooms

— Two full baths

■ The foyer with 12' ceiling leads past decorative columns into the Family room with a center fireplace

■ The Living Room and Dining Room are linked by the Foyer and have windows overlooking the Front Porch

■ The Kitchen has a serving bar and is adjacent to the breakfast nook which has a French door that opens to the backyard

■ The private Master Suite has a tray ceiling and a vaulted Bath with a double vanity

■ An optional basement, slab or a crawl space foundation — please specify when ordering

Main floor — 1,856 sq. ft.
Garage — 429 sq. ft.

Stately Home

No. 96435

This plan features:

— Four bedrooms

— Two full and one half baths

■ An elegant brick exterior and careful detailing

■ Light floods through the arched window in the clerestory dormer above the foyer

■ Great Room topped by a cathedral ceiling boasting built-in cabinets and bookshelves

■ Through glass doors capped by an arched window the Sun Room is access from the Great Room

■ Both the Dining Room and the Bedroom/Study have tray ceilings

■ Master Suite includes a fireplace, access to the deck, his and her vanities, a shower and a whirlpool tub

■ An optional basement or crawl space foundation — please specify when ordering

Main floor — 2,526 sq. ft.
Garage — 611 sq. ft.

© 1992 Donald A. Gardner Architects, Inc.

Total living area 2,526 sq. ft. ■ *Price Code E* ■

Great Room With Cathedral Ceiling

No. 94970

This plan features:

— Three bedrooms

— One full and one three quarter baths

■ A convenient split ranch design with three steps up from the entry to the Great Room

■ Bay window, fireplace and an outstanding volume ceiling highlight the Great Room

■ Dinette's angled shaped accented by windows on the corner angles and a vaulted ceiling

■ Efficient family Kitchen with snack bar/island counter plus a corner sink and built-in pantry

■ Master bedroom is enhanced by a tiered ceiling, three quartered bath and a boxed window

■ Two additional bedrooms share a full bath in the hall

Main floor — 1,385 sq. ft.
Garage — 658 sq. ft.

Total living area 1,385 sq. ft. ■ *Price Code A* ■

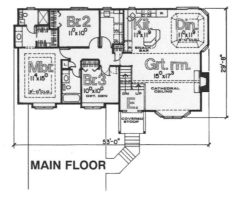

MAIN FLOOR

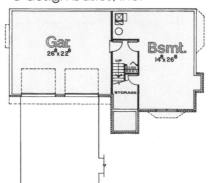

© design basics, inc.

Open Air Ranch

■ *Total living area 1,901 sq. ft.* ■ *Price Code C* ■

No. 84014

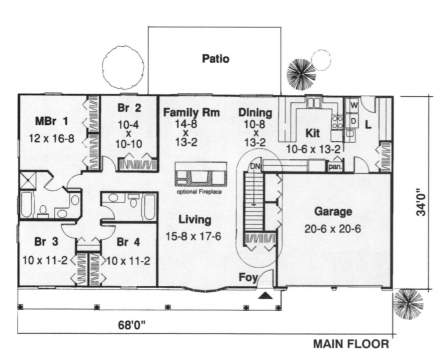

MAIN FLOOR

68'0"

34'0"

Patio

MBr 1
12 x 16-8

Br 2
10-4 x 10-10

Family Rm
14-8 x 13-2

Dining
10-8 x 13-2

Kit
10-6 x 13-2

W
D
L

optional Fireplace

DN

pan.

Living
15-8 x 17-6

Garage
20-6 x 20-6

Br 3
10 x 11-2

Br 4
10 x 11-2

Foy

■ **This plan features:**

— Four bedrooms

— Two full baths

■ Stone fireplace, wood storage and bookshelves separate the Living room from the Family room

■ The Dining room features doors to the rear patio

■ A convenient U-shaped kitchen is highlighted by a double sink, a pantry, and ample counter space

■ A Laundry/Utility room is located off of the two-car Garage

■ Three bedrooms share a full Bath

■ The Master bedroom has two closets and a private Bath with a dual vanity

■ No materials list is available for this plan

Main floor — 1,901 sq. ft.
Garage — 420 sq. ft.

Illusion of Spaciousness

© 1997 Donald A. Gardner Architects, Inc.

■ *Total living area 1,246 sq. ft.* ■ *Price Code B* ■

No. 96484

■ This plan features:

— Three bedrooms

— Two full baths

■ Open living spaces and vaulted ceilings creating an illusion of spaciousness

■ Cathedral ceilings maximize space in Great Room and Dining Room

■ Kitchen features skylight and breakfast bar

■ Well equipped Master Suite in rear for privacy

■ Two additional bedrooms in front share a full bath

Main floor — 1,246 sq. ft.
Garage — 420 sq. ft.

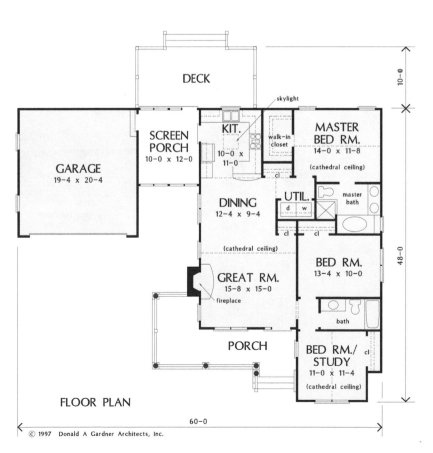

FLOOR PLAN

© 1997 Donald A Gardner Architects, Inc.

Magnificent Master Suite

■ *Total living area 1,702 sq. ft.* ■ *Price Code B* ■

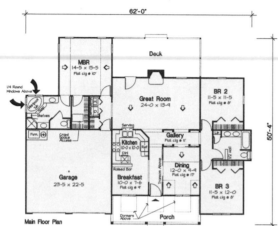

No. 24719

■ **This plan features:**

— Three bedrooms

— Two full baths

■ Soft arches and friendly dormers enhance covered Porch

■ Front hall between Kitchen and Dining Room leads to Gallery and Great Room beyond

■ Formal Dining Room with dormer window and pocket doors

■ Expansive Great Room with a cozy fireplace and Deck access

■ Angled and efficient Kitchen with serving counter, extended raised bar and bright Breakfast area

■ Secluded Master Bedroom with a large walk-in closet and lavish bath with a double vanity and a corner whirlpool tub

■ Two additional bedrooms with ample closets, share a double vanity bath

■ No materials list is available for this plan

Main floor — 1,702 sq. ft.
Garage — 540 sq. ft.

Daytime Delight

■ *Total living area 1,653 sq. ft.* ■ *Price Code B* ■

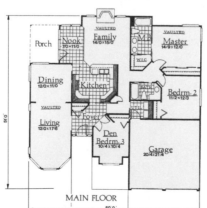

MAIN FLOOR

No. 91607

■ **This plan features:**

— Three bedrooms

— Two full baths

■ A large, vaulted ceiling in the Living Room and Dining Room, that flows together and is accentuated by huge windows

■ A centrally-located Kitchen with a double sink, and ample cabinet and counter space

■ A glass-walled eating Nook with access to a covered porch

■ A vaulted ceiling in the Family Room, with a focal point fireplace

■ An exciting Master Suite with a vaulted ceiling, a walk-in closet and a private double vanity Bath

■ Two additional bedrooms, one with French doors, served by a full hall Bath

Main floor — 1,653 sq. ft.

■ *Total living area 1,884 sq. ft.* ■ *Price Code C* ■

No. 98430

■ This plan features:

— Three bedrooms

— Two full and one half baths

■ Arched openings highlight the hallway accessing the Great Room

■ A French door to the rear yard and decorative columns at its arched entrance

■ Another vaulted ceiling topping the dining room

■ An expansive kitchen features a center work island, a built-in pantry and a breakfast area

■ A Master Suite also has a tray ceiling treatment and has a lavish private bath

■ An optional basement, slab or crawl space foundation — please specify when ordering

Main floor – 1,884 sq. ft.
Basement – 1,908 sq. ft.
Garage – 495 sq. ft.

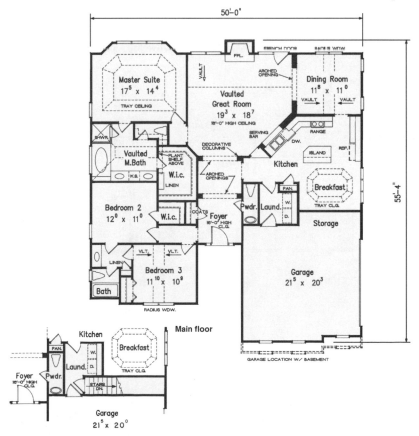

Surprisingly Spacious for a Smaller Home

Total living area 1,958 sq. ft. ■ Price Code C

No. 98743

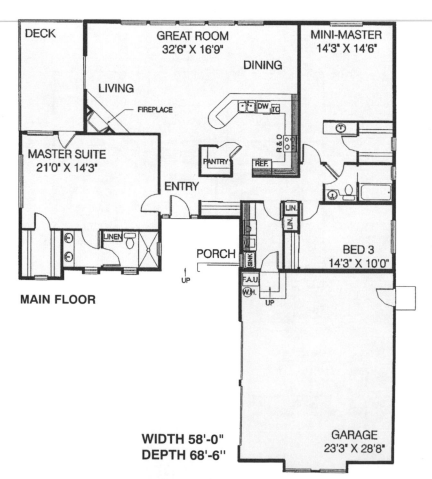

DECK

GREAT ROOM
32'6" X 16'9"

MINI-MASTER
14'3" X 14'6"

DINING

LIVING

FIREPLACE

MASTER SUITE
21'0" X 14'3"

PANTRY

REF.

ENTRY

LIN.

LIN.

LINEN

PORCH

UP

MAIN FLOOR

F.A.U.
W.H.

UP

BED 3
14'3" X 10'0"

WIDTH 58'-0"
DEPTH 68'-6"

GARAGE
23'3" X 28'8"

This plan features:

— Three bedrooms

— Two full baths

■ A vaulted ceiling in the richly illuminated Foyer, which presents three choices of direction

■ An eye-catching Great Room with a vaulted ceiling, a corner fireplace and a bank of windows on the rear wall

■ An efficient U-shaped Kitchen with an angled eating bar

■ A luxurious Master Suite that includes access to the rear deck and a private bath

■ A Mini-Master Suite that includes a walk-in closet with a vanity right outside and private access to the hall bath

■ No materials list is available for this plan

Main floor — 1,958 sq. ft.

■ Total living area 2,280 sq. ft. ■ Price Code D ■

No. 91796

■ **This plan features:**

— Three bedrooms

— Two full baths

■ Covered Deck leads into Entry and expansive Living Room and Deck beyond

■ Living/Dining room area surrounded by windows and Deck also offers a cozy fireplace topped by a vaulted ceiling

■ Open Kitchen with a walk-in pantry and a work island with sink

■ Private Master Suite offers a walk-in closet, a dual vanity and a nearby Office

■ Two additional bedrooms with ample closets, share a full Bath and Utility area

Main floor — 2,280 sq. ft.
Garage — 440 sq. ft.

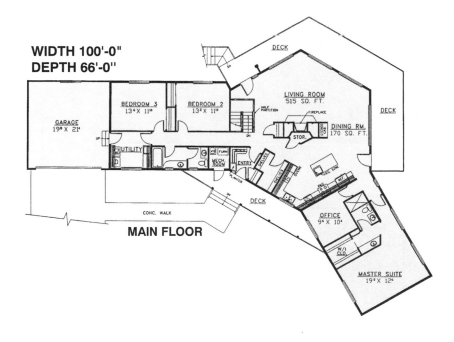

WIDTH 100'-0"
DEPTH 66'-0"

MAIN FLOOR

Relaxed Country Living

© 1997 Donald A. Gardner Architects, Inc.

■ *Total living area 2,027 sq. ft.* ■ *Price Code D* ■

No. 96402

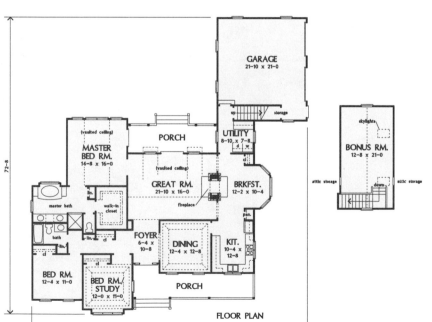

FLOOR PLAN

© 1997 Donald A. Gardner Architects, Inc.

This plan features:

— Three bedrooms

— Two full baths

■ Comfortable country home with deluxe Master Suite, front and back Porches and dual-sided fireplace

■ Vaulted Great Room brightened by two clerestory dormers and fireplace shared with Breakfast bay

■ Dining Room and front Bedroom/Study dressed up with tray ceilings

■ Master Bedroom features vaulted ceiling, and luxurious Bath with over-sized, walk-in closet

■ Skylit Bonus Room over Garage provides extra room for family needs

Main floor — 2,027 sq. ft.
Bonus room — 340 sq. ft.
Garage & storage — 532 sq. ft.

Brick Details Add Class

No. 93165

This plan features:

— Three bedrooms

— Two full baths

- Keystone entrance leads into easy care, tile Entry with plant ledge and convenient closet

- Expansive Great Room with cathedral ceiling over triple window and a corner gas fireplace

- Hub Kitchen accented by arches and columns serving Great Room and Dining area, near laundry area and Garage

- Adjoining Dining area with large windows, access to rear yard and Screen Porch

- Private Master Bedroom suite with a walk-in closet and plush bath with corner whirlpool tub

- Two additional bedrooms share a full bath

- No materials list is available for this plan

Main floor — 1,472 sq. ft.
Basement — 1,472 sq. ft.
Garage — 424 sq. ft.

*This plan is not to be built within a 20 mile radius of Iowa City, IA.

Total living area 1,472 sq. ft. ■ Price Code A

MAIN FLOOR PLAN

An
EXCLUSIVE DESIGN
By Ahmann Design Inc.

Abundance of Closet Space

No. 20204

This plan features:

— Three bedrooms

— Two full baths

- Roomy walk-in closets in all the bedrooms

- A Master Bedroom with decorative ceiling and a private full bath

- A fireplaced Living Room with sloped ceilings and sliders to the deck

- An efficient Kitchen, with plenty of cupboard space and a pantry

Main area —1,532 sq. ft.
Garage — 484 sq. ft.

An
EXCLUSIVE DESIGN
By Karl Kreeger

Total living area 1,532 sq. ft. ■ Price Code B

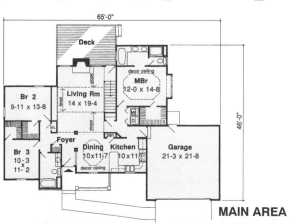

MAIN AREA

137

Champagne Style on a Soda-Pop Budget

Total living area 988 sq. ft. ■ Price Code A

No. 24302

This plan features:

— Three bedrooms

— One full and one three quarter baths

■ Multiple gables, circle-top windows, and a unique exterior setting this delightful Ranch apart in any neighborhood

■ Living and Dining Rooms flowing together to create a very roomy feeling

■ Sliding doors leading from the Dining Room to a covered Patio

■ A Master Bedroom with a private Bath

Main area — 988 sq. ft.
Basement — 988 sq. ft.
Garage — 280 sq. ft
Optional 2-car garage — 384 sq. ft.

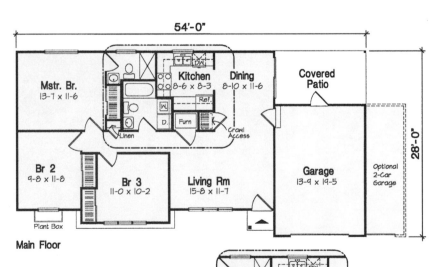

Main Floor

Optional Basement Plan

An EXCLUSIVE DESIGN *By Marshall Associates*

138

■ *Total living area 2,978 sq. ft.* ■ *Price Code E* ■

No. 94242

■ This plan features:

— Three bedrooms

— Two full, one three quarter, and one half baths

■ Wonderfully balanced exterior highlighted by triple arched glass in Entry Porch, leading into the Gallery Foyer

■ Triple arches lead into Formal Living and Dining Room, Verandah and beyond

■ Kitchen, Nook, and Leisure Room area easily flow together

■ Owners' wing has a Master Suite with glass alcove to rear yard, a lavish bath and a Study offering many uses

■ No materials list is available for this plan

Main floor — 2,978 sq. ft
Garage — 702 sq. ft.

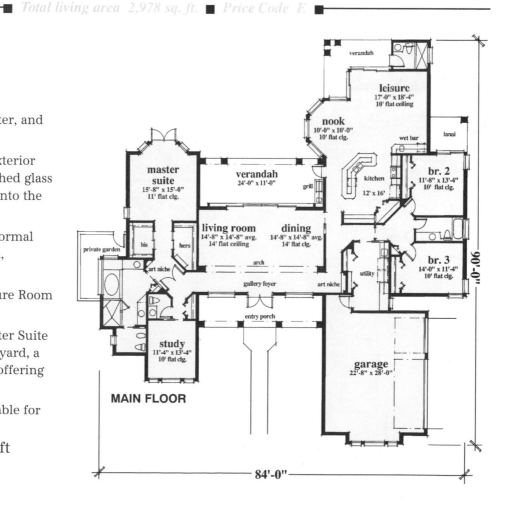

MAIN FLOOR

Attractive Styling

Total living area 1,849 sq. ft. ■ Price Code B

No. 93427

This plan features:

— Three bedrooms

— Two full baths

■ Tremendous style and presence created by windows, sidelights and transoms combined with a dramatic entrance

■ Formal Dining Room, off the Foyer, enjoying a view of the front yard and access to the Family Room

■ A grand fireplace, with windows to either side, serves as a focal point

■ Breakfast Room/Kitchen are open to the Family Room

■ Secluded Master Suite with walk-in closet, recessed ceiling and five-piece bath

■ Two additional bedrooms located at the opposite side of the home

■ No materials lists is available for this plan

Main floor — 1,849 sq. ft.
Garage — 555 sq. ft.

MAIN FLOOR

An
EXCLUSIVE DESIGN
By Greg Marquis

Light and Airy

Total living area 1,643 sq. ft. ■ Price Code B

No. 10745

This plan features:

— Three bedrooms

— One full and one three quarter baths

■ An open plan with cathedral ceilings

■ A fireplaced Great Room flowing into the Dining Room

■ A Master Bedroom with a private Master Bath

■ An efficient Kitchen, with Laundry area and pantry in close proximity

Main area — 1,643 sq. ft.
Basement — 1,643 sq. ft.
Garage — 484 sq. ft.

MAIN AREA

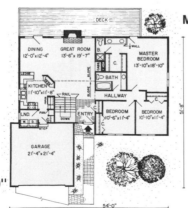

WIDTH 66'-4"
DEPTH 59'-10"

A Home for Today's Lifestyle

■ *Total living area 2,787 sq. ft.* ■ *Price Code E* ■

No. 92902

■ **This plan features:**

— Four bedrooms

— Three full baths

■ Family living area comprised of a family room, breakfast area, and island kitchen

■ Formal Dining Room with easy access from the Kitchen

■ Pampering Master Suite with private Master Bath and an abundance of storage space

■ Three additional full bath, having ample closet space

■ Screened porch and covered patio extending living space outdoors

■ No materials list is available for this plan

Main floor — 2,782 sq. ft.
Garage — 685 sq. ft.

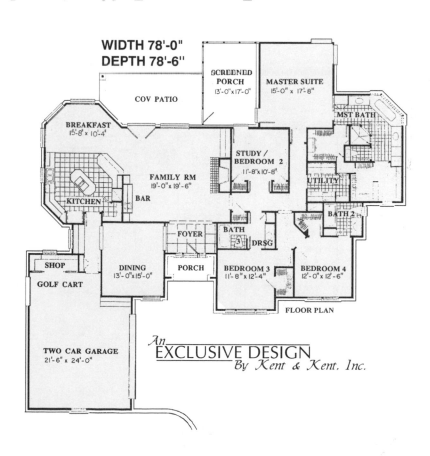

Designed For Easy Building And Easy Living

© 1996 Donald A Gardner Architects, Inc.

■ *Total living area 1,800 sq. ft.* ■ *Price Code C* ■

No. 99814

FLOOR PLAN

© 1996 Donald A Gardner Architects, Inc.

■ **This plan features:**

— Three Bedrooms

— Two full baths

■ Refined, traditional exterior created by brick, double dormers, and a hip roof

■ Foyer opens to a generous Great Room with cathedral ceiling and fireplace

■ Columns define entrance to Kitchen with a center island

■ Master Bedroom, Dining Room, and front Bedroom/Study receive distinction from tray ceilings

Main floor — 1,800 sq. ft.
Garage — 477 sq. ft.

142

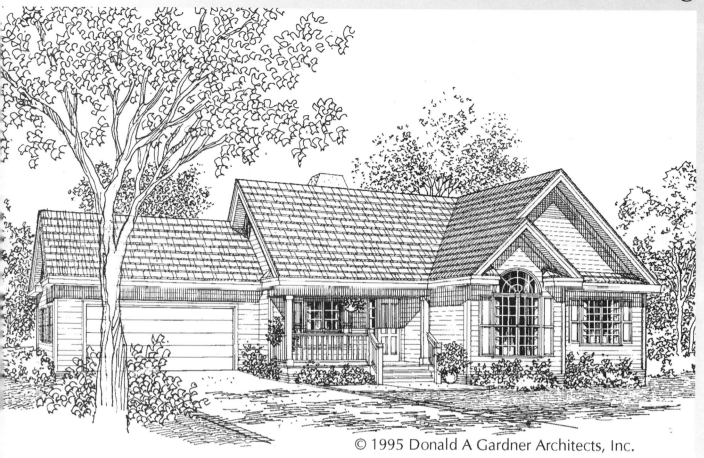

© 1995 Donald A Gardner Architects, Inc.

■ *Total living area 1,417 sq. ft.* ■ *Price Code B* ■

No. 99809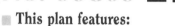

■ This plan features:

— Three bedrooms

— Two full baths

■ Cathedral ceiling expanding the Great room, Dining Room and Kitchen

■ A versatile bedroom or study topped by a cathedral ceiling accented by double circle-top windows

■ Master Suite complete with a cathedral ceiling, including a bath with a garden tub, linen closet and a walk-in closet

Main floor — 1,417 sq. ft.
Garage — 441 sq. ft.

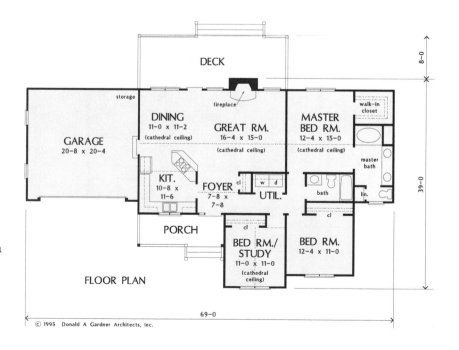

DECK

8-0

storage

DINING
11-0 x 11-2
(cathedral ceiling)

fireplace

GREAT RM.
16-4 x 15-0
(cathedral ceiling)

walk-in closet

MASTER BED RM.
12-4 x 15-0
(cathedral ceiling)

GARAGE
20-8 x 20-4

KIT.
10-8 x 11-6

FOYER
7-8 x 7-8

cl

w d

UTIL.

master bath

bath

lin.

39-0

PORCH

cl

BED RM./ STUDY
11-0 x 11-0
(cathedral ceiling)

cl

BED RM.
12-4 x 11-0

FLOOR PLAN

69-0

© 1995 Donald A Gardner Architects, Inc.

Especially Surprising

Total living area 1,495 sq. ft. ▪ Price Code A

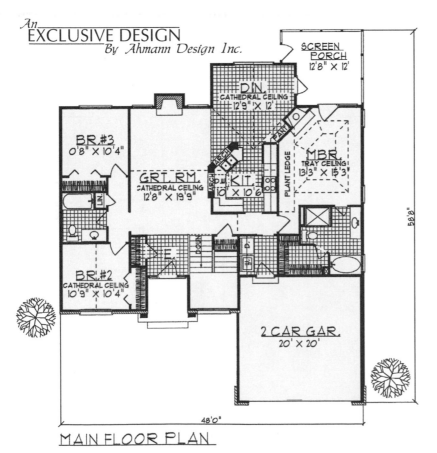

An EXCLUSIVE DESIGN
By Ahmann Design Inc.

MAIN FLOOR PLAN

No. 99106

▪ **This plan features:**

— Three bedrooms

— Two full baths

▪ Graceful columns support the covered entry

▪ The tiled foyer leads directly into the Great room that has a rear wall fireplace, and a cathedral ceiling

▪ The Kitchen has an arched pass through to the Great room and is open to the Dining room with a cathedral ceiling

▪ The Screen Porch is accessed from the Dining room

▪ The Master Suite has a plant ledge, a fireplace, a tray ceiling, a walk in closet, and a fully appointed Bath

▪ No materials list available for this plan

Main floor — 1,495 sq. ft.
Basement — 1,495 sq. ft.

144

Efficient Use of Space

No. 94130

This plan features:

- Three bedrooms
- One full bath
- The Living Room, Dining Room and the Kitchen are laid out in an efficient L-shaped design
- This open floor plan adds to the illusion of more space created in the home
- The Master Bedroom has private access to the full Bath in the hall
- Two additional bedrooms are located in proximity to the full Bath
- No materials list is available for this plan

Main floor — 1,006 sq. ft.
Basement — 1,006 sq. ft.
Garage — 433 sq. ft.

Total living area 1,006 sq. ft. ■ *Price Code C*

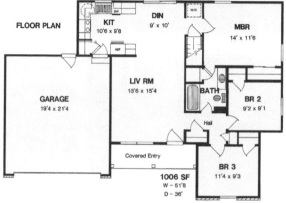

FLOOR PLAN

KIT 10'6 x 9'8
DIN 9' x 10'
MBR 14' x 11'6
GARAGE 19'4 x 21'4
LIV RM 13'6 x 15'4
BATH
BR 2 9'2 x 9'1
Hall
Covered Entry
BR 3 11'4 x 9'3
1006 SF
W – 51'8
D – 36'

Step Saving Ranch

No. 84357

This plan features:

- Three bedrooms
- One full and one three quarter baths
- A column supports the covered Front Porch
- The Living room is expanded by a front bay and included a cozy fireplace
- The Dining room accesses the rear Patio
- The galley Kitchen features a double sink and easy access to the Dining room
- The large Master Bedroom has an attached three quarter Bath
- Two secondary bedrooms share a full Bath in the hall
- No materials list is available for this plan

Main floor — 1,268 sq. ft.

Total living area 1,268 sq. ft. ■ *Price Code A*

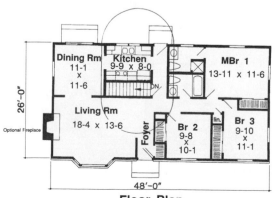

Dining Rm 11-1 x 11-6
Kitchen 9-9 x 8-0
MBr 1 13-11 x 11-6
26'-0"
Living Rm 18-4 x 13-6
Foyer
Br 2 9-8 x 10-1
Br 3 9-10 x 11-1
Optional Fireplace
48'-0"

Floor Plan

Kitchen 9-9 x 11-6
opt. slab/crawl space

Compact Plan

© 1996 Donald A. Gardner Architects, Inc.

Total living area 1,372 sq. ft. ■ Price Code B

No. 99830

■ This plan features:

— Three bedrooms

— Two full baths

■ A Great Room topped by a cathedral ceiling, combining with the openness of the adjoining Dining Room and Kitchen, to create a spacious living area

■ A bay window enlarging the Dining Room and a palladian window allowing ample light into the Great Room

■ An efficient U-shaped Kitchen leading directly to the garage, convenient for unloading groceries

■ A Master Suite highlighted by ample closet space and a private a sky lit bath enhanced by a dual vanity and a separate tub and shower

Main floor — 1,372 sq. ft.
Garage & Storage — 537 sq. ft.

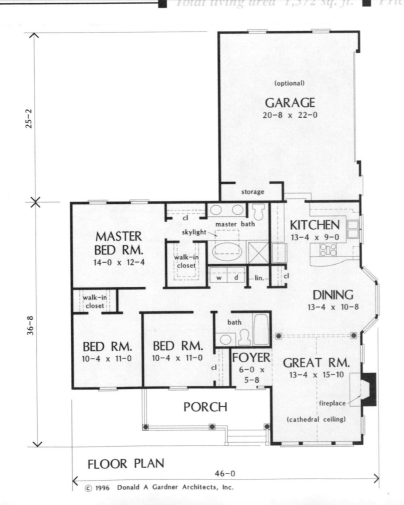

FLOOR PLAN

© 1996 Donald A Gardner Architects, Inc.

Classic Features

■ Total living area 1,530 sq. ft. ■ Price Code B

No. 90691

■ This plan features:

— Three bedrooms

— Two full baths

■ A cathedral ceiling in the Living Room with a heat-circulating fireplace

■ A spectacular bow window and skylight in the Dining Room

■ A sliding glass door and skylight in the Kitchen

■ A Master Bedroom including a private Master Bath with a whirlpool tub

■ Two additional bedrooms that share a full, double-vanity hall bath

Main area— 1,530 sq. ft.
Basement — 1,434 sq. ft.

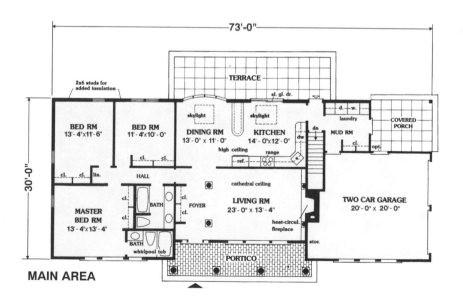

MAIN AREA

Build In Stages

REAR ELEVATION

■ Total living area 1,042 sq. ft. ■ Price Code A ■

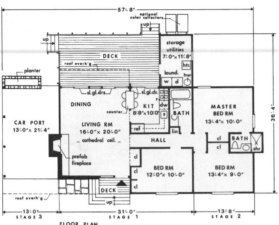

FLOOR PLAN

No. 90638

■ **This plan features:**

— Three bedrooms

— One full and one three quarter baths

■ A covered entrance into spacious Living/Dining Area with a 13 foot cathedral ceiling, fireplace and two sliding glass doors to a huge Deck

■ An efficient L-shaped Kitchen with separate counter space for dining is adjacent to Deck and Laundry/Utility room

■ A Master Bedroom with a private shower bath

■ Two additional bedrooms sharing a full hall Bath

■ An option to build in stages

Main floor — 1,042 sq. ft.

Tailored for a View to the Side

■ Total living area 2,579 sq. ft. ■ Price Code D ■

Main Level Floor Plan

No. 93708

■ **This plan features:**

— Three/Four bedrooms

— Three full and one half baths

■ A large entry Foyer highlighted by a ceiling dome and French doors leading to the private study or guest bedroom with a vaulted ceiling

■ An elegant formal Dining Room with a high ceiling and a columned and arched entrance

■ A sunken Great Room with a high tray ceiling and arched and columned openings and a fireplace

■ A Breakfast Room, with an optional planning desk, opens to the Kitchen via the eating bar

■ An island and walk-in pantry adding to the Kitchen's efficiency

■ A tray ceiling and lavish bath pamper the owner in the Master Suite

■ No materials list is available for this plan

Main floor — 2,579 sq. ft.
Garage — 536 sq. ft.

An EXCLUSIVE DESIGN
By Building Science Associates

For an Established Neighborhood

■ Total living area 1,292 sq. ft. ■ Price Code A ■

No. 93222

■ This plan features:

— Three bedrooms

— Two full baths

■ An expansive Living Room enhanced by natural light streaming in from the large front window

■ A bayed formal Dining Room with direct access to the Sun Deck and the Living Room for entertainment ease

■ An efficient, galley Kitchen, convenient to both formal and informal eating areas

■ An informal Breakfast Room with direct access to the Sun Deck

■ A large Master Suite equipped with a walk-in closet and a full private Bath

Main area — 1,276 sq. ft.
Finished staircase — 16 sq. ft.
Basement — 392 sq. ft.
Garage — 728 sq. ft.

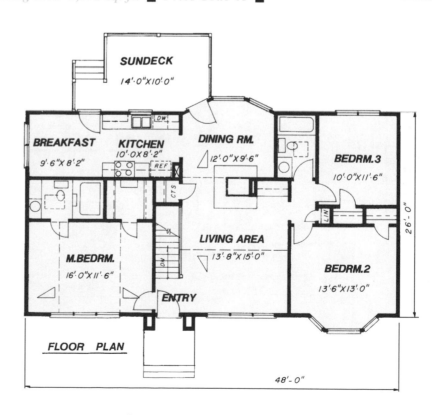

An EXCLUSIVE DESIGN
By Jannis Vann & Associates, Inc.

Amenity-Packed Affordability

Total living area—1,484 sq. ft. ■ Price Code B

No. 92525

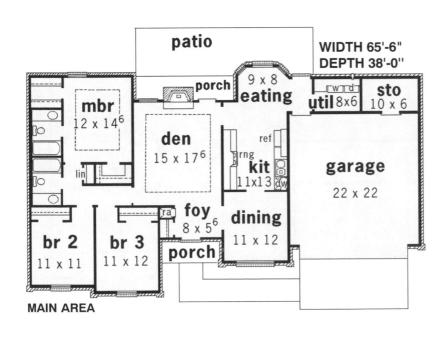

patio

porch

9 x 8
eating

WIDTH 65'-6"
DEPTH 38'-0"

w d
util 8x6

sto
10 x 6

mbr
12 x 14⁶

den
15 x 17⁶

ref

rng

kit
11x13

dw

garage
22 x 22

lin

ra

foy
8 x 5⁶

br 2
11 x 11

br 3
11 x 12

porch

dining
11 x 12

MAIN AREA

This plan features:

— Three bedrooms

— Two full baths

■ A sheltered entrance inviting your guests onward

■ A fireplace in the Den offering a focal point, while the decorative ceiling adds definition to the room

■ A well-equipped Kitchen flowing with ease into the Breakfast bay or Dining Room

■ A Master Bedroom, having two closets and a private Master Bath

■ An optional crawl space or slab foundation — please specify when ordering

Main area — 1,484 sq. ft.
Garage — 544 sq. ft.

Central Courtyard Features Pool

■ *Total living area 2,194 sq. ft.* ■ *Price Code C* ■

No. 10507

■ **This plan features:**

— Three bedrooms

— One full and one three quarter baths

■ A central courtyard complete with a pool

■ A secluded Master Bedroom accented by a skylight, a spacious walk-in closet, and a private bath

■ A convenient Kitchen easily serving the patio for comfortable outdoor entertaining

■ A detached two-car Garage

Main floor — 2,194 sq. ft.
Garage — 576 sq. ft.

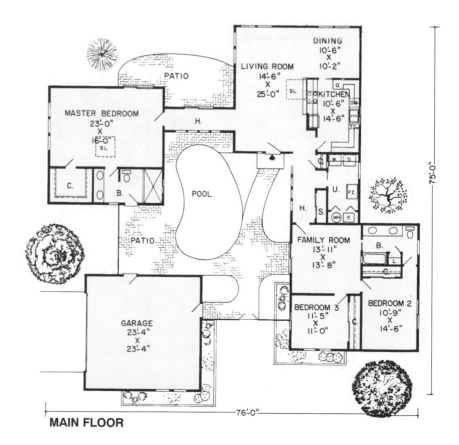

MAIN FLOOR

Spanish Style Affordable Home

Total living area 1,111 sq. ft. ■ Price Code A

No. 91340

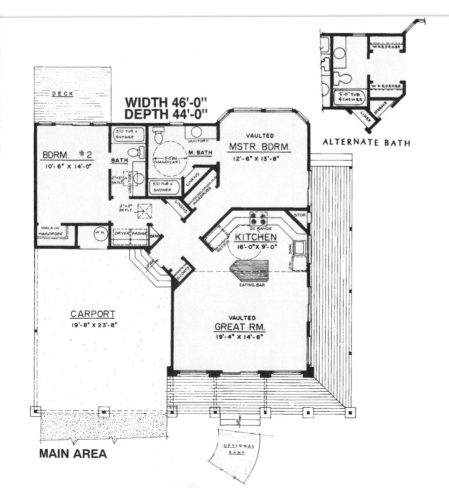

DECK

WIDTH 46'-0"
DEPTH 44'-0"

ALTERNATE BATH

BDRM. #2
10'-6" X 14'-0"

VAULTED
MSTR. BDRM.
12'-6" X 13'-8"

KITCHEN
16'-0" X 9'-0"

EATING BAR

CARPORT
19'-8" X 23'-8"

VAULTED
GREAT RM.
19'-4" X 14'-6"

OPTIONAL RAMP

MAIN AREA

■ **This plan features:**

— Two bedrooms

— Two full baths

■ A large Master Suite with vaulted ceilings and a handicap accessible private bath

■ Vaulted ceilings in the Great Room

■ An open Kitchen area with an eating bar

Main area — 1,111 sq. ft.

Appealing Master Suite

No. 92239

This plan features:

- Three bedrooms
- Two full baths
- Sheltered Entry into spacious Living Room with a corner fireplace and Patio access
- Efficient Kitchen with a serving counter for Dining area and nearby Utility/Garage entry
- Private Master Bedroom offers a vaulted ceiling and pampering bath with a dual vanity and walk-in closets and a garden window tub
- Two additional bedrooms with ample closets, share a full bath
- No materials list is available for this plan

Main floor — 1,198 sq. ft.

Total living area 1,198 sq. ft. ■ *Price Code A*

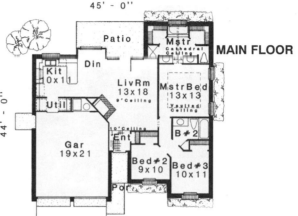

MAIN FLOOR

Compact Home Design

No. 10455

This plan features:

- Three bedrooms
- Two full baths
- An energy saving airlock Entry
- A Living Room with an entire wall of windows, fireplace, built-in bookcases, and a wetbar
- A step-saver Kitchen with an abundance of storage and a convenient peninsula
- A Master Bedroom with separate vanities and walk-in closets

Main area — 1,643 sq. ft.
Garage — 500 sq. ft.

Total living area 1,643 sq. ft. ■ *Price Code B*

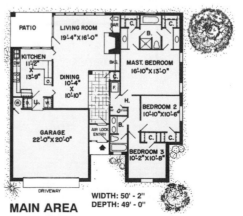

MAIN AREA

WIDTH: 50'- 2"
DEPTH: 49'- 0"

For First Time Buyers

■ *Total living area 1,310 sq. ft.* ■ *Price Code A* ■

No. 93048

WIDTH 49–10

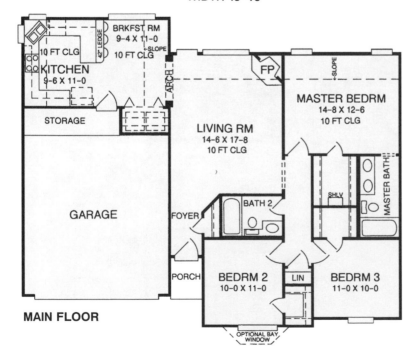

DEPTH 40–6

MAIN FLOOR

BRKFST RM
9-4 X 11-0
10 FT CLG

KITCHEN
9-6 X 11-0

10 FT CLG

42" LEDGE

SLOPE

STORAGE

LIVING RM
14-6 X 17-8
10 FT CLG

ARCH

FP

SLOPE

MASTER BEDRM
14-8 X 12-6
10 FT CLG

MASTER BATH

SHLV

GARAGE

FOYER

BATH 2

PORCH

BEDRM 2
10-0 X 11-0

LIN

BEDRM 3
11-0 X 10-0

OPTIONAL BAY
WINDOW

■ This plan features:

— Three bedrooms

— Two full baths

■ An efficiently designed Kitchen with a corner sink, ample counter space and a peninsula counter

■ A sunny Breakfast Room with a convenient hide-away laundry center

■ An expansive Family Room that includes a corner fireplace and direct access to the Patio

■ A private Master Suite with a walk-in closet and a double vanity Bath

■ Two additional bedrooms, both with walk-in closets, that share a full hall bath

■ No materials list is available for this plan

Main floor — 1,310 sq. ft.
Garage — 449 sq. ft.

Classic Blend of Brick and Stucco

■ *Total living area 1,668 sq. ft.* ■ *Price Code C* ■

No. 92555

■ **This plan features:**

— Three bedrooms

— Two full baths

■ Arch top windows on the front of this home combining with brick and stucco, brick quoins and dentil molding

■ Foyer giving access to the formal dining room accented by columns

■ Den includes a raised ceiling and a focal point fireplace.

■ Kitchen and breakfast nook open into the den creating a feeling of spaciousness

■ Master suite is situated to the left, rear corner and features a five - piece bath and walk-in closet

■ An optional crawl space or slab foundation — please specify when ordering

Main floor — 1,668 sq. ft.
Garage — 537 sq. ft.

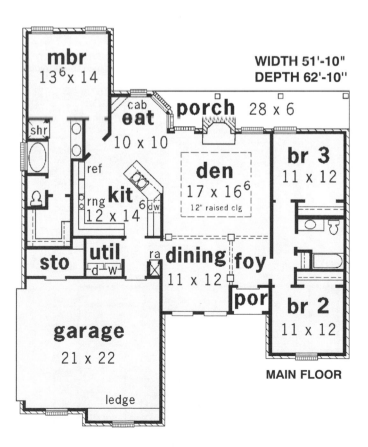

WIDTH 51'-10"
DEPTH 62'-10"

mbr 13⁶ x 14
eat 10 x 10
cab
porch 28 x 6
den 17 x 16⁶
12" raised clg
br 3 11 x 12
shr
ref
rng
kit 12 x 14
dw
sto
util
d w
dining 11 x 12
foy
ra
por
br 2 11 x 12
garage 21 x 22
ledge

MAIN FLOOR

Steep Pitched Roof with Quoins

Total living area 1,556 sq. ft. ■ Price Code C

No. 92556

■ **This plan features:**

— Three bedrooms

— Two full baths

■ Classic brick exterior features a steep pitched roof, and decorative quoins

■ The Foyer leads into the Den which is highlighted by a fireplace

■ The Kitchen is centered between the Dining room and the Eating nook

■ Two secondary bedrooms each have walk-in closets and share a full hall bath

■ The isolated Master bedroom has a walk-in closet and a full bath

■ There is a bonus room over the two-car garage for future expansion

■ An optional slab or a crawl space foundation — please specify when ordering

Main floor — 1,556 sq. ft.
Bonus — 282 sq. ft.
Garage — 565 sq. ft.

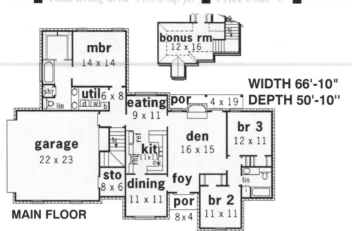

WIDTH 66'-10"
DEPTH 50'-10"

MAIN FLOOR

Step Saving Features

Total living area 1,537 sq. ft. ■ Price Code B

No. 92694

■ **This plan features:**

— Three bedrooms

— Two full baths

■ Charming home has a covered front porch with decorative styling

■ The open foyer is accented by a wood railed staircase to the lower level

■ The Great room is open and has a corner fireplace

■ The Dining room has a sloped ceiling and an access door to the rear porch

■ The L-shaped Kitchen has a center island

■ The large Master bedrooms has a door to the rear porch, a walk in closet, and a private bath

■ Two additional bedrooms have plenty of closet space and share a full bath

■ No materials list is available for this plan

Main floor — 1,537 sq. ft.
Basement — 1,537 sq. ft.
Garage — 400 sq. ft.

MAIN FLOOR

■ *Total living area 1,653 sq. ft.* ■ *Price Code B* ■

No. 92283

■ This plan features:

— Three bedrooms

— Two full baths

■ A sheltered Porch leads into an easy-care tile Entry

■ Spacious Living Room offers a cozy fireplace, triple window and access to Patio

■ An efficient Kitchen with a skylight, work island, Dining area, walk-in pantry and Utility/Garage entry

■ Secluded Master Bedroom highlighted by a vaulted ceiling, access to Patio and a lavish bath

■ Two additional bedrooms, one with a cathedral ceiling, share a full bath

■ No materials list is available for this plan

Main floor — 1,653 sq. ft.
Garage — 420 sq. ft.

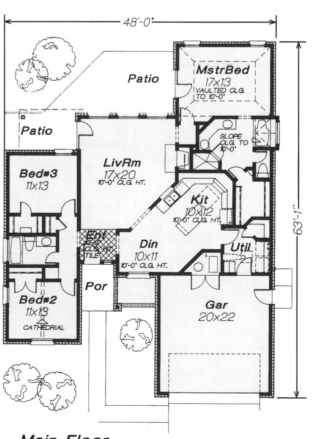

Main Floor

Mixture of Traditional and Country Charm

© 1994 Donald A. Gardner Architects, Inc.

Total living area 1,954 sq. ft. ■ Price Code C

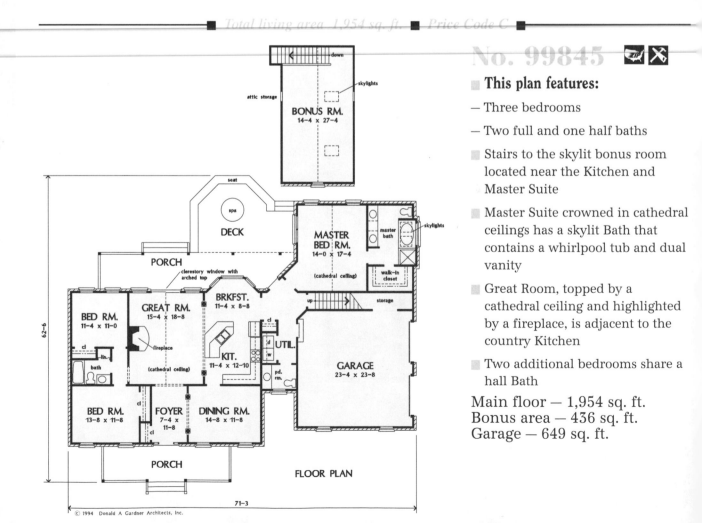

BONUS RM.
14-4 x 27-4

attic storage

skylights

down

DECK

seat

spa

PORCH

clerestory window with
arched top

GREAT RM.
15-4 x 18-8

BRKFST.
11-4 x 8-8

MASTER
BED RM.
14-0 x 17-4

(cathedral ceiling)

master
bath

skylights

walk-in
closet

storage

up

62-6

BED RM.
11-4 x 11-0

fireplace

cl

lin.

bath

KIT.
11-4 x 12-10

(cathedral ceiling)

cl

d
w

UTIL.

pd.
rm.

GARAGE
23-4 x 23-8

BED RM.
13-8 x 11-8

cl

FOYER
7-4 x
11-8

cl

DINING RM.
14-8 x 11-8

PORCH

FLOOR PLAN

71-3

No. 99845

This plan features:

— Three bedrooms

— Two full and one half baths

■ Stairs to the skylit bonus room located near the Kitchen and Master Suite

■ Master Suite crowned in cathedral ceilings has a skylit Bath that contains a whirlpool tub and dual vanity

■ Great Room, topped by a cathedral ceiling and highlighted by a fireplace, is adjacent to the country Kitchen

■ Two additional bedrooms share a hall Bath

Main floor — 1,954 sq. ft.
Bonus area — 436 sq. ft.
Garage — 649 sq. ft.

© 1994 Donald A. Gardner Architects, Inc.

Moderate Ranch Has Features of a Larger Plan

■ *Total living area 1,811 sq. ft.* ■ *Price Code C* ■

No. 90441

■ This plan features:

— Three bedrooms

— Two full baths

■ A large Great Room with a vaulted ceiling and a stone fireplace with bookshelves on either side

■ A spacious Kitchen with ample cabinet space conveniently located next to the large Dining Room

■ A Master Suite having a large bath with a garden tub, double vanity and a walk-in closet

■ Two other large bedrooms, each with a walk-in closet and access to the full bath

■ An optional basement, slab or crawl space combination — please specify when ordering

Main floor — 1,811 sq. ft.

MAIN FLOOR

Secluded Master Suite

■ Total living area 1,680 sq. ft. ■ Price Code C ■

No. 92527

■ **This plan features:**

— Three bedrooms

— Two full baths

■ A convenient one-level design with an open floor plan between the Kitchen, Breakfast area and Great Room

■ A vaulted ceiling and a cozy fireplace in the spacious Great Room

■ A well-equipped Kitchen using a peninsula counter as an eating bar

■ A Master Suite with a luxurious Master Bath

■ Two additional bedrooms having use of a full hall bath

■ An optional crawl space and slab foundation available — please specify when ordering

Main area — 1,680 sq. ft.
Garage — 538 sq. ft.

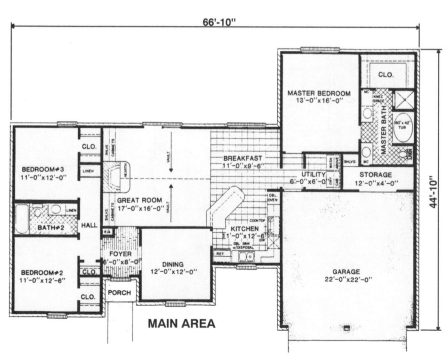

66'-10"

44'-10"

CLO.

MASTER BEDROOM
13'-0"x16'-0"

MASTER BATH

60"x42" TUB

BEDROOM #3
11'-0"x12'-0"

CLO.

LINEN

BREAKFAST
11'-0"x9'-6"

UTILITY
6'-0"x6'-0"

STORAGE
12'-0"x4'-0"

GREAT ROOM
17'-0"x16'-0"

LINEN

BATH #2

HALL

KITCHEN
11'-0"x12'-6"

DBL. OVEN

COOKTOP

DBL. SINK W/DISPOSAL

REF.

FOYER
6'-0"x8'-0"

DINING
12'-0"x12'-0"

GARAGE
22'-0"x22'-0"

BEDROOM #2
11'-0"x12'-6"

CLO.

CLO.

PORCH

MAIN AREA

Refined Country Style

No. 96447

This plan features:

— Four bedrooms

— Two full and one half baths

■ Arched windows and interior columns adding refined style

■ Generous Great Room with soaring cathedral ceiling

■ Well planned angled counter Kitchen with adjoining nook

■ Privately situated Master Bedroom with bath and walk in closet

■ Large secondary bedrooms share a full bath

Main floor—2,207 sq. ft.
Garage—634 sq. ft.
Bonus — 435 sq. ft.

Total living area 2,207 sq. ft. ■ *Price Code D*

Two Separate Dining Areas

No. 91349

This plan features:

— Two bedrooms

— Two full baths

■ A vaulted ceiling entry

■ A Living Room with a vaulted ceiling, accented by a bay window and an optional fireplace

■ A garden window, eating bar, and an abundance of storage space in the efficient Kitchen

■ A Master Bedroom with its own bath, a double sink vanity and a walk-in closet

■ A Library with a vaulted ceiling option and a window seat

Main area — 1,694 sq. ft.

Total living area 1,694 sq. ft. ■ *Price Code B*

MAIN AREA

Columned Keystone Arched Entry

Total living area 2,256 sq. ft. ■ Price Code D

No. 96503

■ This plan features:

— Three bedrooms

— Two full baths

■ Keystone arches and arched transoms above the windows

■ Formal Dining Room and Study flank the Foyer

■ Fireplace in Great Room

■ Efficient Kitchen with a peninsula counter and bayed Nook

■ A step ceiling in the Master Suite and interesting master bath with a triangular area for the oval bath tub

■ The secondary bedrooms share a full bath in the hall.

Main floor — 2,256 sq. ft.
Garage — 514 sq. ft.

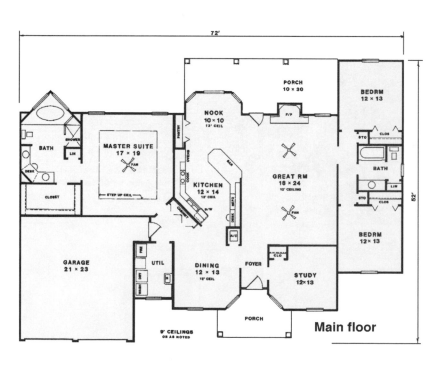

Main floor

■ *Total living area 1,742 sq. ft.* ■ *Price Code B* ■

No. 93061

■ **This plan features:**

— Three bedrooms

— Two full baths

■ Great Room with a fireplace and access to the rear yard

■ Unique Dining Room with an alcove of windows, adjoins the Kitchen

■ Angled counter with an eating bar and a built-in pantry in the Kitchen easily serves the Breakfast area, and Great Room

■ Master Bath with a corner whirlpool tub, a double vanity and a huge walk-in closet

■ An optional slab or crawlspace foundation available — please specify when ordering

■ No materials list is available for this plan

Main floor — 1,742 sq. ft.
Garage — 566 sq. ft.

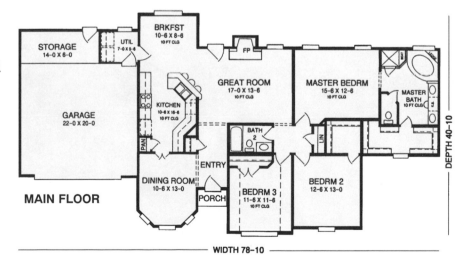

STORAGE
14-0 X 6-0

UTIL
7-0 X 5-6

BRKFST
10-6 X 8-6
10 FT CLG

FP

GARAGE
22-0 X 20-0

KITCHEN
10-6 X 16-6
10 FT CLG

PAN

GREAT ROOM
17-0 X 13-6
10 FT CLG

MASTER BEDRM
15-6 X 12-6
10 FT CLG

MASTER BATH
10 FT CLG

BATH 2

ENTRY

LIN

MAIN FLOOR

DINING ROOM
10-6 X 13-0

PORCH

BEDRM 3
11-6 X 11-6
10 FT CLG

BEDRM 2
12-6 X 13-0

DEPTH 40-10

WIDTH 78-10

Eye-Appealing Balance

Total living area 2,470 sq. ft. ■ Price Code D

Main Floor

No. 92257

This plan features:

— Three bedrooms

— Two full and one half baths

■ Arched Portico enhances entry into Gallery and spacious Living Room, with focal point fireplace surrounded by glass

■ Cathedral ceilings top Family Room and formal Dining Room

■ An efficient Kitchen with breakfast area opens to Family Room, Utility Room with convenient Garage entry

■ Corner Master Bedroom suite with access to covered Patio and private bath with a double vanity and garden window tub

■ Two additional bedrooms with walk-in closets share a full bath

■ No materials list is available for this plan

Main Floor — 2,470 sq. ft.
Garage — 483 sq. ft.

An Open Plan

Total living area 1,605 sq. ft. ■ Price Code B

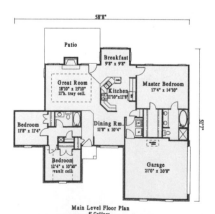

Main Level Floor Plan
8' Ceilings

No. 93702

This plan features:

— Three bedrooms

— Two full baths

■ An open floor plan giving the appearance of spaciousness even through the home is small in square footage

■ A sheltered entrance that leads to a short Foyer with a coat closet

■ A large front window adding to the elegance of the Dining Room

■ A tray ceiling in the Living Room which is also enhanced by a fireplace

■ An octagonal Kitchen including a dining bar and open to the Breakfast Room

■ A large and private Master Bedroom with an oversized walk-in closet

■ A secondary bedroom located at the front of the house with a vaulted ceiling and a circle-topped window

■ No materials list is available for this plan

Main floor — 1,605 sq. ft.
Garage — 436 sq. ft.

An EXCLUSIVE DESIGN
By Building Science Associates

Sloped Ceiling Is Attractive Feature of Design

■ Total living area 1,688 sq. ft. ■ Price Code B ■

No. 10548

An
EXCLUSIVE DESIGN
By Karl Kreeger

■ **This plan features:**

— Three bedrooms

— Two and one half baths

■ A fireplace and sloped ceiling in
the Living Room

■ A Master Bedroom complete with
a full bath, shower and dressing
area

■ A decorative ceiling in the Dining
Room

Main area — 1,688 sq. ft.
Basement — 1,688 sq. ft.
Screened porch — 120 sq. ft.
Garage — 489 sq. ft.

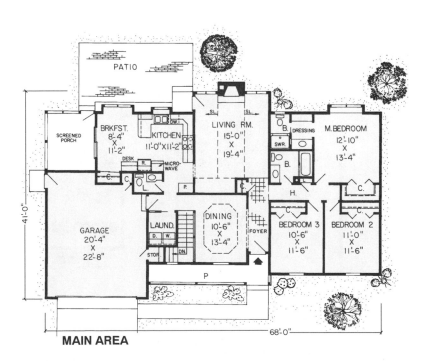

MAIN AREA

Quaint Starter Home

Total living area 1,050 sq. ft. ■ Price Code A

No. 92400

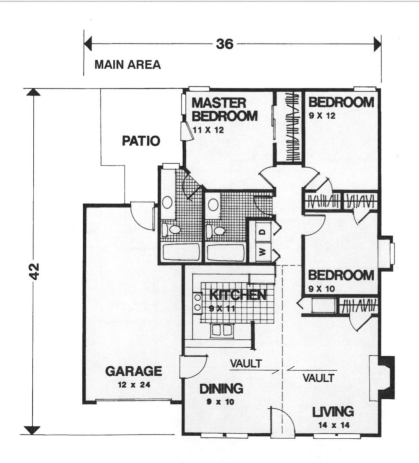

■ **This plan features:**

— Three bedrooms

— Two full baths

■ A vaulted ceiling giving an airy feeling to the Dining and Living Rooms

■ A streamlined Kitchen with a comfortable work area, a double sink and ample cabinet space

■ A cozy fireplace in the Living Room

■ A Master Suite with a large closet, French doors leading to the patio and a private bath

■ Two additional bedrooms sharing a full bath

■ No materials list is available for this plan

Main area — 1,050 sq. ft.

L-Shaped Front Porch

■ *Total living area 1,280 sq. ft.* ■ *Price Code A* ■

No. 98747

■ This plan features:

— Three bedrooms

— Two full baths

■ Attractive wood siding and a large L-shaped covered porch

■ Front entry leading to generous living room with a vaulted ceiling

■ Large two-car garage with access through utility room

■ Roomy secondary bedrooms share the full bath in the hall

■ Kitchen highlighted by a built-in pantry and a garden window

■ Vaulted ceiling adds volume to the Dining Room

■ Master Suite in an isolated location enhanced by abundant closet space, separate vanity, and linen storage

Main floor — 1,280 sq. ft.

FLOOR PLAN
WIDTH 52'-0"
DEPTH 47'-0"

OPT. MSTR. BATH

Nostalgia Returns

■ *Total living area 1,368 sq. ft.* ■ *Price Code A* ■

No. 99321

■ **This plan features:**

— Three bedrooms

— Two full baths

■ A half-round transom window with quarter-round detail and a vaulted ceiling in the Great Room

■ A cozy corner fireplace which brings warmth to the Great Room

■ A vaulted ceiling in the Kitchen/Breakfast area

■ A Master Suite with a walk-in closet and a private Master Bath

■ Two additional bedrooms which share a full hall bath

Main area — 1,368 sq. ft.

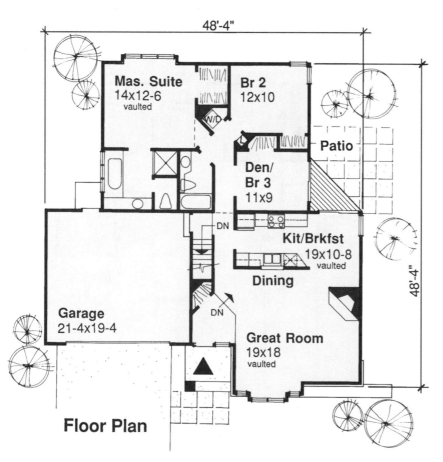

Floor Plan

Loads of Light

No. 10466

This plan features:

— Four bedrooms

— Three full baths

■ Bright Entry with transom and sidelight windows leads into Living Room with a beamed ceiling above a hearth fireplace

■ Formal Dining Room with delightful window convenient for entertaining

■ Greenhouse corner window highlights Kitchen with a pantry, laundry closet, serving counter and glass eating Nook beyond

■ Glass walls enhance Family Room with access to Kitchen, Patio and Garage

■ Master Bedroom accented by a corner window seat, double vanity bath and a huge walk-in closet with a skylight

■ Three more bedrooms with ample closets and access to a full bath

Main floor — 2,285 sq. ft.
Garage — 483 sq. ft.

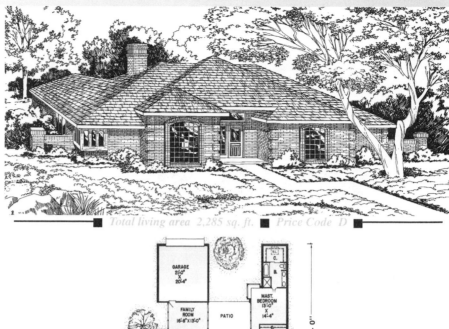

Total living area 2,285 sq. ft. ■ Price Code D

MAIN FLOOR

Simple Comfort

No. 93429

This plan features:

— Three bedrooms

— Two full baths

■ Welcoming front porch sheltering the entrance

■ Family Room highlighted by a fireplace and adjoins with the Dining Room

■ Efficient Kitchen is laid out in an convenient U-shape and has easy access to the Dining Room

■ Master Suite includes a decorative ceiling treatment and a private Master Bath

■ Two additional bedrooms feature ample closet space and easy access to a full bath in the hall

■ No materials list is available for this plan

Main floor — 1,496 sq. ft.
Basement — 752 sq. ft.
Garage — 744 sq. ft.

An EXCLUSIVE DESIGN *By Greg Marquis*

Total living area 1,496 sq. ft. ■ Price Code A

MAIN FLOOR

Elegant Brick Exterior

Total living area 1,390 sq. ft. ■ Price Code B

No. 92557

■ **This plan features:**

—Three bedrooms

—Two full baths

■ Detailing and accenting columns enhance the covered front porch

■ Den has a corner fireplace and adjoins with the Dining Room

■ Efficient Kitchen is well-appointed and with easy access to the utility/laundry room

■ Master Bedroom topped by a vaulted ceiling and pampered by a private bath and a walk-in closet

■ Two secondary bedrooms are located at the opposite end of home sharing a full bath

■ An optional slab or crawl space foundation — please specify when ordering

Main floor — 1,390 sq. ft.
Garage — 590 sq. ft.

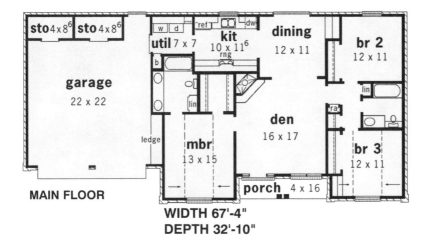

MAIN FLOOR

WIDTH 67'-4"
DEPTH 32'-10"

Cathedral Ceiling Enlarges Great Room

© 1996 Donald A Gardner Architects, Inc.

■ *Total living area 1,699 sq. ft.* ■ *Price Code B* ■

No. 99811

■ This plan features:

— Three bedrooms

— Two full baths

■ Two dormers add volume to the Foyer

■ Great Room, topped by a cathedral ceiling, is open to the Kitchen and Breakfast area

■ Accent columns define the Foyer, Great Room, Kitchen, and Breakfast area

■ Private Master Suite crowned in a tray ceiling and highlighted by a skylit bath

■ Front bedroom topped by a tray ceiling

Main floor — 1,699 sq. ft.
Garage — 498 sq. ft.
Bonus — 336 sq. ft.

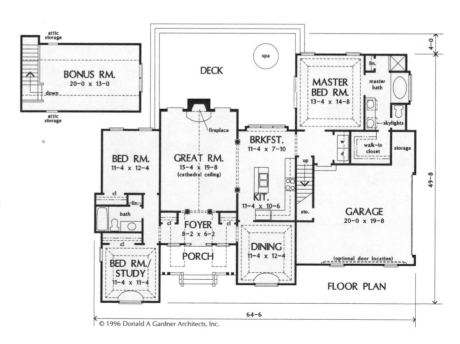

© 1996 Donald A Gardner Architects, Inc.

Soaring Ceilings Add Space and Drama

MAIN AREA

Total living area 1,387 sq. ft. ■ Price Code A

No. 90288

■ **This plan features:**

— Two bedrooms (with optional third bedroom)

— Two full baths

■ A sunny Master Suite with a sloping ceiling, private terrace entry, and luxurious garden bath with an adjoining Dressing Room

■ A Gathering Room with a fireplace, study and formal Dining Room, flowing together for a more spacious feeling

■ A convenient pass-through that adds to the efficiency of the galley Kitchen and adjoining Breakfast Room

Main area — 1,387 sq. ft.
Garage — 440 sq. ft.

Appealing Brick Elevation

Total living area 2,172 sq. ft. ■ Price Code C

MAIN AREA

No. 94971

■ **This plan features:**

— Three bedrooms

— Two full and one three quarter bath

■ Formal Living and Dining Room flanking the Entry

■ Impressive Great Room topped by an eleven foot ceiling and enhanced by picture window

■ Awning windows framing the raised hearth fireplace

■ Attractive kitchen/dinette area includes an island, desk, wrapping counters, a walk-in pantry and access to the covered patio

■ Pampering master suite with a skylight dressing area, a walk-in closet, double vanity, a whirlpool tub and a decorative plant shelf

Main floor — 2,172 sq. ft.
Garage — 680 sq. ft.

Expansive Living Room

■ *Total living area 1,346 sq. ft.* ■ *Price Code A* ■

No. 98434

■ This plan features:

— Three bedrooms

— Two full baths

■ Vaulted ceiling crowns spacious Living Room highlighted by a fireplace

■ Built-in pantry and direct access from the garage adding to the conveniences of the Kitchen

■ Walk-in closet and a private five piece bath topped by a vaulted ceiling in the Master Bedroom suite

■ Proximity to the full bath in the hall from the secondary bedrooms

■ An optional basement, slab or crawl space foundation available — please specify when ordering

Main floor — 1,346 sq. ft.
Garage — 395 sq. ft.

MAIN FLOOR

Practical Layout

■ *Total living area 1,114 sq. ft.* ■ *Price Code A* ■

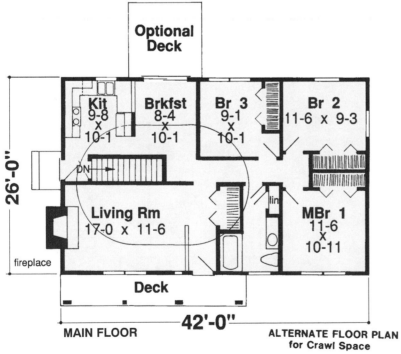

Optional Deck

Kit
9-8
x
10-1

Brkfst
8-4
x
10-1

Br 3
9-1
x
10-1

Br 2
11-6 x 9-3

DN

Living Rm
17-0 x 11-6

MBr 1
11-6
x
10-11

lin

fireplace

26'-0"

Deck

42'-0"

MAIN FLOOR

ALTERNATE FLOOR PLAN
for Crawl Space

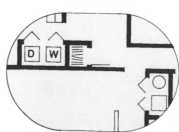

No. 84330

■ **This plan features:**

— Three bedrooms

— One full bath

■ The Living room is enhanced by a fireplace and bright front window

■ The U-shaped Kitchen has plenty of counter space for ease in meal preparation

■ The Breakfast nook is adjacent to the Kitchen and has sliding door to the rear deck

■ All three Bedrooms have large closets

■ There is a full bath in the hall

■ No materials list is available for this plan

Main floor — 1,114 sq. ft.

Great As A Mountain Retreat

© 1996 Donald A Gardner Architects, Inc.

■ *Total living area 1,912 sq. ft.* ■ *Price Code D* ■

No. 99815

■ This plan features:

— Three bedrooms

— Two full baths

■ Board and batten siding, stone, and stucco combine to give this popular plan a casual feel

■ User friendly Kitchen with huge pantry for ample storage and island counter

■ Casual family meals in sunny Breakfast bay; formal gatherings in the columned Dining area

■ Master Suite is topped by a deep tray ceiling, has a large walk-in closet, an extravagant private bath and direct access to back porch

Main floor — 1,912 sq. ft.
Garage — 580 sq. ft.
Bonus — 398 sq. ft.

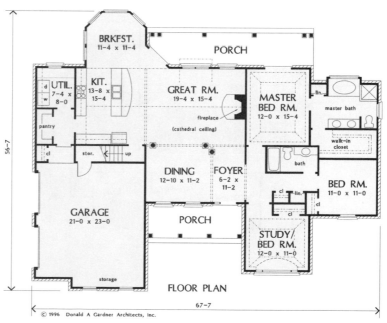

FLOOR PLAN

© 1996 Donald A Gardner Architects, Inc.

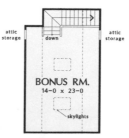

BONUS RM.
14-0 x 23-0

Designed for Today's Family

© 1995 Donald A. Gardner Architects, Inc.

■ *Total living area 2,192 sq. ft.* ■ *Price Code D* ■

No. 99838

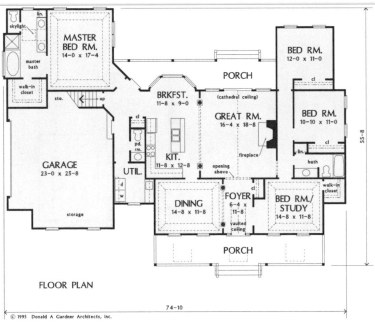

FLOOR PLAN

© 1995 Donald A Gardner Architects, Inc.

MASTER BED RM.
14-0 x 17-4

skylight

lin.

master bath

walk-in closet

BRKFST.
11-8 x 9-0

PORCH

(cathedral ceiling)

GREAT RM.
16-4 x 18-8

BED RM.
12-0 x 11-0

cl

BED RM.
10-10 x 11-0

55-8

cl

lin.

bath

fireplace

opening above

KIT.
11-8 x 12-8

pd. rm.

cl

UTIL.

d   w

GARAGE
23-0 x 25-8

storage

sto.

up

DINING
14-8 x 11-8

FOYER
6-4 x 11-8

vaulted ceiling

BED RM./ STUDY
14-8 x 11-8

cl

walk-in closet

PORCH

74-10

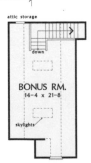

attic storage

down

BONUS RM.
14-4 x 21-8

skylights

■ This plan features:

— Three bedrooms

— Two full and one half baths

■ Volume and 9' ceilings add elegance to a comfortable, open floor plan

■ Secluded bedrooms designed for pleasant retreats at the end of the day

■ Airy Foyer topped by a vaulted dormer sends natural light streaming in

■ Formal Dining Room delineated from the Foyer by columns topped with a tray ceiling

■ Extra flexibility in the front bedroom which could double as a study

■ Tray ceiling, skylights and a garden tub, in the bath highlight the Master Suite

Main floor — 2,192 sq. ft.
Garage & Storage — 582 sq. ft.
Bonus — 390 sq. ft.

Cute Cottage

No. 93414

This plan features:

— Three bedrooms

— Two full baths

- A cute covered front porch adds character to this cottage plan

- The Large Living room has a 10' ceiling and a side wall fireplace

- The Kitchen is open to the Dining room

- The Kitchen is equipped with a center island, a planning desk, and a cooktop

- A convenient laundry room is located off of the Kitchen

- The Master bedroom has a walk in closet and a full bath

- Two secondary bedrooms are identical in size and share a bath in the hall

- There is a detached two-car garage with this plan

- No materials list available for this plan

Main floor — 1,393 sq. ft.
Garage — 528 sq. ft.

Total living area 1,393 sq. ft. ■ Price Code A

An EXCLUSIVE DESIGN *By Greg Marquis*

MAIN FLOOR

Terrace Doubles Living Space

No. 90683

This plan features:

— Three bedrooms

— Two full baths

- Wood and stone exterior enhanced by welcoming covered Porch

- Heat circulating fireplace adds warmth to spacious Living Room

- Skylights in high sloping ceilings above Family Room, Dining area and Kitchen provide natural light and space

- Family Room/Dining area with a built-in entertainment center and sliding glass doors to Terrace

- Pass-through convenience from the efficient Kitchen to the Dining Area

- Bay window with cozy seat enhances the Master Bedroom

- Two additional bedrooms share a double vanity bath

Main floor — 1,567 sq. ft.
Basement — 1,413 sq. ft.
Garage — 490 sq. ft.

Total living area 1,567 sq. ft. ■ Price Code B

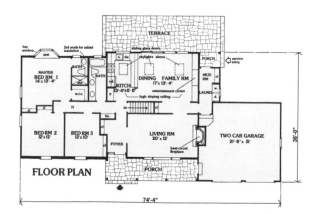

FLOOR PLAN

Style and Convenience

Total living area - 1,373 sq. ft. ■ Price Code A

No. 98411

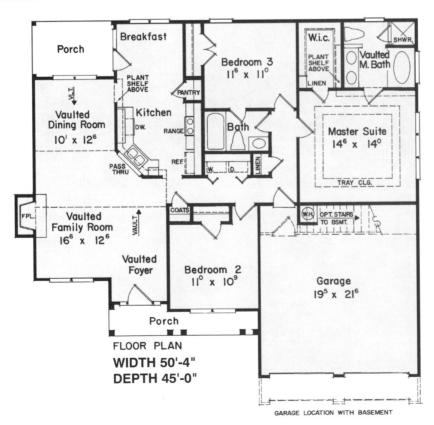

FLOOR PLAN
WIDTH 50'-4"
DEPTH 45'-0"

GARAGE LOCATION WITH BASEMENT

This plan features:

— Three bedrooms

— Two full baths

■ Large front windows, dormers and an old-fashioned porch

■ A vaulted ceiling in the Foyer

■ A Formal Dining Room crowned in an elegant vaulted ceiling

■ An efficient Kitchen enhanced by a pantry, a pass through to the Family Room

■ A decorative tray ceiling, a five piece private bath and a walk-in closet in the Master Suite

■ An optional basement or crawl space foundation available — please specify when ordering

Main floor — 1,373 sq. ft.
Basement — 1,386 sq. ft.

■ *Total living area 1,735 sq. ft.* ■ *Price Code B* ■

No. 94969

This plan features:

— Three bedrooms

— Two full baths

■ A welcoming front Porch leads to the Entry that is topped by a 10' ceiling

■ The Great Room and Dining Room both have a 10' ceiling, and transom windows

■ The L-shaped Kitchen has a center island and is open to the angled Breakfast Room

■ The Master Bedroom features a bay window, decorative ceiling, and a private bath with a whirlpool tub

Main floor — 1,735 sq. ft.
Garage — 488 sq. ft.

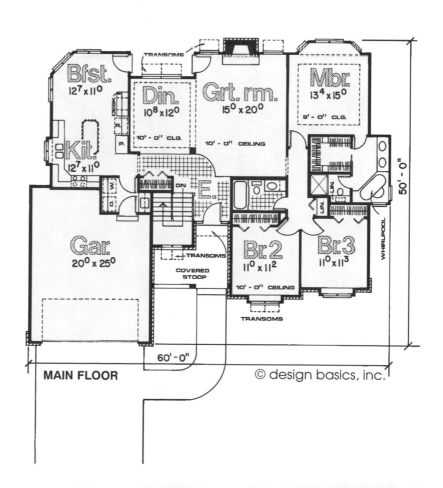

MAIN FLOOR   © design basics, inc.

Tasteful Elegance Aim of Design

No. 22020

This plan features:

— Three bedrooms

— Two full baths

- A charming exterior French Provincial
- A semi-circular Dining area overlooking the patio
- An island Kitchen efficiently designed with ample cabinets and counter areas
- A Family Room with a woodburning fireplace
- A Master Bedroom with a dressing area and a private bath

Main floor — 1,772 sq. ft.
Garage — 469 sq. ft.

■ *Total living area 1,772 sq. ft.* ■ *Price Code B* ■

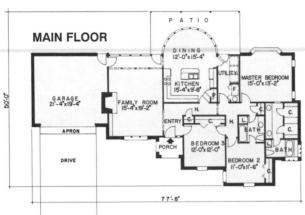

MAIN FLOOR

Sophisticated Country Style

No. 92558

This plan features:

— Three bedrooms

— Two full baths

- Covered porches both front and rear add country style
- The Den has a fireplace, built-in cabinets and is crowned by a vaulted ceiling
- The U-shaped Kitchen is open to the Dining area which accesses the rear porch
- Two identically sized bedrooms share a bath in their hall
- The Master bedroom has a raised ceiling, a walk-in closet, and a full bath
- An optional crawl space or a slab foundation—please specify when ordering

Main floor — 1,294 sq. ft.
Garage — 477 sq. ft.

■ *Total living area 1,294 sq. ft.* ■ *Price Code B* ■

WIDTH 51'-10"
DEPTH 47'-0"

MAIN FLOOR

© 1997 Donald A. Gardner Architects, Inc.

■ *Total living area 1,903 sq. ft.* ■ *Price Code D* ■

No. 96405

■ This plan features:

— Four bedrooms

— Two full baths

■ This home combines Victorian charm with today's lifestyle needs

■ Ceilings vaulted in Great Room and ten feet height in Foyer, Dining Room, Kitchen/Breakfast bay and Bedroom/Study

■ Secluded Master Bedroom suite features tray ceiling, walk-in closet and private, skylit bath

■ Two additional bedrooms, located in separate wing, share a full bath

■ Front and rear Porches extend living area outdoors

Main floor — 1,903 sq. ft.
Garage & storage — 531 sq. ft.

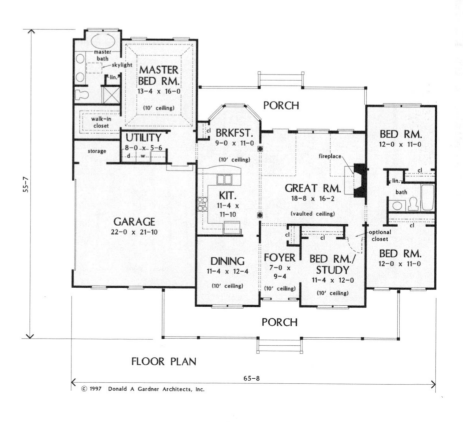

FLOOR PLAN

© 1997 Donald A Gardner Architects, Inc.

Perfect Plan for Busy Family

Total living area 1,756 sq. ft. ■ Price Code B

An EXCLUSIVE DESIGN
By Ahmann Design Inc.

No. 93191

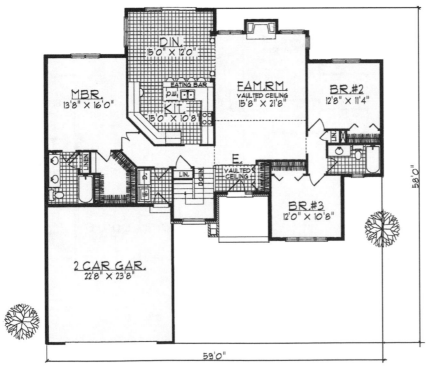

MAIN FLOOR PLAN

This plan features:

— Three bedrooms

— Two full baths

▪ Covered Entry opens to vaulted Foyer and Family Room

▪ Family Room with a vaulted ceiling and central fireplace

▪ Angular Kitchen with an eating bar, built-in desk and nearby laundry and Garage entry

▪ Secluded Master Bedroom with a large walk-in closet and double vanity bath

▪ Two additional bedrooms with easy access to a full bath

▪ Plenty of room for growing family to expand on lower level

▪ No materials list is available for this plan

Main floor — 1,756 sq. ft.

Carefree Comfort

■ *Total living area 1,492 sq. ft.* ■ *Price Code A* ■

No. 90692

■ **This plan features:**

— Three bedrooms

— Two full baths

■ Cedar shingle siding and flowerboxes

■ A heat-circulating fireplace

■ A central Foyer separating active areas from the bedroom wing

■ A sunny Living Room with an arched window, fireplace, and soaring cathedral ceilings

■ A formal Dining Room adjoining the Living Room

Main area — 1,492 sq. ft.

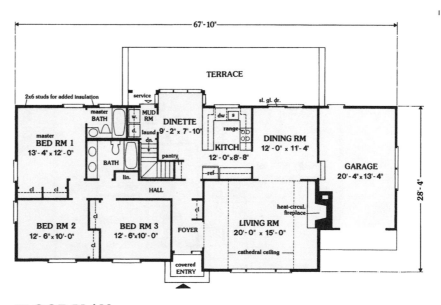

FLOOR PLAN

Easy Maintenance

■ *Total living area 786 sq. ft.* ■ *Price Code A* ■

No. 94307

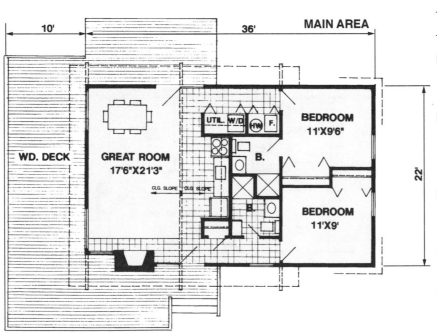

MAIN AREA

10'

36'

WD. DECK

GREAT ROOM
17'6"X21'3"

CLG. SLOPE   CLG. SLOPE

UTIL. W/D HW F.

B.

B.

BEDROOM
11'X9'6"

BEDROOM
11'X9'

22'

■ **This plan features:**

— Two bedroom

— Two three quarter baths

■ Abundant glass and a wrap-around Deck to enjoy the outdoors

■ A tiled entrance into a large Great Room with a fieldstone fireplace and dining area below a sloped ceiling

■ A compact tiled Kitchen open to a Great Room and adjacent to the Utility area

■ Two bedrooms, one with a private bath, offer ample closet space

■ No materials list is available for this plan

Main Area — 786 sq. ft.

An
EXCLUSIVE DESIGN
By Marshall Associates

Super Starter

No. 10791

This plan features:

- Three Bedrooms

- One full bath

- Entrance into spacious Living Room with an over-sized coat closet is brightened by triple window

- Efficient Kitchen/Dining combination features laundry closet and access to side and back yard

- Three bedrooms with ample closet space share a full bath

- Optional alternate plan with Crawl Space and U-shaped Kitchen available

Main area — 1,092 sq. ft.
Basement — 1,092 sq. ft.

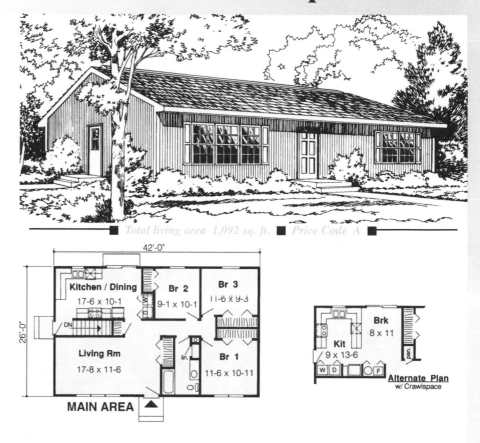

■ Total living area 1,092 sq. ft. ■ Price Code A ■

Kitchen / Dining 17-6 x 10-1

Br 2 9-1 x 10-1

Br 3 11-6 x 9-3

Living Rm 17-8 x 11-6

Br 1 11-6 x 10-11

42'-0"

26'-0"

MAIN AREA

Brk 8 x 11

Kit 9 x 13-6

Alternate Plan w/ Crawlspace

Keystones, Arches and Gables

No. 93171

This plan features:

- Three bedrooms

- Two full and one half baths

- Tiled Entry opens to Living Room with focal point fireplace

- U-shaped Kitchen with a built-in pantry, eating bar and nearby laundry/Garage entry

- Comfortable Dining Room with bay window and French doors to Screen Porch expanding living area outdoors

- Corner Master Bedroom offers a great walk-in closet and private bath

- Two additional bedrooms with ample closets and double windows, share a full bath

- No materials list is available for this plan

Main floor — 1,642 sq. ft.
Basement — 1,642 sq. ft.

■ Total living area 1,642 sq. ft. ■ Price Code B ■

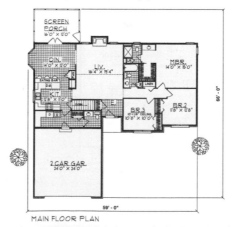

SCREEN PORCH

DIN. 14'0" x 9'0"

LIV. 16'-4" x 19'4"

MBR. 14'0" x 15'0"

KIT.

BR 3 10'-8" x 10'0"

BR 2 11'8" x 12'8"

2 CAR GAR. 24'0" x 24'0"

MAIN FLOOR PLAN

59' - 0"

An **EXCLUSIVE DESIGN** *By Ahmann Design Inc.*

185

Economical Three Bedroom

© 1993 Donald A. Gardner Architects, Inc.

Total living area 1,322 sq. ft. ■ Price Code B

No. 99849

FLOOR PLAN

This plan features:

— Three bedrooms

— Two full baths

■ Dormers above the covered porch casting light into the Foyer

■ Columns punctuating the entrance to the open Great Room/Dining Room area with a shared cathedral ceiling and a bank of operable skylights

■ Kitchen with a breakfast counter, open to the Dining Area

■ Private Master Bedroom suite with a tray ceiling and luxurious bath featuring a double vanity, separate shower, and skylights over the whirlpool tub

Main floor — 1,322 sq. ft.
Garage & Storage — 413 sq. ft.

© 1993 Donald A Gardner Architects, Inc.

Affordable Living

■ *Total living area 984 sq. ft.* ■ *Price Code A* ■

No. 24303

■ This plan features:

— Three bedrooms

— Two full baths

■ A simple, yet gracefully designed exterior

■ A sheltered entrance into a roomy Living Room graced with a large front window

■ U-shaped Kitchen with double sinks and adequate storage

■ A Master Bedroom equipped with a full Bath

■ Two additional bedrooms that share a full hall bath complete with a convenient laundry center

Main area — 984 sq. ft.
Basement — 960 sq. ft.
Garage — 280 sq. ft.
Opt. 2-car Garage — 400 sq. ft.

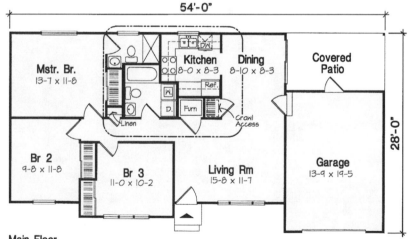

Main Floor
Plan # 24303

An EXCLUSIVE DESIGN
By Marshall Associates

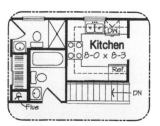

Optional Basement Plan

Designed for Informal Life Style

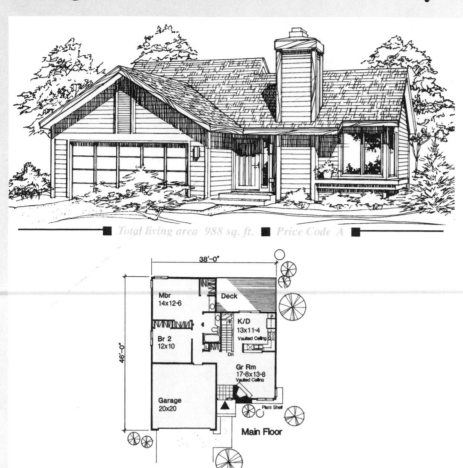

Total living area 988 sq. ft. ■ Price Code A

Main Floor

■ **This plan features:**

— Two bedrooms

— One full bath

■ A Great Room and Kitchen accented by vaulted ceilings

■ A conveniently arranged L-shaped food preparation center

■ A Dining Room overlooking a deck through sliding doors

■ A Great Room highlighted by a corner fireplace

■ A Master Bedroom including a separate vanity and dressing area

Main floor — 988 sq. ft.
Basement — 988 sq. ft.
Garage — 400 sq. ft.

Ranch with Country Appeal

Total living area 1,539 sq. ft. ■ Price Code B

MAIN AREA

No. 24721

■ **This plan features:**

— Three bedrooms

— Two full baths

■ Tiled foyer leading into the Living Room

■ Sloped ceiling topping the Living Room also accented by a fireplace

■ Built-in shelves on either side of the arched opening between the Living Room and the Dining Room

■ Efficient U-shaped Kitchen highlighted by breakfast bar

■ French door accessing rear deck from Dining Area

■ Master Suite crowned with a decorative ceiling, and contains a private whirlpool bath

■ Roomy secondary bedrooms share a full bath in the hall

■ No materials list is available for this plan

Main floor — 1,539 sq. ft.
Basement — 1,530 sq. ft.

Country Ranch

■ *Total living area 1,485 sq. ft.* ■ *Price Code A* ■

No. 91797

■ This plan features:

— Three bedrooms

— Two full baths

▪ A railed and covered wrap-around porch, adding charm to this country-styled home

▪ A high vaulted ceiling in the Living Room

▪ A smaller Kitchen with ample cupboard and counter space, that is augmented by a large pantry

▪ An informal Family Room with access to the wood deck

▪ A private Master Suite with a spa tub and a walk-in closet

▪ Two family bedrooms that share a full hall bath

▪ A shop and storage area in the two-car garage

Main area — 1,485 sq. ft.
Garage — 701 sq. ft.

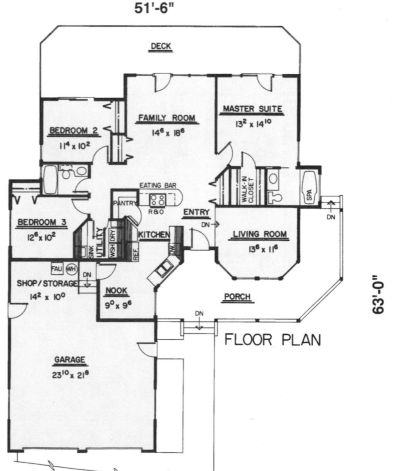

51'-6"

63'-0"

DECK

BEDROOM 2
11⁴ x 10²

FAMILY ROOM
14⁶ x 18⁶

MASTER SUITE
13² x 14¹⁰

WALK-IN CLOSET

SPA

EATING BAR

PANTRY

R&O

ENTRY

DN

BEDROOM 3
12⁶ x 10²

SINK

UTILITY

WSH DRY

KITCHEN

REF.

DW

LIVING ROOM
13⁶ x 11⁶

DN

FAU WH

DN

SHOP/STORAGE
14² x 10⁰

NOOK
9⁰ x 9⁶

PORCH

DN

GARAGE
23¹⁰ x 21⁸

FLOOR PLAN

189

Cozy Traditional

Total living area 1,862 sq. ft. ■ Price Code C

No. 93000

■ **This plan features:**

— Three bedrooms

— Two full baths

■ An angled eating bar separating the Kitchen, Breakfast Room and Great Room, while leaving these areas open for easy entertaining

■ An efficient, well-appointed Kitchen that is convenient to both the formal Dining Room and the sunny Breakfast Room

■ A spacious Master Suite with oval tub, step-in shower, double vanity and walk-in closet

■ Two additional bedrooms with ample closet space that share a full hall bath

■ No materials list is available for this plan

Main floor — 1,862 sq. ft.
Garage — 520 sq. ft.

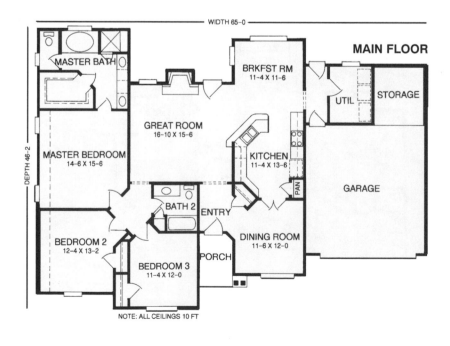

MAIN FLOOR

WIDTH 65-0

DEPTH 46-2

MASTER BATH

MASTER BEDROOM
14-6 X 15-6

BEDROOM 2
12-4 X 13-2

BEDROOM 3
11-4 X 12-0

BATH 2

ENTRY

PORCH

GREAT ROOM
16-10 X 15-6

BRKFST RM
11-4 X 11-6

KITCHEN
11-4 X 13-6

PAN

UTIL

STORAGE

GARAGE

DINING ROOM
11-6 X 12-0

NOTE: ALL CEILINGS 10 FT

■ Total living area 1,345 sq. ft. ■ Price Code A ■

No. 91342

■ This plan features:

— Three bedrooms

— Two full baths

■ A handicaped Master Bath plan is available

■ Vaulted Great Room, Dining Room and Kitchen areas

■ A Kitchen accented with angles and an abundance of cabinets for storage

■ A Master Bedroom with an ample sized wardrobe, large covered private deck, and private bath

Main area — 1,345 sq. ft.
Width — 47'-8"
Depth — 56'-0"

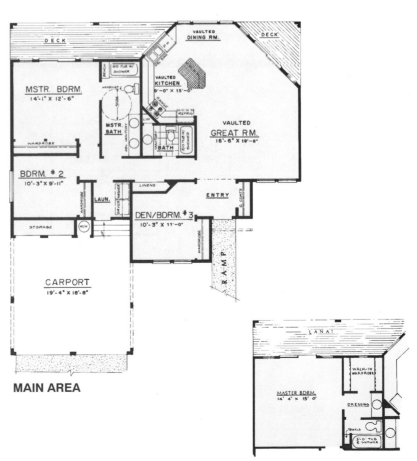

MAIN AREA

ALTERNATE BATH

Amenities Normally Found In Larger Homes

© 1995 Donald A Gardner Architects, Inc.

■ *Total living area—1,253 sq. ft.* ■ *Price Code B* ■

No. 99858

FLOOR PLAN

© 1995 Donald A Gardner Architects, Inc.

■ **This plan features:**

—Three bedrooms

—Two full baths

■ A continuous cathedral ceiling in the Great Room, Kitchen, and Dining Room giving a spacious feel to this efficient plan

■ Skylighted Kitchen with a seven foot high wall by the Great Room and a popular plant shelf

■ Master Bedroom suite opens up with a cathedral ceiling and contains walk-in and linen closets and a private bath with garden tub and dual vanity

■ Cathedral ceiling as the crowing touch to the front bedrooms/study

Main floor — 1,253 sq. ft.
Garage & Storage — 420 sq. ft.

Multiple Peaks

No. 96450

This plan features:

— Three bedrooms

— Two full baths

■ Stucco and tile with a dramatic arched entrance and large windows

■ Fireplace and built-in cabinets accent the large Great Room with a cathedral ceiling

■ Smart island Kitchen with skylit Breakfast area opens to the Great Room

■ Master Suite highlighted by a skylit bath and access to the rear deck

■ Cathedral and tray ceilings plus 9' ceilings throughout the home add dramatic vertical proportion

Main floor — 2,090 sq. ft.

Garage — 568 sq. ft.

■ *Total living area 2,090 sq. ft.* ■ *Price Code D*

Intelligent Use of Space

No. 10483

This plan features:

— Three bedrooms

— Two full baths

■ Lots of living packed into this well-designed home

■ A combined Kitchen and Dining Room

■ A highly functional Kitchen, including a corner sink under double windows

■ A Living Room accentuated by a large fireplace and well-placed skylight

■ A sleeping area containing three bedrooms and two full baths

Main area — 1,025 sq. ft.

Garage — 403 sq. ft.

■ *Total living area 1,025 sq. ft.* ■ *Price Code A*

An EXCLUSIVE DESIGN *By Karl Kreeger*

Beautiful From Front to Back

© 1995 Donald A. Gardner Architects, Inc.

B. NATHAN

■ *Total living area — 1,632 sq. ft.* ■ *Price Code C* ■

No. 99840

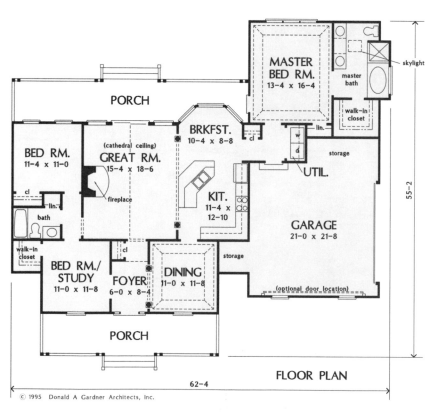

FLOOR PLAN

© 1995 Donald A. Gardner Architects, Inc.

■ This plan features:

—Three bedrooms

—Two full baths

■ Porches front and back, gables and dormers providing special charm

■ Central Great Room with a cathedral ceiling, fireplace, and a clerestory window which bringing natural light

■ Columns dividing the open Great Room from the Kitchen and the Breakfast Bay

■ A tray ceiling and columns dressing up the formal Dining Room

■ Skylighted Master Bath with shower, whirlpool tub, dual vanity and spacious walk-in closet

Main floor — 1,632 sq. ft.
Garage & Storage — 561 sq. ft.

Compact Home is Surprisingly Spacious

■ *Total living area 1,314 sq. ft.* ■ *Price Code A* ■

No. 90905

■ This plan features:

— Three bedrooms

— One full and one three quarter baths

■ A spacious Living Room warmed by a fireplace

■ A Dining Room flowing off the Living Room, with sliding glass doors to the deck

■ An efficient, well-equipped Kitchen with a snack bar, double sink, and ample cabinet and counter space

■ A Master Suite with a walk-in closet and private full bath

■ Two additional, roomy bedrooms with ample closet space and protection from street noise from the two-car garage

Main area — 1,314 sq. ft.
Basement — 1,488 sq. ft.
Garage — 484 sq. ft.
Width — 50'-0"
Depth — 54'-0"

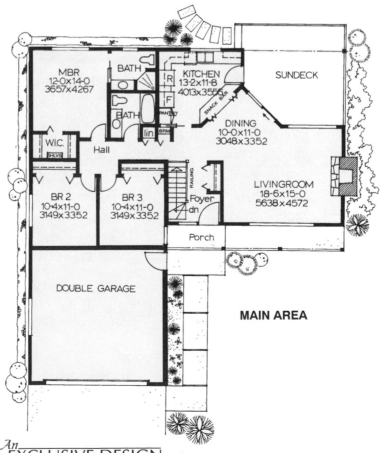

MAIN AREA

An EXCLUSIVE DESIGN
By Westhome Planners, Ltd.

Contemporary Convenience

No. 20008

This plan features:

— Three bedrooms

— Two full baths

- A Living Room with vaulted ceilings and a fireplace
- A Master Suite with vaulted ceilings, walk-in closet and the privacy of a Master Bath
- An open Kitchen with a Breakfast Bay arrangement

Main floor — 1,545 sq. ft.
Basement — 1,545 sq. ft.
Garage — 396 sq. ft.

Total living area 1,545 sq. ft. ■ Price Code B

MAIN FLOOR

A Unique Look

No. 93415

This plan features:

— Three bedrooms

— Two full baths

- The covered front porch leads into the foyer that has a 12-foot ceiling
- The Dining room is punctuated by columns at it's entrance
- The Family room also has a 12-foot ceiling, plus a fireplace and a rear window wall
- The Breakfast bay opens into the Kitchen which features an angled counter serving bar
- The Master bedrooms has a 9-foot ceiling, two closets, a full bath, and access to a private rear porch
- Two additional bedrooms on the other side of the home both have walk in closets and share a hall bath
- A covered walkway leads to a two-car garage in the rear
- No materials list is available for this plan

Main floor — 1,714 sq. ft.
Garage — 528 sq. ft.

Total living area 1,714 sq. ft. ■ Price Code B

An **EXCLUSIVE DESIGN** *By Greg Marquis*

MAIN FLOOR

WIDTH 55'-0"
DEPTH 40'-0"

Covered Front and Rear Porches

■ *Total living area 1,660 sq. ft.* ■ *Price Code C* ■

No. 92560

■ **This plan features:**

—Three bedrooms

—Two full baths

■ Traditional country styling with front and rear covered porches

■ Peninsula counter/eating bar in Kitchen for meals on the go

■ Formal Dining room with built-in cabinet

■ Vaulted ceiling and cozy fireplace highlighting Den

■ Private Master Bedroom suite pampered by five-piece bath

■ Two bedrooms at the opposite of home sharing a full bath

■ An optional slab or crawl space foundation available — please specify when ordering

Main floor — 1,660 sq. ft.
Garage — 544 sq. ft.

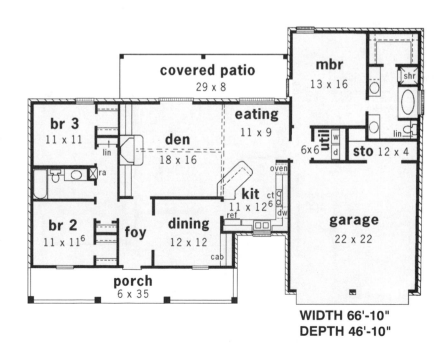

WIDTH 66'-10"
DEPTH 46'-10"

Four Bedroom Charmer

Total living area 2,185 sq. ft. ■ Price Code C

MAIN FLOOR

WIDTH — 58'-0"
DEPTH — 60'-0"

No. 91346

■ This plan features:

— Four bedrooms

— Two full baths

■ A Living Room with a masonry fireplace, large windowed bay and vaulted ceiling

■ A coffered ceiling and built-in china cabinet in the Dining Room

■ A large Family Room with a wood stove alcove

■ An island cook top, built-in pantry and a telephone desk in the efficient Kitchen

■ A luxurious Master Bedroom with whirlpool garden tub, walk-in closet and double sink vanity

■ Two bedrooms share a full bath

■ A Study with a window seat and built-in bookshelves

Main floor — 2,185 sq. ft.

Casually Elegant

© 1995 Donald A. Gardner Architects, Inc.

■ *Total living area 1,561 sq. ft.* ■ *Price Code C* ■

No. 96417

■ This plan features:

— Three bedrooms

— Two full baths

■ Arched windows, dormers and charming front and back porches with columns creating country flavoring

■ Central Great Room topped by a cathedral ceiling, a fireplace and a clerestory window

■ Breakfast bay for casual dining is open to the Kitchen

■ Columns accenting the entryway into the formal Dining Room

■ Cathedral ceiling crowning the Master Bedroom

■ Master Bath with skylights, whirlpool tub, shower, and a double vanity

Main floor – 1, 561 sq. ft.
Garage & Storage – 346 sq. ft.

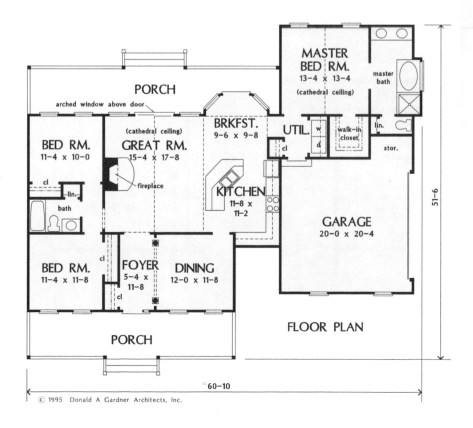

© 1995 Donald A Gardner Architects, Inc.

Great Room Heart of Home

Total living area 1,087 sq. ft. ■ *Price Code A*

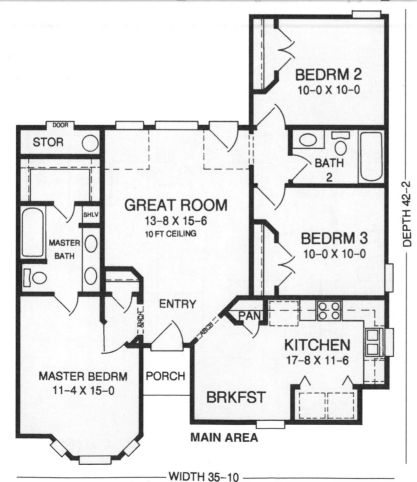

MAIN AREA

WIDTH 35-10

No. 93015

This plan features:

— Three bedrooms

— Two full baths

■ Sheltered porch leads into the Entry with arches and a Great Room

■ Spacious Great Room with a ten foot ceiling above a wall of windows and rear yard access

■ Efficient Kitchen with a built-in pantry, a laundry closet and a Breakfast area accented by a decorative window

■ Bay of windows enhances the Master Bedroom suite with a double vanity bath and a walk-in closet

■ Two additional bedrooms with ample closets, share a full bath

■ No materials list is available for this plan

Main area — 1,087 sq. ft.

Be in Tune with the Elements

No. 24240

This plan features:

— Two bedrooms

— Two full baths

- Cozy front porch to enjoy three seasons
- A simple design allowing breezes to flow from front to back, heat to rise to the attic and cool air to settle
- A fireplaced Living Room
- A formal Dining Room next to the Kitchen
- A compact Kitchen with a breakfast nook and a pantry
- A rear entrance with a covered porch
- A Master Suite with a private bath

Main area — 964 sq. ft.

■ *Total living area 964 sq. ft.* ■ *Price Code A* ■

Main Floor

Impressive Two-Sided Fireplace

No. 94972

This plan features:

— Three bedrooms

— Two full baths

- Foyer directs traffic flow into the Great Room enhanced by an impressive two-sided fireplace
- Formal Dining area is open to the great room offering a view of the fireplace
- French doors off entry access Kitchen with a large pantry, a planning desk and a snack bar
- Dinette accesses a large comfortable screen porch
- Laundry room is strategically located off the Kitchen providing direct access from the garage
- French doors provide access to the master suite topped by an elegant, decorative ceiling and highlighted by a pampering bath

Main floor — 1,580 sq. ft.
Garage — 456 sq. ft.

■ *Total living area 1,580 sq. ft.* ■ *Price Code B* ■

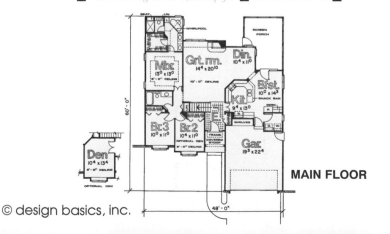

MAIN FLOOR

201

Three Bedroom Ranch

■ Total living area 1,575 sq. ft. ■ Price Code B

No. 98414

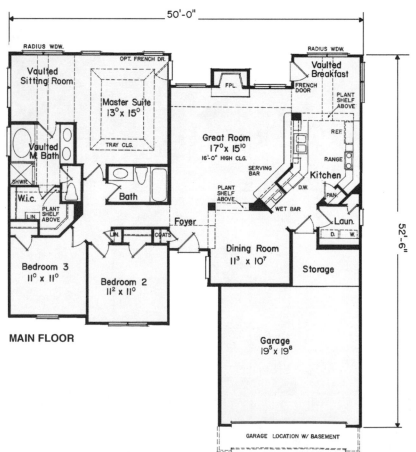

MAIN FLOOR

This plan features:

— Three bedrooms

— Two full baths

■ Formal Dining Room enhanced by a plant shelf and a side window

■ Wetbar located between the Kitchen and the Dining Room

■ Built-in pantry, a double sink and a snack bar highlight the Kitchen

■ Breakfast Room containing a radius window and a French door to the rear yard

■ Large cozy fireplace framed by windows in the Great Room

■ Master Suite with a vaulted ceiling over the sitting area, a master bath and a walk-in closet

■ An optional basement or crawl space foundation available — please specify when ordering

Main floor — 1,575 sq. ft.
Garage — 459 sq. ft.
Basement — 1,658 sq. ft.

Large Living in a Small Space

■ *Total living area 993 sq. ft.* ■ *Price Code A* ■

No. 24304

■ This plan features:

— Three bedrooms

— Two full baths

■ A sheltered entrance leads into an open Living Room with a corner fireplace and a wall of windows

■ A well-equipped Kitchen features a peninsula counter with a Nook, a laundry and clothes closet, and a built-in pantry

■ A Master Bedroom with a private bath

■ Two additional bedrooms that share full hall bath

Main floor — 993 sq. ft.
Garage — 390 sq. ft.
Optional Basement — 987 sq. ft.

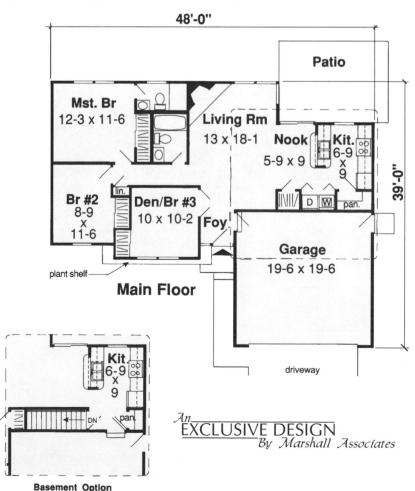

48'-0"

Patio

Mst. Br
12-3 x 11-6

Living Rm
13 x 18-1

Nook
5-9 x 9

Kit.
6-9 x 9

39'-0"

Br #2
8-9 x 11-6

Den/Br #3
10 x 10-2

Foy

D W pan.

Garage
19-6 x 19-6

plant shelf

lin.

Main Floor

driveway

Kit
6-9 x 9

DN pan.

Basement Option

An
EXCLUSIVE DESIGN
By Marshall Associates

Perfect for Your Corner Lot

No. 93192

■ **This plan features:**

– Three bedrooms

– Two full and one half baths

■ Pillars and decorative windows highlight front entrance into Foyer with cathedral ceiling and a large closet

■ Spacious Living Room enhanced by a central fireplace and decorative window

■ Convenient Kitchen with a work island, Dining area with outdoor access, and nearby laundry/Garage entry

■ Corner Master Suite offers direct access to back yard, a large walk-in closet and a pampering bath

■ Two additional bedrooms with ample closet space and easy access to a full bath

■ No materials list is available for this plan

Main floor — 1,868 sq. ft.

■ Total living area 1,868 sq. ft. ■ Price Code C ■

MAIN FLOOR PLAN

An
EXCLUSIVE DESIGN
By Ahmann Design Inc.

Small in Size, Not Style

No. 93430

■ **This plan features:**

– Three bedrooms

– Two full baths

■ Formal Foyer area leading to a spacious Family Room topped by a sloped ceiling and enhanced by a fireplace

■ Kitchen highlighted by an island and open to the Dining Area

■ Built-in pantry expanding storage space in the Kitchen

■ Master Bedroom, accented by a recessed ceiling and enjoying a walk-in closet and a five piece, private bath

■ Two additional bedrooms sharing the full bath in the hall

■ No material list is available for this plan

Main floor — 1,562 sq. ft.
Basement — 1,562 sq. ft.
Garage — 506 sq. ft.

■ Total living area 1,562 sq. ft. ■ Price Code B ■

MAIN FLOOR

An
EXCLUSIVE DESIGN
By Greg Marquis

Bay Windows and a Terrific Front Porch

■ *Total living area 1,778 sq. ft.* ■ *Price Code B* ■

No. 93261

■ **This plan features:**

— Three bedrooms

— Two full baths

■ A country front porch

■ An expansive Living Area that includes a fireplace

■ A Master Suite with a private Master Bath and a walk-in closet, as well as a bay window view of the front yard

■ An efficient Kitchen that serves the sunny Breakfast Area and the Dining Room with equal ease

■ A built-in pantry and a desk add to the conveniences in the Breakfast Area

■ Two additional bedrooms that share the full hall bath

■ A convenient main floor Laundry Room

An
EXCLUSIVE DESIGN
By Jannis Vann & Associates, Inc.

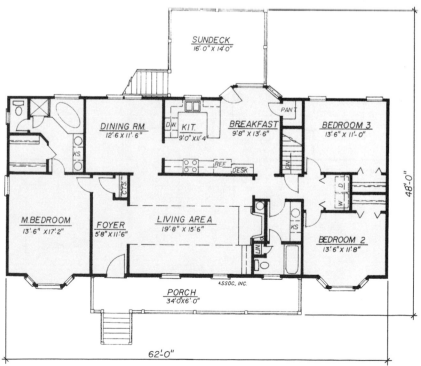

Main area — 1,778 sq. ft.
Basement — 1,008 sq. ft.
Garage — 728 sq. ft.

Sunny Dormer Brightens Foyer

© 1996 Donald A Gardner Architects, Inc.

■ *Total living area 1,386 sq. ft.* ■ *Price Code B* ■

No. 99812

■ This plan features:

—Three bedrooms

—Two full baths

■ Today's comforts with cost effective construction

■ Open Great room, Dining Room, and Kitchen topped by a cathedral ceiling emphasizing spaciousness

■ Adjoining Deck providing extra living or entertaining room

■ Front bedroom crowned in cathedral ceiling and pampered by a private bath with garden tub, dual vanity and a walk-in closet

■ Skylighted Bonus Room above the garage offering flexibility and opportunity for growth

Main floor — 1,386 sq. ft.
Garage — 517 sq. ft.
Bonus room — 314 sq. ft.

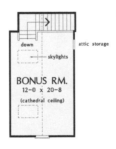

© 1996 Donald A Gardner Architects, Inc.

A Special Kind of Coziness

■ *Total living area 1,089 sq. ft.* ■ *Price Code A* ■

No. 98805

■ This plan features:

— Three bedrooms

— One full and one half baths

■ An open rail staircase compliments the central Foyer

■ The Living room with it's warm fireplace combines with the Dining area

■ The Kitchen is highlighted by a desk, a pantry, and a serving bar

■ Laundry conveniently located near the bedrooms

■ The Master suite includes a private half bath

■ Two secondary bedrooms have ample closet space

Main floor — 1,089 sq. ft.
Basement — 1,089 sq. ft.
Garage — 462 sq. ft.

MAIN FLOOR

44'0"

50'0"

DINING AREA
9' x 11'

covered deck

KITCHEN
11'6 x 9'

dw

desk   pntry   f

MASTER BEDROOM
11' x 11'

dn

linen

railing

LIVING ROOM
11' x 16'

coats

BEDROOM
9' x 9'

w   d

BEDROOM
9' x 9'

covered entry

TWO-CAR GARAGE
20' x 21'6

An
EXCLUSIVE DESIGN
By Weinmaster Home Design

Home Builders on a Budget

© 1996 Donald A. Gardner Architects, Inc.

■ *Total living area 1,498 sq. ft* ■ *Price Code B* ■

No. 99860

■ **This plan features:**

— Three bedrooms

— Two full baths

■ Down-sized country plan for home builder on a budget

■ Columns punctuate open, one-level floor plan and connect Foyer with clerestory window dormers

■ Front Porch and large, rear Deck extend living space outdoors

■ Tray ceilings decorate Master Bedroom, Dining Room and Bedroom/Study

■ Private Master Bath features garden tub, double vanity, separate shower and skylights

Main floor — 1,498 sq. ft.
Garage & storage — 427 sq. ft.

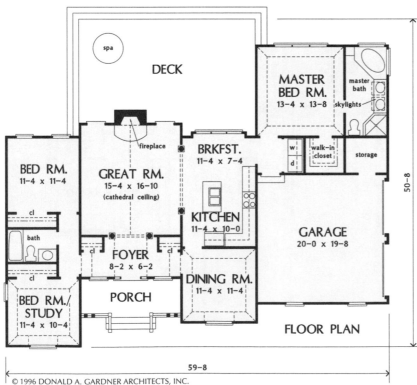

© 1996 DONALD A. GARDNER ARCHITECTS, INC.

A Compact Home

No. 93018

This plan features:

— Three bedrooms

— Two full baths

■ Siding with brick wainscoting distinguishing the elevation

■ A large Family Room with a corner fireplace and direct access to the outside

■ An arched opening leading to the Breakfast Area

■ A bay window illuminating the Breakfast Area with natural light

■ An efficiently designed, U-shaped Kitchen with ample cabinet and counter space

■ A Master Suite with a private Master Bath

■ Two additional bedrooms that share a full hall bath

■ No materials list is available for this plan

Main floor — 1,142 sq. ft.
Garage — 428 sq. ft.

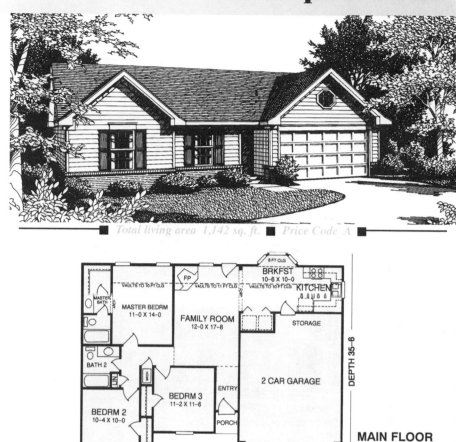

Total living area 1,142 sq. ft. ■ Price Code A

MAIN FLOOR

Superbly Styled

No. 92268

This plan features:

— Four bedrooms

— Two full baths

■ A covered Porch and an Entry with a 9' ceiling greet you

■ The Living room has a rear wall fireplace and access to the covered Patio

■ The L-shaped Kitchen which features a center island opens into the Dining room

■ The Master bedroom has a 10' vaulted ceiling, plus a private bath with a cathedral ceiling

■ Two secondary bedrooms share a hall bath, while a fourth bedroom can be used as a Study

■ This plan has a two-car garage

■ No materials list available for this plan

Main floor — 1,706 sq. ft.
Garage — 399 sq. ft.

Total living area 1,706 sq. ft. ■ Price Code B

Floor Plan

One Floor Convenience

Total living area — 1,359 sq. ft. ■ Price Code A

No. 98443

■ This plan features:

— Three bedrooms

— Two full baths

■ Vaulted Foyer blending with the vaulted Great Room giving a larger feeling to the home

■ Formal Dining Room opening into the Great Room

■ Kitchen including a serving bar, flowing into the Breakfast Room

■ Master Suite topped by a decorative tray ceiling and a vaulted ceiling in the Master Bath

■ Two additional bedrooms sharing the full bath in the hall

■ An optional crawl space or slab foundation available — please specify when ordering

■ No materials list is available for this plan

Main floor — 1,359 sq. ft.
Garage — 439 sq. ft.

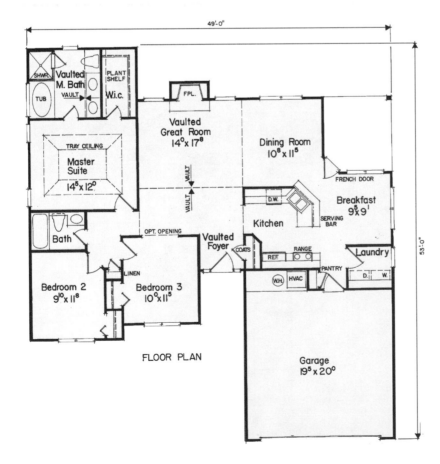

An Affordable Floor Plan

■ *Total living area 1,410 sq. ft.* ■ *Price Code A* ■

No. 91807 ✄

■ This plan features:

— Three bedrooms

— One full and one three quarter baths

■ A covered porch entry

■ An old-fashioned hearth fireplace in the vaulted ceiling Living Room

■ An efficient Kitchen with U-shaped counter that is accessible from the Dining Room

■ A Master Bedroom with a large walk-in closet and private bath

■ An optional crawl space and slab foundation available — please specify when ordering

Main floor — 1,410 sq. ft.
Garage — 484 sq. ft.

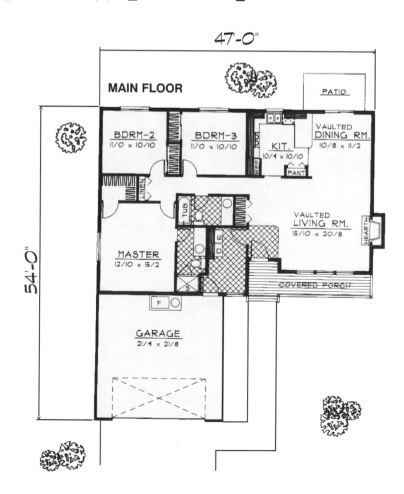

MAIN FLOOR

47'-0"

54'-0"

BDRM-2
11/0 x 10/10

BDRM-3
11/0 x 10/10

KIT.
10/4 x 10/10

PANT.

PATIO

VAULTED
DINING RM.
10/8 x 11/2

LINEN

TUB

MASTER
12/10 x 15/2

VAULTED
LIVING RM.
15/10 x 20/8

HEARTH

COVERED PORCH

GARAGE
21/4 x 21/8

Large Home with a Cottage Feeling

Total living area 3,947 sq. ft. ■ Price Code F

Main Floor

Lower Floor

An
EXCLUSIVE DESIGN
By Britt J. Willis

No. 24803

■ **This plan features:**

— Four bedrooms

— Two full and one half baths

■ Exterior detail of this home has a cottage like charm

■ Two entrances to the Dining room are punctuated by columns

■ The Great room is the centerpiece of this home and features a gas fireplace, built-ins, and a decorator ceiling

■ The sunny Breakfast room has windows on three of it's walls, plus an access door to the deck

■ The Kitchen has many special features such as, a desk, a pantry, and an island counter

■ The Master suite and it's adjoining bath and closet are spacious and luxurious

■ The finished lower level includes three bedrooms, a full bath, a Family room, and storage space

■ No materials list is available for this plan

Main level — 2,414 sq. ft.
Lower level — 1,533 sq. ft.
Basement — 881 sq. ft.
Garage — 816 sq. ft.

Quoins and Arch Window Accents

Total living area 1,704 sq. ft. ■ Price Code B

MAIN AREA

No. 94602

■ **This plan features:**

— Three bedrooms

— Two full bathrooms

■ Sheltered entry leads into pillared Foyer defining Living and Dining room areas

■ A cozy fireplace and access to Covered Porch featured in Living Room

■ Efficient Kitchen offers a work island, Utility and bright Breakfast area

■ Master Bedroom wing enhanced by a luxurious bath with a walk-in closet, double vanity and spa tub

■ Two additional bedrooms with over-sized closets, share a double vanity bath

■ An optional crawl space and slab foundation available — please specify when ordering

■ No materials list is available for this plan

Main area —1,704 sq. ft.

Private Master Suite

■ *Total living area 2,069 sq. ft.* ■ *Price Code D* ■

No. 96505

■ This plan features:

— Three bedrooms

— Two full and one half bath

■ Secluded Master Bedroom suite tucked into the rear left corner of the home with a five-piece bath and two walk-in closets

■ Two additional bedrooms at the opposite side of the home sharing the full bath in the hall

■ Expansive Living Room highlighted by a corner fireplace and access to the rear porch

■ Kitchen is sandwiched between the bright, bayed nook and the formal Dining Room providing ease in serving

Main floor — 2,069 sq. ft.
Garage — 481 sq. ft.

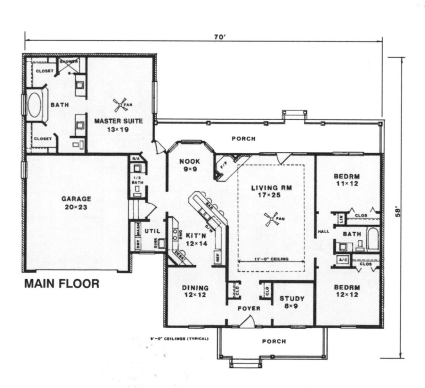

MAIN FLOOR

Traditional Ranch

Total living area 2,275 sq. ft. ■ Price Code D

No. 92404

I like tub

DECK

BR.#2
14x11

BREAKFAST

KITCHEN
10x10

MASTER
14x18

FAMILY ROOM
16X18

Trey Clg.

BR.#3
13x12

Stairs
Down

DINING
12x13

FOYER

LIVING
13x13

Cathedral

UTILITY

Trey Clg.

Cathedral

Cathedral

WORKSHOP

MAIN FLOOR

60'

62'

GARAGE
22x19

Drive

Music Den etc.?

This plan features:

— Three bedrooms

— Two full baths

■ A tray ceiling in the Master Suite that is equipped with his -n- her walk-in closets and a private Master Bath with a cathedral ceiling

■ A formal Living Room with a cathedral ceiling

■ A decorative tray ceiling in the elegant formal Dining Room

■ A spacious Family Room with a vaulted ceiling and a fireplace

■ A modern, well-appointed Kitchen with snack bar and bayed Breakfast area

■ Two additional bedrooms that share a full hall bath each having a walk-in closet

Main floor — 2,275 sq. ft.
Basement — 2,207 sq. ft.
Garage — 512 sq. ft.

Columned Elegance

■ *Total living area 2,485 sq. ft.* ■ *Price Code D* ■

No. 90461

■ This plan features:

— Three bedrooms

— Two full baths

■ Elegant columns on the front Porch

■ The Study and the Dining room both overlook the front Porch

■ The Great room has a fireplace, built-in book shelves and access to the rear Deck

■ The Kitchen has an angled serving bar with a double sink

■ The secluded Master suite has dual walk-in closets, and a bath with a spa tub

■ An optional basement or crawl space foundation available — please specify when ordering

Main floor — 2,485 sq. ft.
Basement — 2,485 sq. ft.
Garage — 484 sq. ft.

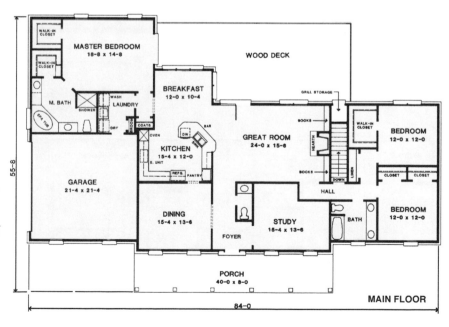

Warm and Inviting

■ *Total living area 1,363 sq. ft.* ■ *Price Code B* ■

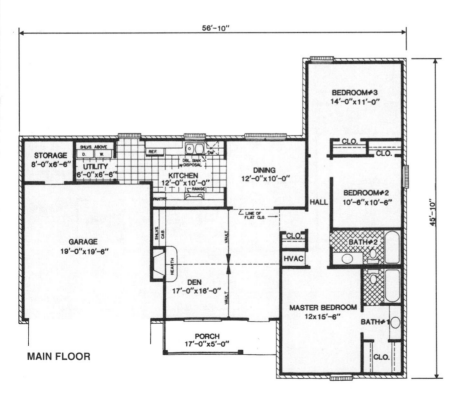

MAIN FLOOR

STORAGE
8'-0"x6'-6"

UTILITY
6'-0"x6'-6"

KITCHEN
12'-0"x10'-0"

REF.

DBL. SINK
w/DISPOSAL

RANGE

PANTRY

DINING
12'-0"x10'-0"

BEDROOM #3
14'-0"x11'-0"

CLO.

CLO.

HALL

BEDROOM #2
10'-6"x10'-6"

GARAGE
19'-0"x19'-6"

SHLVS
CAB

HEARTH

LINE OF
FLAT CLG.

CLO.

BATH #2

HVAC

DEN
17'-0"x16'-0"

VAULT

MASTER BEDROOM
12x15'-6"

PORCH
17'-0"x5'-0"

BATH #1

CLO.

56'-10"

45'-10"

No. 92528

■ **This plan features:**

— Three bedrooms

— Two full baths

■ A Den with a cozy fireplace and vaulted ceiling

■ A well-equipped Kitchen having a windowed double sink and built-in pantry

■ A spacious Master Bedroom with a private Master Bath and walk-in closet

■ Additional bedrooms sharing full hall bath

■ An optional crawl space and slab foundation available — please specify when ordering

Main floor — 1,363 sq. ft.
Garage — 434 sq. ft.

Another Nice Ranch Design

No. 90354

This plan features:

— Three bedrooms

— One full and one three quarter baths

- A vaulted ceiling in the Great Room, that includes a fireplace and access to the rear deck

- Double door entrance into the Den/third bedroom

- A Kitchen and breakfast area with a vaulted ceiling and an efficient layout

- A Master Suite crowned by a vaulted ceiling and pampered by a private bath and dressing area

- A full hall bath that serves the two additional bedrooms

Main area — 1,360 sq. ft.

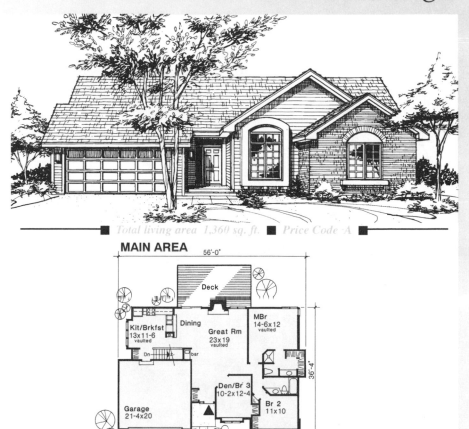

Total living area 1,360 sq. ft. ■ Price Code A

MAIN AREA

Classically Appointed

No. 92561

This plan features:

— Three bedrooms

— Two full baths

- The recessed front entry leads into a formal foyer

- The Dining room has a bright front window and directly accesses the Kitchen

- The Kitchen is U-shaped and features a wall oven, and an angled counter eating bar

- There is an eating bay that overlooks the back porch and is open to the Kitchen

- The Den has a 12-foot raised ceiling and a fireplace

- The Master suite features a raised ceiling, a full bath, and a walk in closet

- Two large secondary bedrooms share a bath in the hall

- An optional slab or a crawl space foundation available — please specify when ordering

Main floor — 1,856 sq. ft.
Garage — 521 sq. ft.

Total living area 1,856 sq. ft. ■ Price Code D

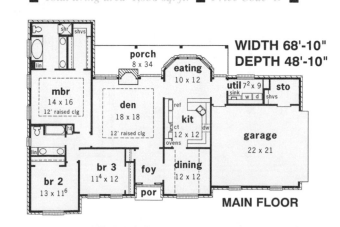

WIDTH 68'-10"
DEPTH 48'-10"

MAIN FLOOR

Pleasing to the Eye

Total living area 1,202 sq. ft. ■ Price Code A

No. 93073

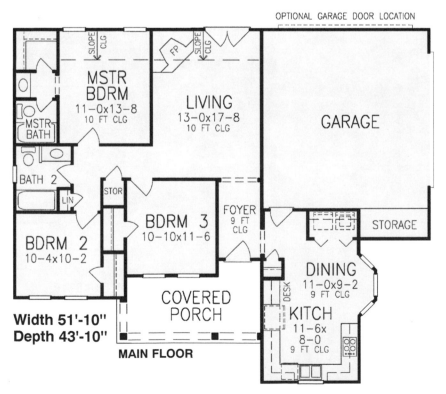

MAIN FLOOR

Width 51'-10"
Depth 43'-10"

MSTR BDRM
11-0x13-8
10 FT CLG

LIVING
13-0x17-8
10 FT CLG

GARAGE

MSTR BATH

BATH 2

STOR

LIN

BDRM 3
10-10x11-6

FOYER
9 FT CLG

STORAGE

BDRM 2
10-4x10-2

COVERED PORCH

DINING
11-0x9-2
9 FT CLG

DESK

KITCH
11-6x 8-0
9 FT CLG

OPTIONAL GARAGE DOOR LOCATION

■ This plan features:

— Three Bedrooms

— Two full baths

■ A large front porch opening to a foyer with 9' ceilings

■ Kitchen with a dining area with a bay window, built-in desk and a sunny window over the sink

■ Living room including a corner fireplace and 10' ceilings

■ Master suite with a sloped ceiling, a private bath and walk-in closet

■ Two car garage with optional door location at the rear of the home

■ An optional crawl space or slab foundation available — please specify when ordering

■ No materials list is available for this plan

Main floor — 1,202 sq. ft.
Garage — 482 sq. ft.

Elegant Entertaining Indoors and Out

■ *Total living area 2,177 sq. ft.* ■ *Price Code C* ■

No. 90001

■ This plan features:

— Four bedrooms

— Two full and one half baths

■ Gracious double doors lead into the Reception Foyer with a unique bridge over a moat to the Living Room

■ Huge, stone fireplace, a concealed bar and French doors enhance this Living Room

■ Gracious Dining Room equipped with an open grill

■ Efficient Kitchen with an eating bar as part of the Family Room, highlighted by a corner fireplace

■ Sunken Master Bedroom suite with a decorative window topped by a cathedral ceiling

■ Three large bedrooms with ample closet space share a full bath

Main floor — 2,177 sq. ft

MAIN FLOOR

219

Window Boxes Add Romantic Charm

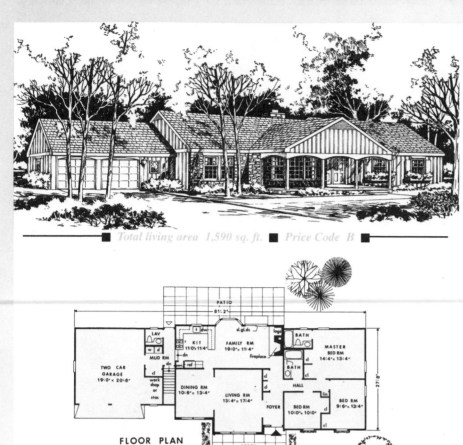

■ *Total living area 1,590 sq. ft.* ■ *Price Code B* ■

No. 90684

■ **This plan features:**

— Three bedrooms

— Two full and one half baths

■ A spacious Living Room and formal Dining Room combination that is perfect for entertaining

■ A Family Room with a large fireplace and an expansive glass wall that overlooks the patio

■ An informal Dining bay, convenient to both the Kitchen and the Family Room

■ An efficient and well-equipped Kitchen with a peninsula counter dividing it from the Family Room

■ A Master Bedroom with his-n-her closets and a private Master Bath

Main area — 1590 sq. ft.
Basement — 900 sq. ft.

FLOOR PLAN

Accent on Privacy

■ *Total living area 2,591 sq. ft.* ■ *Price Code D* ■

No. 91436

■ **This plan features:**

— Three bedrooms

— Two full and one half bath

■ Stucco exterior and arched windows create a feeling of grandeur

■ Sunken living room has a fireplace and elegant decorative ceiling

■ Sweeping views of the backyard and direct access to the rear deck from the Family Room, Kitchen and Breakfast Nook

■ Gourmet Kitchen with two pantries, full height shelving, and a large island snack bar

■ Master bedroom suite enjoys its privacy on the opposite side of the home from the other bedrooms

■ Fabulous Master bath with recessed tub and corner shower

■ Continental bath connecting the two secondary bedrooms

■ An optional basement, crawl space, and slab foundation available — please specify when ordering

Main floor — 2,591 sq. ft.
Basement — 2,591 sq. ft.

OPTIONAL BASEMENT

MAIN FLOOR

A Comfortable Informal Design

■ Total living area 1,300 sq. ft. ■ Price Code B ■

No. 94801

■ This plan features:

— Three bedrooms

— Two full baths

■ Warm, country front Porch with wood details

■ Spacious Activity Room enhanced by a pre-fab fireplace

■ Open and efficient Kitchen/Dining area highlighted by bay window, adjacent to Laundry and Garage entry

■ Corner Master Bedroom offers a pampering bath with a garden tub and double vanity topped by a vaulted ceiling

■ Two additional bedrooms with ample closets, share a full bath

■ An optional crawl space or slab foundation available — please specify when ordering

Main floor — 1,300 sq. ft.
Garage — 576 sq. ft.

Greek Revival

Total living area—1,528 sq. ft. ■ Price Code B

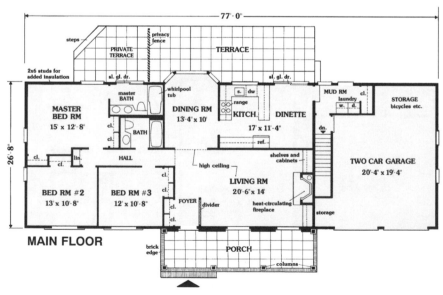

MAIN FLOOR

No. 99610

■ **This plan features:**

— Three bedrooms

— Two full baths

■ A large front porch with pediment and columns

■ A stunning, heat-circulating fireplace flanked by cabinetry and shelves in the Living Room

■ A formal Dining Room enhanced by a bay window

■ An efficient, U-shaped Kitchen with a peninsula counter and informal Dinette area

■ A Master Suite with a private Master Bath and direct access to the private terrace

■ Two additional bedrooms sharing a full hall bath

Main floor — 1,460 sq. ft.
Laundry/mudroom — 68 sq. ft.
Basement — 1,367 sq. ft.
Garage & storage — 494 sq. ft.

Carefree Convenience

■ *Total living area 1,600 sq. ft.* ■ *Price Code B* ■

No. 10674

■ This plan features:

— Three bedrooms

— Two full baths

■ A galley Kitchen, centrally-located between the Dining, Breakfast and Living Room areas

■ A huge Family Room which exits onto the patio

■ A Master Suite with double closets and vanities with two additional bedrooms share a full-half bath

Main area — 1,600 sq. ft.
Garage — 465 sq. ft.

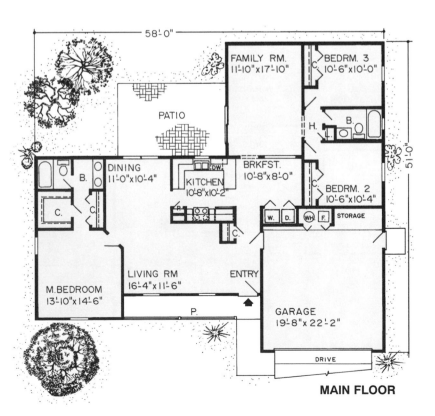

MAIN FLOOR

Split Bedroom Ranch

Total living area — 1,804 sq. ft. ■ *Price Code C*

Main floor — 1,804 sq. ft.
Basement — 1,804 sq. ft.
Garage — 506 sq. ft.

No. 90476

This plan features:

— Three bedrooms

— Two full baths

■ The formal Foyer opens into the Great room which features a vaulted ceiling and a hearth fireplace

■ The U-shaped Kitchen is located between the Dining Room and the Breakfast nook

■ The secluded Master Bedroom is spacious and includes amenities such as walk-in closets and a full bath

■ Two secondary bedrooms have ample closet space and share a full bath

■ The covered front Porch and rear Deck provide additional space for entertaining

■ An optional basement, slab or a crawl space foundation — please specify when ordering

MAIN FLOOR

Charming with Drama

No. 96478

This plan features:

- Four bedrooms
- Three full baths
- Transom windows and gables charm the exterior
- Decorative columns and dramatic ceiling treatments highlighting the interior
- Sharing a cathedral ceiling, the Great Room and Kitchen are open to each other as well as the Breakfast Bay
- A sliding pocket door separates the Kitchen from the formal Dining Room, topped by a tray ceiling
- Master Suite also includes a tray ceiling and a luxurious bath with a skylit garden tub and a walk-in closet
- Three additional bedrooms, including one with a private bath and optional arrangement for the physically changed, are located on the opposite side of the home

Main floor — 2,203 sq. ft.
Garage & storage — 551 sq. ft.
Bonus room — 395 sq. ft.

Total living area 2,203 sq. ft. ■ Price Code D

Small Yet Sophisticated

No. 92281

This plan features:

- Three bedrooms
- Two full baths
- Spacious Great Room highlighted by a fireplace and built-in shelving
- Efficient, U-shaped Kitchen with ample work and storage space, sliding glass door to Covered Patio and a Dining area with a window seat
- Spacious Master Bedroom suite enhanced by window seats, vaulted ceiling, a lavish bath and large walk-in closet
- Two additional bedrooms share a full bath
- Convenient Utility area and Garage entry
- No materials list is available for this plan

Main floor — 1,360 sq. ft.
Garage — 380 sq. ft.

Total living area 1,360 sq. ft. ■ Price Code A

MAIN FLOOR

Outdoor-Lovers' Delight

Total living area 1,540 sq. ft. ■ Price Code B

No. 10748

This plan features:

— Three bedrooms

— Two full baths

■ A roomy Kitchen and Dining Room

■ A massive Living Room with a fireplace and access to the wrap-around porch via double French doors

■ An elegant Master Suite and two additional spacious bedrooms closely located to the laundry area

Main Area — 1,540 sq. ft.
Porches — 530 sq. ft.

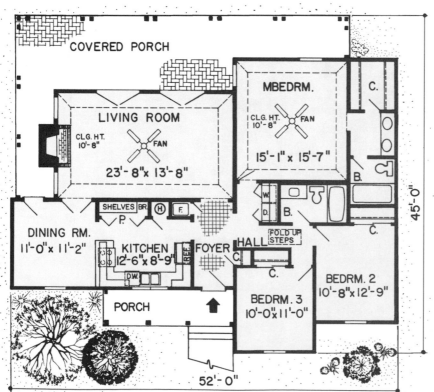

COVERED PORCH

LIVING ROOM
CLG. HT. 10'-8"
FAN
23'-8"x 13'-8"

MBEDRM.
CLG. HT. 10'-8"
FAN
15'-1"x 15'-7"

C.

B.

SHELVES BR. (H) F.
P.

W
D.
B.

C.

DINING RM.
11'-0"x 11'-2"

KITCHEN
12'-6"x 8'-9"
REF.
DW

FOYER
C.

HALL
FOLD UP STEPS

C.

BEDRM. 2
10'-8"x 12'-9"

PORCH

BEDRM. 3
10'-0"x 11'-0"

45'-0"

52'-0"

MAIN AREA

Enhanced by a Columned Porch

■ *Total living area 1,754 sq. ft.* ■ *Price Code C* ■

No. 92531

■ This plan features:

— Three bedrooms

— Two full baths

■ A Great Room with a fireplace and decorative ceiling

■ A large efficient Kitchen with Breakfast area

■ A Master Bedroom with a private Master Bath and walk-in closet

■ A formal Dining Room conveniently located near the Kitchen

■ Two additional bedrooms with walk-in closets and use of full hall bath

■ An optional crawl space or slab foundation available — please specify when ordering

Main floor — 1,754 sq. ft.
Garage — 552 sq.ft.

MAIN FLOOR

Contemporary Ranch Design

No. 26740

This plan features:

— Three bedrooms

— Two full baths

- Sloping cathedral ceilings

- An efficient, centrally-located Kitchen

- A Daylight Room for dining pleasure

- A secluded Master Bedroom with Master Bath and access to private Deck

- A Great Hall with fireplace

Main floor — 1,512 sq. ft.
Garage — 478 sq. ft.

■ *Total living area 1,512 sq. ft.* ■ *Price Code B* ■

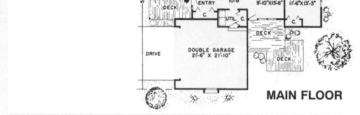

MAIN FLOOR

Welcoming Gables and Porch

No. 93033

This plan features:

— Four bedrooms

— Two full and one half baths

- The large Master bedroom has an attached bath with dual vanity and a walk in closet

- Three additional bedrooms each have plenty of closet space and share a full bath

- The Dining room and Great room share a double sided fireplace

- The island Kitchen has a walk-in pantry

- Have a relaxing meal in the Nook or on the back Porch

- No materials list is available for this plan

Main floor — 2,389 sq. ft.
Garage — 543 sq. ft.

■ *Total living area 2,389 sq. ft.* ■ *Price Code D* ■

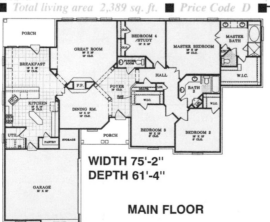

WIDTH 75'-2"
DEPTH 61'-4"

MAIN FLOOR

■ *Total living area 1,388 sq. ft.* ■ *Price Code A* ■

No. 93279

■ This plan features:

— Three bedrooms

— Two full baths

■ A central, double fireplace adding warmth and atmosphere to the Family Room, Kitchen and the Breakfast area

■ An efficient Kitchen highlighted by a peninsula counter that doubles as a snack bar

■ A Master Suite that includes a walk-in closet, a double vanity, separate shower and tub in the bath

■ Two additional bedrooms sharing a full hall bath

■ A wooden deck that can be accessed from the Breakfast Area

■ An optional crawl space or slab foundation — please specify when ordering

Main floor — 1,388 sq. ft.
Garage — 400 sq. ft.

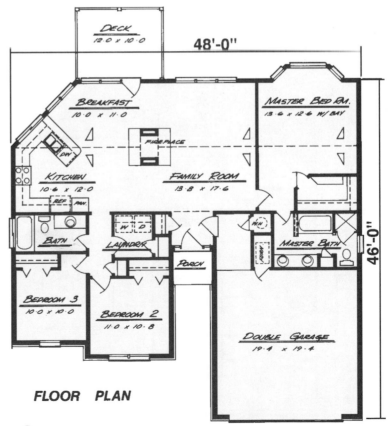

FLOOR PLAN

An
EXCLUSIVE DESIGN
By Jannis Vann & Associates, Inc.

Compact Three Bedroom

© 1990 Donald A. Gardner Architects, Inc.

No. 96418

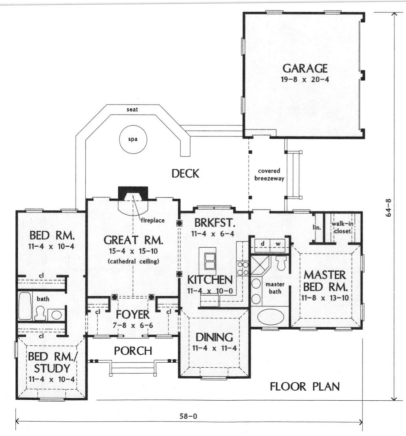

FLOOR PLAN

© 1990 Donald A. Gardner Architects, Inc.

This plan features:

—Three bedrooms

—Two full baths

■ Contemporary interior punctuated by elegant columns

■ Dormers above the covered porch light the foyer leading to the dramatic Great Room crowned in a cathedral ceiling and enhanced by a fireplace

■ Great Room opens to the island Kitchen with Breakfast area and access to a spacious rear deck

■ Tray ceilings adding interest to the Bedroom/Study, Dining Room and the Master Bedroom

■ Luxurious Master Bedroom suite highlighted by a walk-in closet and a bath with dual vanity, separate shower and a whirlpool tub

Main floor — 1,452 sq. ft.
Garage & storage — 427 sq. ft.

Flexible Plan Creates Many Options

■ *Total living area 1,016 sq. ft.* ■ *Price Code A* ■

No. 90324

■ This plan features:

— Two bedrooms with optional third bedroom/den

— Two full baths

■ A Great Room featuring vaulted ceiling, fireplace, and built-in bookcase

■ An eat-in Kitchen opening onto a partially enclosed deck through sliding doors

■ An L-shaped design of the Kitchen providing for easy meal preparation

■ A Master Bedroom with private bath, large walk-in closet, and window seat

Main floor — 1,016 sq. ft.

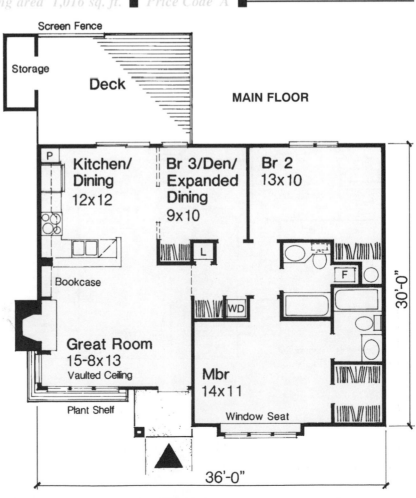

Screen Fence

Storage

Deck

MAIN FLOOR

Kitchen/ Dining
12x12

Br 3/Den/ Expanded Dining
9x10

Br 2
13x10

P

L

WD

Bookcase

Great Room
15-8x13
Vaulted Ceiling

Mbr
14x11

F

Plant Shelf

Window Seat

30'-0"

36'-0"

Attractive Ceiling Treatments and Open Layout

■ *Total living area — 1,654 sq. ft.* ■ *Price Code B* ■

No. 96506

This plan features:

— Three bedrooms

— Two full and one half baths

■ Great Room and Master Suite with step-up ceiling treatments

■ A cozy fireplace providing warm focal point in the Great Room

■ Open layout between Kitchen, Dining and Great Room lending a more spacious feeling

■ Five-piece, private bath and walk-in closet pampering Master Suite

■ Two additional bedrooms located at opposite end of home

■ Master Suite sharing the full bath in the hall

Main floor — 1,654 sq. ft.
Garage — 480 sq. ft.

MAIN FLOOR

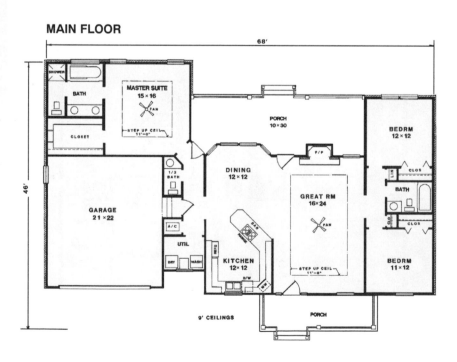

Detailed Ranch Design

No. 90360

This plan features:

- Three bedrooms
- Two full baths
- A Breakfast area with a vaulted ceiling and access to the deck
- An efficient Kitchen with built-in pantry and appliances
- A Master bedroom with private bath and ample closet space
- A large Great Room with a vaulted ceiling and cozy fireplace

Main area — 1,283 sq. ft.

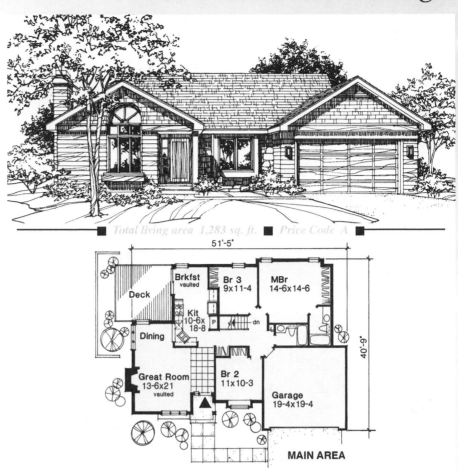

■ *Total living area 1,283 sq. ft.* ■ *Price Code A* ■

51'-5"

40'-9"

Deck

Brkfst
vaulted

Br 3
9x11-4

MBr
14-6x14-6

Kit
10-6x
18-8

Dining

dn

Great Room
13-6x21
vaulted

Br 2
11x10-3

Garage
19-4x19-4

MAIN AREA

Elegant Brick Styling

No. 92563

This plan features:

- Three bedrooms
- Two full baths
- The covered front porch opens into the foyer
- The Den has a vaulted ceiling, and a fireplace with built in cabinets and shelves on either side of it
- The L-shaped Kitchen can be accessed from either the Dining room or the Eating nook
- The Master suite is isolated and features a sumptuous bath and a walk in closet
- Two additional bedrooms are located on the other side of the home, each has a walk in closet
- This home is completed by a two-car garage and storage space
- An optional slab or a crawl space foundation — please specify when ordering this plan

Main floor — 1,680 sq. ft.
Garage — 538 sq. ft.

■ *Total living area 1,680 sq. ft.* ■ *Price Code C* ■

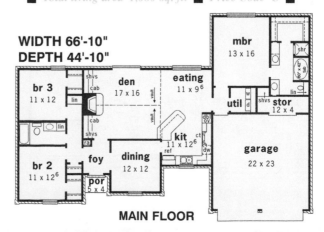

WIDTH 66'-10"
DEPTH 44'-10"

mbr
13 x 16

br 3
11 x 12

den
17 x 16

eating
11 x 9⁶

util

stor
12 x 4

kit
11 x 12⁶

garage
22 x 23

br 2
11 x 12⁶

foy

dining
12 x 12

por
5 x 4

MAIN FLOOR

European Flair

Total living area 1,544 sq. ft. ■ *Price Code B*

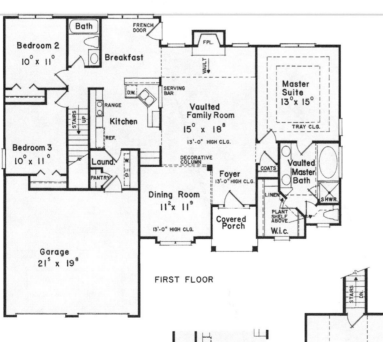

FIRST FLOOR

OPT. BASEMENT STAIR LOCATION

OPTIONAL BONUS ROOM

Main floor — 1,544 sq. ft.
Bonus room — 284 sq. ft.
Garage — 440 sq. ft.
Width 54'-0"
Depth 47'-6"

■ This plan features:

— Three bedrooms

— Two full baths

■ Large fireplace serving as an attractive focal point for the vaulted Family Room

■ Decorative column defining the elegant Dining Room

■ Kitchen including a serving bar for the Family Room and a Breakfast area

■ Master Suite topped by a tray ceiling over the bedroom and a vaulted ceiling over the five-piece Master Bath

■ Optional bonus room for future expansion

■ An optional basement or crawl space foundation — please specify when ordering

■ No materials list is available for this plan

Accented by Vaulted Ceilings & Columns

■ *Total living area 2,094 sq. ft.* ■ *Price Code C* ■

No. 98421

■ This plan features

—Three bedrooms

—Two full and one half baths

■ Columns defining the entrances of the Dining Room, Family Room and the Breakfast Room

■ Vaulted ceilings adding volume to the Foyer, Dining Room, Living Room, Family Room, Breakfast Room and the Master Bath

■ An efficient and well-appointed Kitchen highlighted by serving bar to the Family Room

■ A large focal point fireplace enhancing the Family Room

■ Private Master Suite topped by a tray ceiling and enhanced by a walk-in closet and lavish bath

■ Two additional bedrooms sharing the full bath in the hall

■ An optional basement, crawl space or slab foundation — please specify when ordering

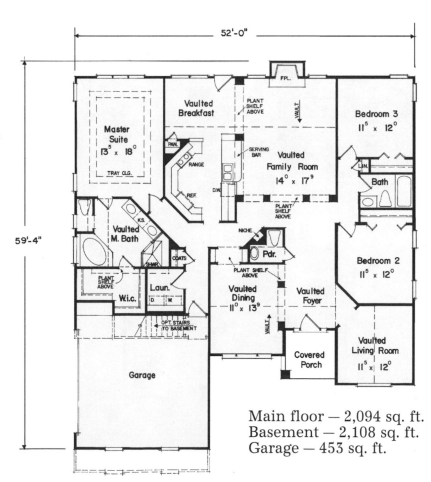

Main floor — 2,094 sq. ft.
Basement — 2,108 sq. ft.
Garage — 453 sq. ft.

Carefree Contemporary

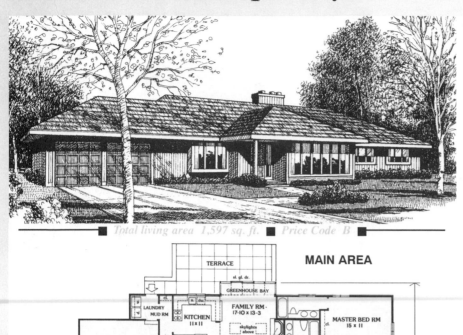

Total living area 1,597 sq. ft. ● Price Code B

MAIN AREA

TERRACE

sl. gl. dr.

GREENHOUSE BAY

LAUNDRY MUD RM

KITCHEN 11 x 11

FAMILY RM. 17-10 x 13-3

skylights above

high sloping ceiling

MASTER BED RM 15 x 11

TWO CAR GARAGE

DINING RM 14-4 x 11

HALL

heat-circulating fireplace

BED RM 11 x 10

BED RM 12-4 x 10

storage

window alcove

FOYER

LIVING RM 20 x 13

38'-8"

75'-4"

No. 90697

■ This plan features:

— Three bedrooms

— Two full baths

■ A corner fireplace adding intrigue to the sunny Living Room

■ Skylights in the high sloping ceiling of the Family Room, which also has a greenhouse bay window and a heat-circulating fireplace

■ An elegant formal Dining Room with a window alcove

■ A Master Bedroom with a private Master Bath and two closets

■ Two additional bedrooms which share a full hall bath

Main area — 1,597 sq. ft.
Basement — 1,512 sq. ft.

Classic Columns Accent Porch

Total living area 1,417 sq. ft. ● Price Code A

Patio

Mstr 14⁰x16⁰

Din 9⁰x13²

Kit 9⁰x13⁴

Gar 22⁰x22⁰

Bed 10¹⁰x10⁰

Bed 10¹⁰x10⁰

Grt 17²x19²

Porch

40'-5"

64'-8"

MAIN FLOOR

No. 94729

■ **This plan features:**

— Three bedrooms

— Two full baths

■ Classic columns accenting the entry Porch of this home achieving an elegant style

■ An open floor plan incorporating twelve foot ceilings in the main living areas

■ Sliding glass doors opening to a rear patio for extended living space

■ Large Kitchen including a peninsula counter/eating bar, convenient for meals on the go

■ Master Suite designed to take advantage of the rear views and has a large walk-in closet

■ Master Bath with a garden tub and a double vanity

■ Two additional bedrooms sharing a full family bath

Main floor — 1,417 sq. ft.
Garage — 522 sq. ft.
Deck — 288 sq. ft.

An
EXCLUSIVE DESIGN
By United Design Associates

Simply Cozy

■ *Total living area 1,325 sq. ft.* ■ *Price Code A* ■

No. 98912

This plan features:

— Three bedrooms

— Two full baths

■ Quaint front porch sheltering Entry into the Living Area showcased by a massive fireplace and built-ins below a vaulted ceiling

■ Formal Dining Room accented by a bay of glass with Sun Deck access

■ Efficient, galley Kitchen with Breakfast area, laundry facilities and outdoor access

■ Secluded Master Bedroom offers a roomy walk-in closet and plush bath with two vanities and a garden window tub

■ Two additional bedrooms with ample closets, share a full skylit bath

Main floor — 1,325 sq. ft.

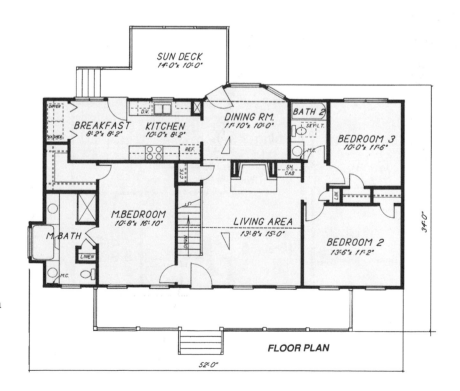

FLOOR PLAN

An
EXCLUSIVE DESIGN
By Jannis Vann & Associates, Inc.

Inviting Entrance Welcomes All

■ Total living area—863 sq. ft. ■ Price Code A ■

No. 92026

■ **This plan features:**

— Two bedrooms

— One full bath

■ A covered front porch

■ A large Living Room/Dining Room combination

■ An efficient U-shaped Kitchen with a double sink and ample cabinet and counter space

■ Two bedrooms that share the full hall bath and have ample storage space

Main area — 863 sq. ft.

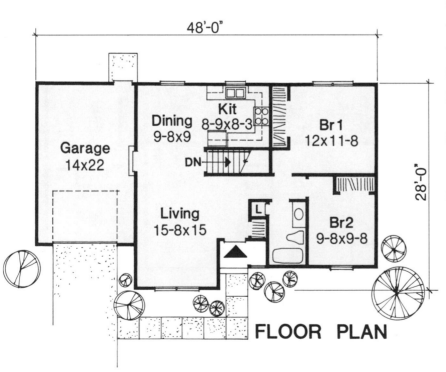

FLOOR PLAN

48'-0"

28'-0"

Garage
14x22

Dining
9-8x9

Kit
8-9x8-3

Br 1
12x11-8

DN

Living
15-8x15

Br2
9-8x9-8

One Story Country Home

■ Total living area 1,367 sq. ft. ■ Price Code A ■

No. 99639 ⚒

■ This plan features:

— Three bedrooms

— Two full baths

■ A Living Room with an imposing high ceiling that slopes down to a normal height of eight feet, focusing on the decorative heat-circulating fireplace at the rear wall

■ An efficient Kitchen that adjoins the Dining Room that views the front Porch

■ A Dinette Area for informal eating in the Kitchen that can comfortably seat six people

■ A Master Suite arranged with a large dressing area that has a walk-in closet plus two linear closets and space for a vanity

Main area — 1,367 sq. ft.
Basement — 1,267 sq. ft.
Garage — 431 sq. ft.

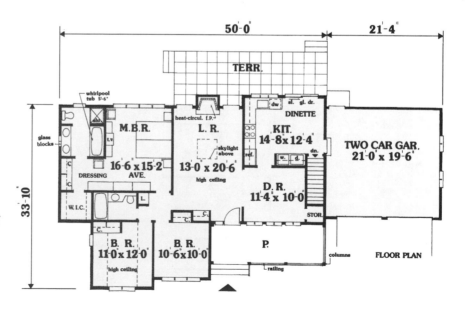

Clever Use of Interior Space

© 1994 Donald A. Gardner Architects, Inc.

No. 99844

■ This plan features:

— Three bedrooms

— Two full baths

■ Efficient interior with cathedral and tray ceilings create feeling of space

■ Great Room boosts cathedral ceiling above cozy fireplace, built-in shelves and columns

■ Octagon Dining Room and Breakfast alcove bathed in light and easily access Porch

■ Open Kitchen features island counter sink and pantry

■ Master Bedroom suite enhance by tray ceiling and plush bath

Main floor — 1,737 sq. ft.
Garage & storage — 517 sq. ft.

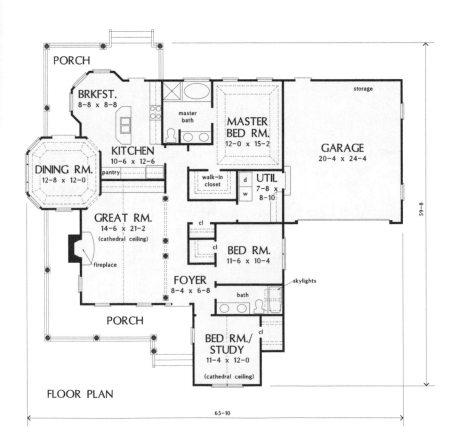

FLOOR PLAN

240

Vaulted Ceilings Enhance Plan

No. 91527

This plan features:

- Three bedrooms

- Two full baths

■ A formal Living Room with a vaulted ceiling that flows into the formal Dining Room

■ An efficient Kitchen with a built-in pantry and a peninsula counter that doubles as an eating bar and adjoins the sunny Eating Nook

■ A Family Room with a cozy fireplace and a vaulted ceiling

■ A Master Suite that includes a walk-in closet and a private bath with a spa tub and double vanity

■ Two additional bedrooms that share a full bath

Main floor — 1,565 sq. ft.
Garage — 440 sq. ft.

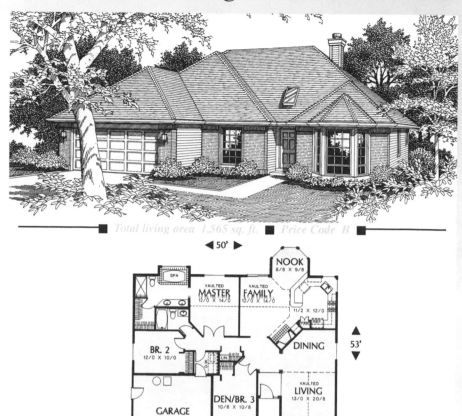

Total living area 1,565 sq. ft. ■ Price Code B

MAIN FLOOR

Bricks and Arches Detail this Ranch

No. 94973 ✕

This plan features:

- Two bedrooms

- Two full and one half baths

■ A Master Bedroom with a vaulted ceiling, luxurious bath, complimented by a skylit walk-in closet

■ A second bedroom that shares a full bath with the den/optional bedroom, which has built-in curio cabinets

■ Columns and arched windows defining the elegant Dining Room

■ A Great Room sharing a see-through fireplace with the Hearth Room, which also has a built in entertainment center

■ A gazebo-shaped nook opening into the Kitchen with a center island, snack bar and desk

Main floor — 2,512 sq. ft.
Garage — 783 sq. ft.

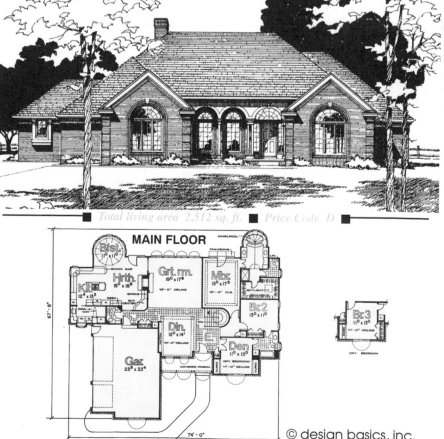

Total living area 2,512 sq. ft. ■ Price Code D

MAIN FLOOR

Easy, Economical Building

© 1996 Donald A Gardner Architects, Inc.

Total living area 1,959 sq. ft. ■ Price Code C

No. 99813

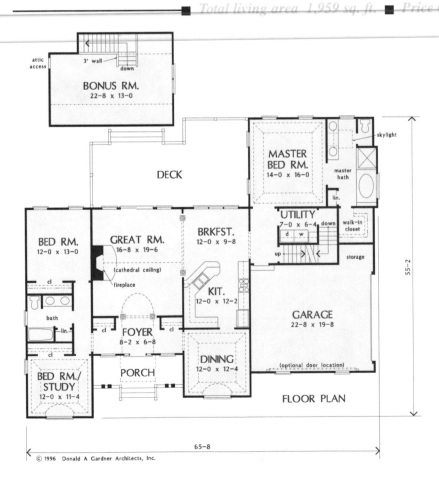

attic access

3' wall
down

BONUS RM.
22-8 x 13-0

DECK

MASTER BED RM.
14-0 x 16-0

skylight

master bath

lin.

UTILITY
7-0 x 6-4

down

d   w

up

walk-in closet

storage

BED RM.
12-0 x 13-0

GREAT RM.
16-8 x 19-6

(cathedral ceiling)

fireplace

BRKFST.
12-0 x 9-8

cl

bath

lin.

KIT.
12-0 x 12-2

GARAGE
22-8 x 19-8

cl

FOYER
8-2 x 6-8

cl

cl

BED RM./STUDY
12-0 x 11-4

PORCH

DINING
12-0 x 12-4

(optional door location)

FLOOR PLAN

55-2

65-8

© 1996 Donald A Gardner Architects, Inc.

This plan features:

— Three bedrooms

— Two full baths

■ Many architectural elements offer efficient and economical design

■ Great Room vaulted ceiling gracefully arches to include arched window dormer

■ Open Kitchen with angled counter easily serves Breakfast area

■ Tray ceilings enhance Dining Room, front bedroom and Master Bedroom

■ Private Master Bath includes garden tub, double vanity and skylight

■ An optional basement or crawl space foundation — please specify when ordering

Main floor — 1,959 sq. ft.
Bonus room — 385 sq. ft.
Garage & storage — 484 sq. ft.

■ *Total living area 2,445 sq. ft.* ■ *Price Code D* ■

No. 98511

■ This plan features:

— Four bedrooms

— Three full and one half baths

■ Entertaining in grand style in the formal Living Room, the Dining Room, or under the covered patio in the backyard

■ A Family Room crowned in a cathedral ceiling, enhanced by a center fireplace and built-in book shelves

■ An efficient Kitchen highlighted by a wall oven, plentiful counter space and a pantry

■ A Master Bedroom with a sitting area, huge walk in closet, private bath and access to a covered lanai

■ A secondary bedroom wing containing three additional bedrooms with ample closet space and two full baths

■ No materials list is available for this plan

Main floor — 2,445 sq. ft.
Garage — 630 sq. ft.

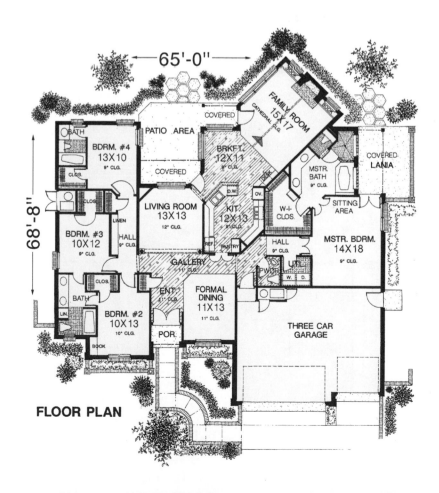

FLOOR PLAN

243

Beautiful Combination of Old and New

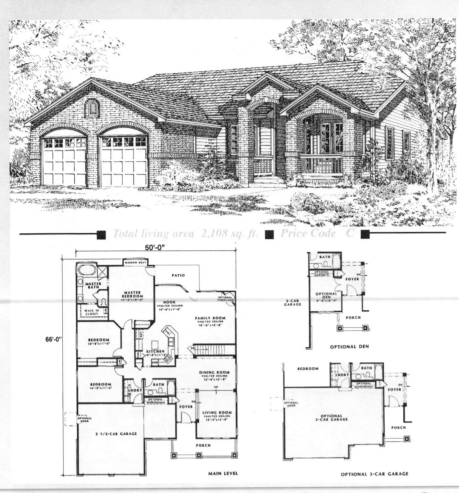

Total living area 2,108 sq. ft. ■ Price Code C

No. 24256

■ This plan features:

— Three bedrooms

— Two full baths

■ Vaulted ceilings in the family living areas; Living Room, Dining Room, Family Room and Eating Nook

■ An open layout between the Kitchen, Nook, and Family Room, making the rooms appear even more spacious

■ A corner fireplace in the Family Room, which also has access to the patio

■ A peninsula counter in the island Kitchen that doubles as an eating bar

■ A lavish Master Suite that is equipped with a private bath and walk-in closet

■ Two family bedrooms that share a full hall bath

Main Area — 2,108 sq. ft.

An
EXCLUSIVE DESIGN
By Energetic Enterprises

Family Room is the Center of Attention

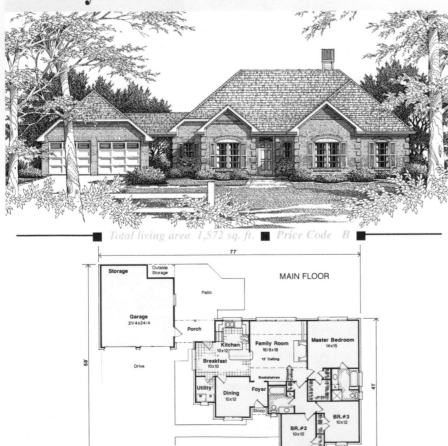

Total living area 1,572 sq. ft. ■ Price Code B

No. 93431

■ This plan features:

— Three bedrooms

— Two full baths

■ Spacious Family Room enhanced by a cozy fireplace and adjoining with the Breakfast/Kitchen allowing for interaction between the rooms

■ Dining Room, to the left of the Foyer and in proximity to the Breakfast/Kitchen area

■ Master Suite including two closets, including a walk-in, and a private Master Bath

■ Two additional bedrooms sharing the full bath in the hall

■ No materials list is available for this plan

Main floor — 1,572 sq. ft.
Garage — 550 sq. ft.

An
EXCLUSIVE DESIGN
By Greg Marquis

Quoin Accents Distinguish this Plan

Total living area 1,142 sq. ft. ■ *Price Code A* ■

No. 93017

■ **This plan features:**

— Three bedrooms

— Two full baths

■ A traditional brick elevation with quoin accents

■ A large Family Room with a corner fireplace and direct access to the outside

■ An arched opening leading to the Breakfast Area

■ A bay window illuminating the Breakfast Area with natural light

■ An efficiently designed, U-shaped kitchen with ample cabinet and counter space

■ A Master Suite with a private Master Bath

■ Two additional bedrooms that share a full hall bath

■ No materials list is available for this plan

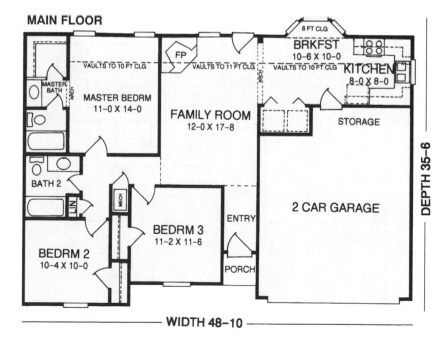

MAIN FLOOR

Main floor — 1,142 sq. ft.
Garage — 428 sq. ft.

Clerestory Windows Add Light

■ Total living area 1,589 sq. ft. ■ Price Code B

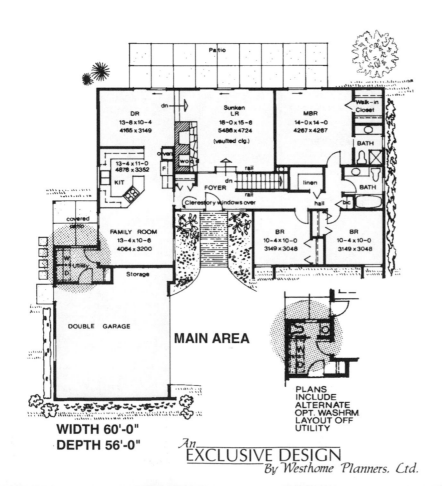

Patio

DR
13-8 x 10-4
4165 x 3149

Sunken
LR
18-0 x 15-6
5486 x 4724
(vaulted clg.)

MBR
14-0 x 14-0
4267 x 4267

Walk-in
Closet

BATH

13-4 x 11-0
4876 x 3352

KIT

oven

w.o.

F

rail

FOYER

dn

rail

linen

BATH

b.c.

hall

Clerestory windows over

covered
patio

FAMILY ROOM
13-4 x 10-6
4064 x 3200

BR
10-4 x 10-0
3149 x 3048

BR
10-4 x 10-0
3149 x 3048

W
D

Utility

Storage

DOUBLE GARAGE

MAIN AREA

PLANS
INCLUDE
ALTERNATE
OPT. WASHRM.
LAYOUT OFF
UTILITY

WIDTH 60'-0"
DEPTH 56'-0"

An
EXCLUSIVE DESIGN
By Westhome Planners, Ltd.

No. 90926

■ **This plan features:**

– Three bedrooms

– One full and one three quarter baths

■ Striking contemporary exterior compliments an exceptional design

■ Open Foyer leads to Sunken Living Room with a vaulted ceiling, a hearth fireplace and sliding glass doors to Patio

■ Hub Kitchen easily serves Dining Room, Family Room and Covered Patio

■ Comfortable Family Room with Patio and Utility/Garage access

■ Master Bedroom offers Patio access, a walk-in closet and private bath

■ Two additional bedrooms with ample closets, share a full bath

Main area — 1,589 sq. ft.
Garage — 474 sq. ft.

Step Saving Convenience

■ *Total living area 1,955 sq. ft.* ■ *Price Code C* ■

No. 92617

■ This plan features:

— Three bedrooms

— Two full baths

■ A covered Porch leading into the Foyer

■ A corner fireplace and a wall of windows with an atrium door to the Patio in the Great Room

■ An efficient Kitchen with a built-in pantry, a peninsula counter/snack bar separating it from the Breakfast alcove

■ Topped by a tray ceiling, a private Master Bedroom offers an ultra bath with a walk-in closet, a double vanity and a window tub

■ Two additional bedrooms, one with a sloped ceiling, sharing a full hall bath

■ No materials list is available for this plan

Main floor — 1,955 sq. ft.

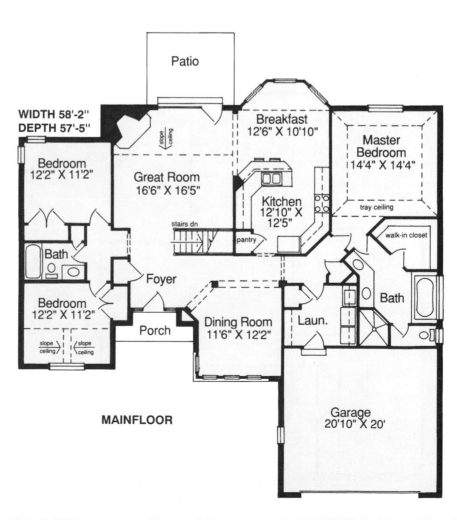

WIDTH 58'-2"
DEPTH 57'-5"

Patio

Breakfast
12'6" X 10'10"

Master Bedroom
14'4" X 14'4"

tray ceiling

Bedroom
12'2" X 11'2"

Great Room
16'6" X 16'5"

Kitchen
12'10" X 12'5"

walk-in closet

slope ceiling

stairs dn

pantry

Bath

Foyer

Bath

Bedroom
12'2" X 11'2"

Dining Room
11'6" X 12'2"

Laun.

slope ceiling

Porch

Garage
20'10" X 20'

MAINFLOOR

Timeless Appeal

■ *Total living area 1,170 sq. ft.* ■ *Price Code A* ■

No. 93075

Width 51'-10"
Depth 53'-6"

GARAGE

STORAGE

SLOPE CLG

FP

SLOPE CLG

MSTR
BDRM
11-0x13-8
10 FT CLG

LIVING
13-0x17-8
10 FT CLG

DESK

DINING
11-0x
9-2

MSTR
BATH

KITCH
11-6x
8-0

BATH 2

STOR

LIN

FOYER

BDRM 2
10-4x10-2

BDRM 3
10-10x11-6

COVERED
PORCH

MAIN FLOOR

This plan features:

— Three bedrooms

— Two full baths

■ Ten foot ceilings giving the Living Room an open feel

■ Cozy corner fireplace and access to the rear yard highlight the Living Room

■ Dining area enhanced by a sunny bay window and is open to the Kitchen

■ Bedrooms conveniently grouped and include roomy closets

■ Master bedroom features a private bath

■ Garage is located on the rear and not visible from the front

■ An optional crawl space or slab foundaiton — please specify when ordering

■ No materials list is available for this plan

Main floor — 1,170 sq. ft.
Garage — 478 sq. ft.

Old World Flavor

No. 93416

This plan features:

— Three bedrooms

— Two full baths

Timely floor plan easily supports a busy family's contemporary lifestyle

Generous center island Kitchen facilitates quick meal preparation

Twelve foot ceiling in the Family Room Entry leads into the Dining Room framed by columns

Vaulted ceiling in the flexible Living Room/Study

Two walk-in closets, a tray ceiling and a private bath compliment the Master Suite

No materials list is available for this plan

Main floor — 1,475 sq ft

Garage & Storage — 455 sq. ft.

Width 43'-0"

Depth 43'-0"

An **EXCLUSIVE DESIGN** By Greg Marquis

■ Total living area 1,475 sq. ft. ■ Price Code A ■

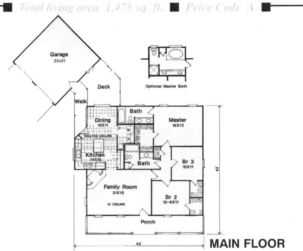

MAIN FLOOR

Options Abound

No. 20061

This plan features:

— Three bedrooms

— Two full baths

A striking exterior featuring vertical siding, shake shingles and stone

A Kitchen with built-in pantry and appliances

An open beamed Master Bedroom

Main floor — 1,674 sq. ft.

Basement — 1,656 sq. ft.

Garage — 472 sq. ft.

■ Total living area 1,674 sq. ft. ■ Price Code B ■

An **EXCLUSIVE DESIGN** By Karl Kreeger

MAIN FLOOR

One-Story Home Brimming With Amenities

Total living area 2,079 sq. ft. ■ Price Code C

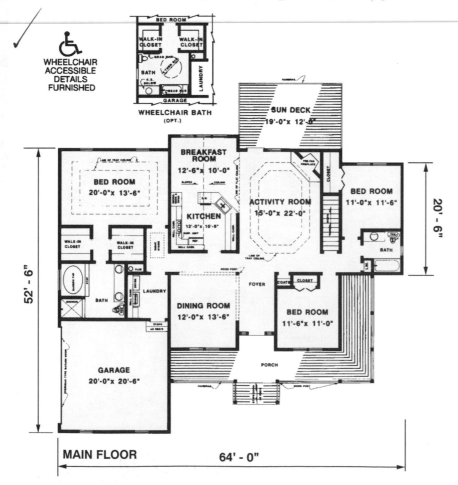

WHEELCHAIR
ACCESSIBLE
DETAILS
FURNISHED

WHEELCHAIR BATH
(OPT.)

BED ROOM

WALK-IN CLOSET

WALK-IN CLOSET

BATH

LAUNDRY

GARAGE

SUN DECK
19'-0" x 12'-0"

BREAKFAST ROOM
12'-6" x 10'-0"

KITCHEN
12'-0" x 10'-8"

ACTIVITY ROOM
15'-0" x 22'-0"

BED ROOM
11'-0" x 11'-6"

BED ROOM
20'-0" x 13'-6"

WALK-IN CLOSET

WALK-IN CLOSET

BATH

BATH

LAUNDRY

DINING ROOM
12'-0" x 13'-6"

FOYER

CLOSET

BED ROOM
11'-6" x 11'-0"

GARAGE
20'-0" x 20'-6"

PORCH

MAIN FLOOR

52' - 6"

20' - 6"

64' - 0"

No. 94805

This plan features:

— Three bedrooms

— Two full baths

■ Pleasant country look with double dormer windows and wrap around Porch

■ Foyer opens to Dining Room and Activity Room enhanced by tray ceiling, corner fireplace and Sun Deck access

■ Kitchen/Breakfast Room topped by a sloped ceiling, offers an angular serving counter and lots of storage space

■ Secluded Master Bedroom graced with twin walk-in closets and a garden tub bath

■ Two additional bedrooms with easy access to full bath

Main floor — 2,079 sq. ft.
Garage — 438 sq. ft.
Basement — 2,079 sq. ft.

Natural Light Gives Bright Living Spaces

■ *Total living area 1,620 sq. ft.* ■ *Price Code B* ■

No. 24317

■ **This plan features:**

— Three bedrooms

— One full and one three quarter baths

■ A generous use of windows throughout the home, creating a bright living space

■ A center work island and a built-in pantry in the Kitchen

■ A sunny Eating Nook for informal eating and a formal Dining Room for entertaining

■ A large Living Room with a cozy fireplace to add atmosphere to the room as well as warmth

■ A Master Bedroom with a private bath and double closets

■ Two additional bedrooms that share a full, compartmented hall bath

Main area — 1,620 sq. ft.

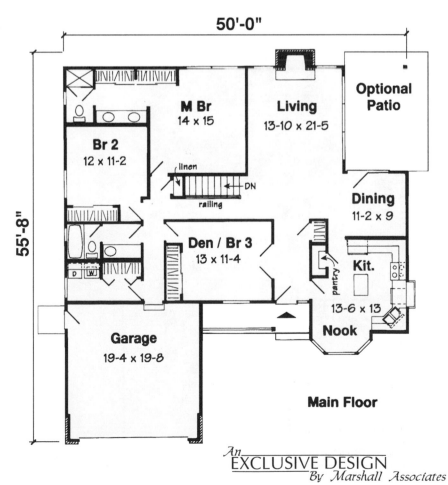

An EXCLUSIVE DESIGN *By Marshall Associates*

Features Found in Large Homes

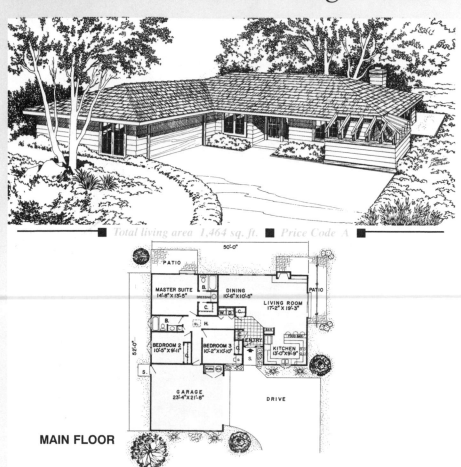

Total living area 1,464 sq. ft. ■ Price Code A

MAIN FLOOR

■ **This plan features:**

— Three bedrooms

— Two full baths

■ A tiled Entry leading into a spacious Living Room

■ A Living Room/Dining area featuring a fireplace with an extended hearth flanked by glass windows and sliding doors

■ An efficient Kitchen with plenty of counter space and a food bar adjacent to the Living Room

■ An inviting Master Suite with a dressing area, a walk-in closet and a private bath

■ Two additional bedrooms, one with a built-in dressing table, sharing a full hall bath

Main floor — 1,464 sq. ft.
Garage — 528 sq. ft.

Wonderful One Level Living

Total living area 1,802 sq. ft. ■ Price Code C

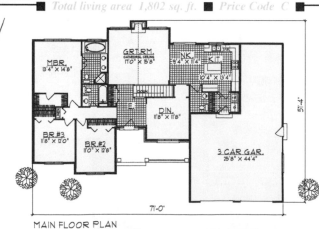

MAIN FLOOR PLAN

No. 93193

■ **This plan features:**

— Three bedrooms

— Two full and one half baths

■ Charming front porch accesses easy-care Entry with archway to Dining Room

■ Central Great Room enhanced by a cathedral ceiling over a cozy fireplace set in a wall of windows

■ Large and convenient Kitchen with work island/snackbar, eating Nook with sliding glass door to backyard, and nearby Laundry/Garage entry

■ Corner Master Bedroom features a walk-in closet and plush bath with a double vanity and spa tub

■ Two additional bedrooms with ample closets and double windows, share a full bath

■ No materials list is available for this plan

Main floor — 1,802 sq. ft.
Basement — 1,802 sq. ft.

An EXCLUSIVE DESIGN
By Ahmann Design Inc.

Perfect for a First Home

■ Total living area 1,544 sq. ft. ■ Price Code B ■

No. 92405

■ This plan features:

— Three bedrooms

— Two full baths

■ A spacious Master Suite including a separate Master Bath with a garden tub and shower

■ A Dining Room and Family Room highlighted by vaulted ceilings

■ An oversized patio accessible from the Master Suite, Family Room and Breakfast Room

■ A well planned Kitchen measuring 12' x 11'

■ No materials list available for this plan

Main area — 1,544 sq. ft.
Garage & Storage — 476 sq. ft.

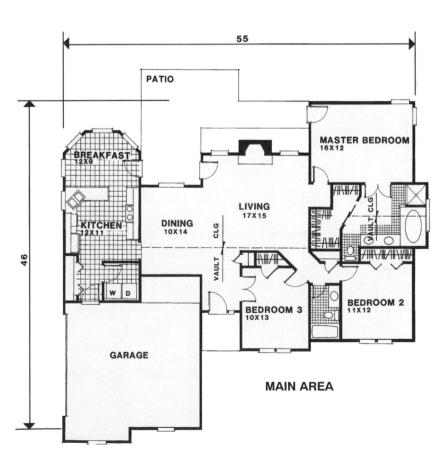

MAIN AREA

Perfect for Family Gatherings

© 1994 Donald A. Gardner Architects, Inc.

Total living area — 1,346 sq. ft. ■ *Price Code B*

No. 99826

■ This plan features:

— Three bedrooms

— Two full baths

■ An open layout between the Great Room, Kitchen, and Breakfast Bay sharing a cathedral ceiling and a fireplace

■ Master Bedroom suite with a soaring cathedral ceiling, direct access to the deck and a well appointed bath with a large walk-in closet

■ Additional bedrooms sharing a full bath in the hall

■ Centrally located utility and storage spaces

Main floor — 1,346 sq. ft.
Garage & storage — 462 sq. ft.

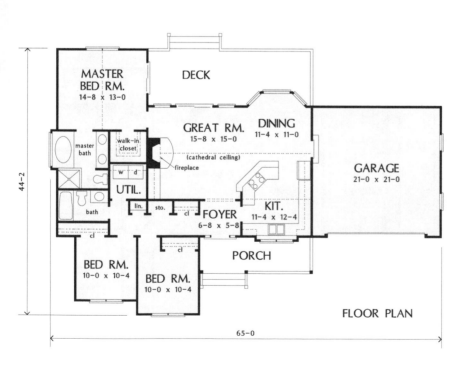

FLOOR PLAN

Carefree Comfort

■ *Total living area 1,665 sq. ft.* ■ *Price Code B* ■

No. 91418

■ This plan features:

— Three bedrooms

— Two full baths

■ A dramatic vaulted Foyer

■ A range-top island Kitchen with a sunny eating Nook surrounded by a built-in planter

■ A vaulted ceiling in the Great Room with a built-in bar and corner fireplace

■ A bayed Dining Room that combines with the Great Room for a spacious feeling

■ A Master Bedroom with a private reading nook, vaulted ceiling, walk-in closet and a well-appointed private Bath

■ Two additional bedrooms sharing a full hall bath

■ An optional basement, crawl space or slab foundation — please specify when ordering

Main area — 1,665 sq. ft.
Garage — 2-car

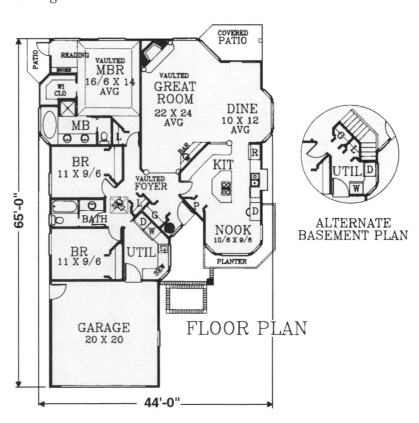

ALTERNATE BASEMENT PLAN

FLOOR PLAN

Easy One Floor Living

Total living area 1,671 sq. ft. ■ Price Code B

WIDTH 50'-0"
DEPTH 51'-0"

No. 98423

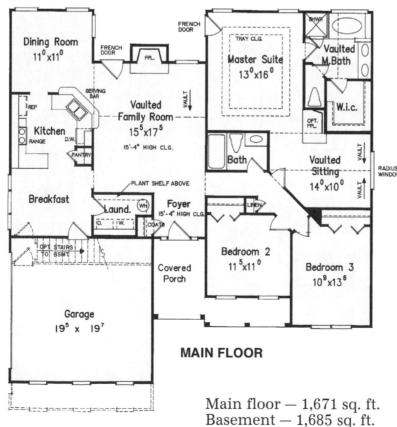

MAIN FLOOR

Main floor — 1,671 sq. ft.
Basement — 1,685 sq. ft.
Garage — 400 sq. ft.

This plan features:

—Three bedrooms

—Two full baths

■ A spacious Family Room topped by a vaulted ceiling and highlighted by a large fireplace and a French door to the rear yard

■ A serving bar open to the Family Room and the Dining Room, a pantry and a peninsula counter adding more efficiency to the Kitchen

■ A crowning tray ceiling over the Master Bedroom and a vaulted ceiling over the Master Bath

■ A vaulted ceiling over the cozy Sitting Room in the Master Suite

■ Two additional bedrooms, roomy in size sharing the full bath in the hall

■ An optional basement, crawl space or slab foundation — please specify when ordering

Clean and Convenient Design

No. 93231

This plan features:

- Three bedrooms
- Two full baths
- Arched entrance into Foyer and central Living Area with fireplace and access to Patio/Sundeck
- Kitchen with peninsula counter/snackbar, convenient to formal Dining Room, Breakfast alcove, Laundry and Garage entry
- Private Master Bedroom with decorative ceiling, walk-in closet and lavish bath with corner whirlpool tub and two vanities
- Two additional bedrooms share a double vanity bath
- An optional crawl space or slab foundation — please specify when ordering
- No materials list is available for this plan

Main floor — 1,781 sq. ft.
Garage — 558 sq. ft.

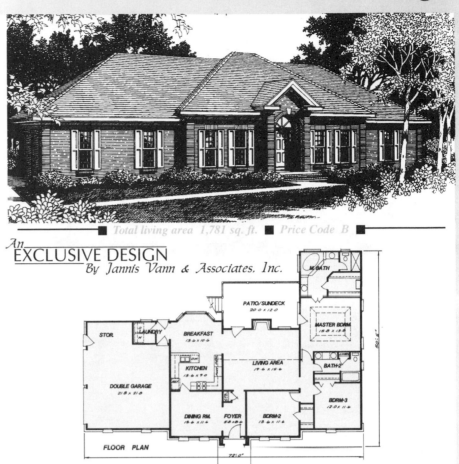

Total living area 1,781 sq. ft. ■ Price Code B

An EXCLUSIVE DESIGN
By Jannis Vann & Associates, Inc.

Outstanding Four Bedroom

No. 98435

This plan features:

- Four bedrooms
- Two full baths
- Radius window highlighting the exterior and the formal Dining Room
- High ceiling topping the Foyer for a grand first impression
- Vaulted ceiling enhances the Great Room further accented by a fireplace framed by windows to either side
- Arched opening to the Kitchen from the Great Room
- Breakfast Room topped by a vaulted ceiling and enhanced by elegant French door to the rear yard
- Tray ceiling and a five-piece compartmental bath gives luxurious presence to the Master Suite
- Three additional bedrooms share a full, double vanity bath in the hall
- An optional basement or crawl space foundation — please specify when ordering

Main floor — 1,945 sq. ft.

Total living area 1,945 sq. ft. ■ Price Code C

Stucco Captures Shade

Total living area—1,642 sq. ft. ■ Price Code B

No. 90502

■ This plan features:

— Three bedrooms

— Two full baths

■ Sheltered Entry opens to airy Living/Dining Room with an inviting fireplace

■ Central Family Room with another fireplace opens to glass Nook with access to covered Patio

■ Open Kitchen easily serves nearby Dining area, Nook and Patio beyond

■ French doors open to Master Suite with Patio access and a private bath

■ Two additional bedrooms with ample closets, share a full bath and laundry

Main floor — 1,642 sq. ft.

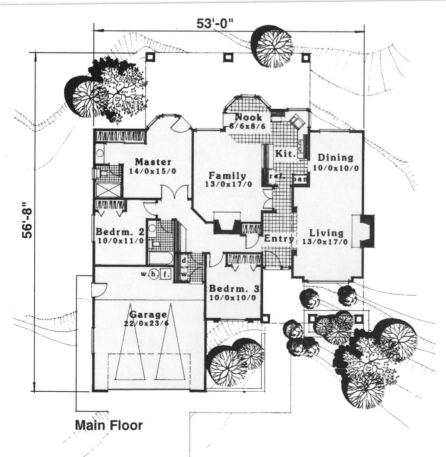

Main Floor

Inviting Wrap-Around Porch

■ *Total living area 1,716 sq. ft.* ■ *Price Code B* ■

No. 93909

■ This plan features:

— Three bedrooms

— Two full baths

■ A warm and inviting welcome, achieved by a wrap-around porch

■ A corner gas fireplace and two skylights highlighted in the Great Room

■ Flowing from the Great Room, the Dining Room naturally lighted by the sliding glass doors to a rear deck and a skylight above

■ A well-appointed, U-shaped Kitchen separated from the Dining Room by a breakfast bar contains another skylight

■ A luxurious Master Bedroom equipped with a plush bath

■ Two additional bedrooms sharing the full bath in the hall and receiving light from the dormers

■ No materials list is available for this plan

Main floor — 1,716 sq. ft.

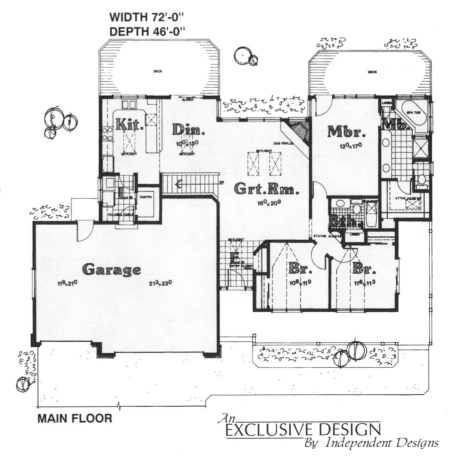

WIDTH 72'-0"
DEPTH 46'-0"

MAIN FLOOR

An EXCLUSIVE DESIGN
By Independent Designs

259

Little Charmer with Side Patio

Total living area 1,412 sq. ft. • Price Code A

No. 90857

This plan features:

— Three bedrooms

— Two full baths

A Utility Room entrance from the Garage into the large Family Room conveniently located just off the Kitchen

A roomy Kitchen including a Breakfast Nook for informal dining

A formal Dining Room combining with the Living Room to yield a good size area for formal entertaining

Main floor — 1,412 sq. ft.
Garage — 365 sq. ft.
Width — 39'-0"
Depth — 60'-0"

MAIN FLOOR

An EXCLUSIVE DESIGN
By Westhome Planners, Ltd.

Living Areas Gather Around Fireplace

Total living area 2,404 sq. ft. • Price Code D

No. 94979

This plan features:

— Three bedrooms

— Two full and one half baths

A see-through fireplace situated between the Hearth Room and the Great Room

Open layout between the Kitchen, Hearth Room and the Breakfast Room creating a terrific informal living space

Built-in pantry, work island and a peninsula counter/snack bar highlighting the Kitchen

Great Room is directly across the hall from the Dining Room and is at the heart of the home

Master Bedroom features two walk-in closets and a five-piece bath

Two additional bedrooms have private access to a full bath

Main floor — 2,404 sq. ft.
Garage — 696 sq. ft.

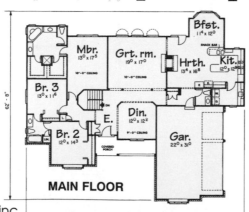

MAIN FLOOR

Stone and Siding

■ *Total living area 2,690 sq. ft.* ■ *Price Code E* ■

No. 94810 ✖

■ This plan features:

—Four bedrooms

—Three full and one half baths

■ Attractive styling using a combination of stone and siding and a covered porch add to the curb appeal

■ Former foyer giving access to the bedroom wing, library or activity room

■ Activity room showcasing a focal point fireplace and including direct access to the rear deck and the breakfast room

■ Breakfast room is topped by a vaulted ceiling and flows into the kitchen

■ A secluded guest bedroom suite is located off the kitchen area

■ Master Suite topped by a tray ceiling and pampered by five piece bath

Main floor — 2,690 sq. ft.
Basement — 2,690 sq. ft.
Garage — 660 sq. ft.

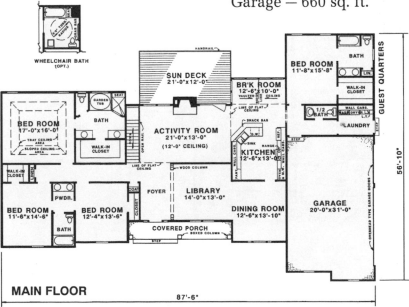

Attractive Exterior

Total living area — 2,167 sq. ft. ■ Price Code C

No. 98512

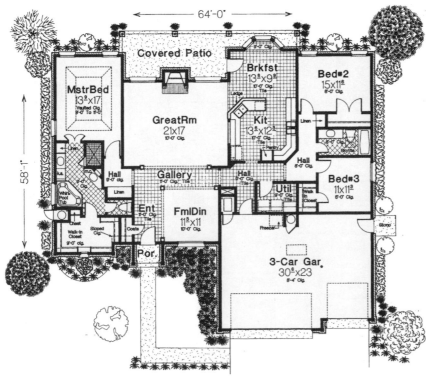

MAIN FLOOR

This plan features:

— Three bedrooms

— Two full baths

■ In the gallery, columns separate space between the Great Room and the Dining Room

■ Access to backyard covered patio from bayed Breakfast Nook

■ The large Kitchen is a chef's dream with lots of counter space and a pantry

■ The Master Bedroom is removed from traffic areas and contains a luxurious Master Bath

■ A hall connects the two secondary bedrooms which share a full skylit bath

■ No materials list is available for this plan

Main floor — 2,167 sq. ft.
Garage — 690 sq. ft.

Multiple Roof Lines Add to Charm

Total living area 3,292 sq. ft. ■ *Price Code F*

No. 92209

■ This plan features:

— Four bedrooms

— Three full baths

■ Entry opens to Gallery, formal Dining and Living rooms with decorative ceilings

■ Spacious Kitchen with a work island opens to Dining alcove, Family Room and Patio beyond

■ Comfortable Family Room offers vaulted ceiling above fireplace and a wetbar

■ Corner Master Bedroom suite enhanced by a vaulted ceiling, double vanity bath and huge walk-in closet

■ Three additional bedrooms with walk-in closets have access to full baths

■ No materials list is available for this plan

Main floor – 3,292 sq. ft.
Garage – 670 sq. ft.

Main Floor
WIDTH — 101'-1"
DEPTH — 73'-10"

European Style

Total living area 2,727 sq. ft. ■ *Price Code F*

No. 92501

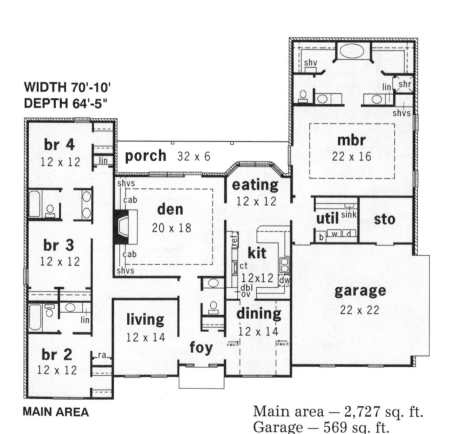

WIDTH 70'-10'
DEPTH 64'-5"

br 4
12 x 12

porch 32 x 6

mbr
22 x 16

den
20 x 18

eating
12 x 12

util sto

br 3
12 x 12

kit
12x12

garage
22 x 22

br 2
12 x 12

living
12 x 14

dining
12 x 14

foy

MAIN AREA

Main area — 2,727 sq. ft.
Garage — 569 sq. ft.

This plan features:

— Four bedrooms

— Three full and one half baths

■ Central Foyer between spacious Living and Dining rooms with arched windows

■ Hub Kitchen with extended counter and nearby Utility/Garage entry, easily serves Breakfast area and Dining Room

■ Spacious Den with a hearth fireplace between built-ins and sliding glass doors to Porch

■ Master Bedroom wing with decorative ceiling, plush bath with two walk-in closets

■ Three additional bedrooms with ample closets and private access to a full bath

■ An optional basement or crawl space foundation — please specify when ordering

Decorative Ceilings Add Accents

No. 96525

This plan features:

- Three bedrooms
- Two full baths
- The cozy front porch leads into the formal Foyer
- A secluded Study to the right of the Foyer
- Colonial columns and a half wall separate the Dining area from the Foyer
- The Great Room is accented by a fireplace and a tray ceiling
- The Kitchen is laid out in an efficient U-shape and features an extended counter/eating bar
- The Master Suite is tucked into the left rear corner of the home
- A tray ceiling highlights the bedroom area of the Master Suite
- Two additional bedrooms, located on the opposite side of the home, share a full bath in the hall

Main floor — 1,771 sq. ft.
Garage — 480 sq. ft.

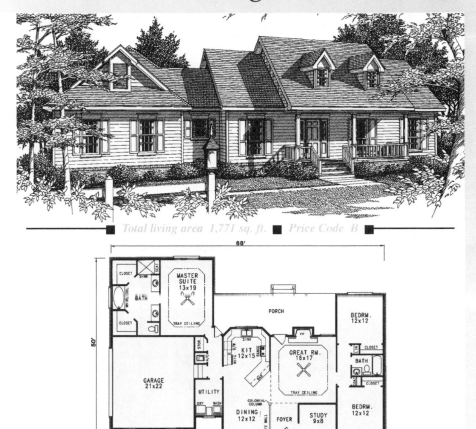

Total living area 1,771 sq. ft. ■ Price Code B

MAIN FLOOR

Cozy Corners and Open Spaces

No. 93418

This plan features:

- Three bedrooms
- Two full baths
- A covered front porch supported by columns
- Foyer with a 9-foot ceiling
- The entrance to the Living room is accented by columns, while a fireplace lies beyond them
- The Kitchen is separated from the Dining room by an angled counter
- A porch and deck in the rear are accessed by a door in the Dining Room
- The Master bedroom has a decorative 10-foot ceiling, a walk in closet and a private bath
- Two additional bedrooms are brightened by front wall windows and share a hall bath
- A two-car drive under garage completes this plan
- No materials list is available for this plan

Main floor — 1,631 sq. ft.
Basement — 1,015 sq. ft.
Garage — 616 sq. ft.

Total living area 1,631 sq. ft. ■ Price Code B

Floor Plan

An EXCLUSIVE DESIGN
By Greg Marquis

Cathedral Window Graced by Massive Arch

No. 20066

■ **This plan features:**

— Three bedrooms

— Two full baths

■ A tiled threshold providing a distinctive entrance

■ A comfortable Living Room with a wood-burning fireplace and tiled hearth

■ A Dining Room with vaulted ceiling

■ A Kitchen with central work island, pantry, planning desk, and Breakfast area

■ A Master Suite with decorative ceilings, Master Bath and bow window

Main area — 1,850 sq. ft.
Basement — 1,850 sq. ft.
Garage — 503 sq. ft.

An
EXCLUSIVE DESIGN
By Karl Kreeger

■ *Total living area 1,850 sq. ft.* ■ *Price Code C*

Living Room Features Exposed Beams

No. 98503

■ **This plan features:**

— Three bedrooms

— Two full baths

■ A covered Porch shelters the entry to this home

■ The large Living room with exposed beams includes a fireplace and built ins

■ The bright Dining room is located next to the Kitchen which features a center island

■ The bedroom wing features three spacious Bedrooms and two full baths

■ The two-car Garage has a handy workshop area

■ An optional crawl space or slab foundation — please specify when ordering

■ No materials list is available for this plan

Main floor — 1,876 sq. ft.
Garage — 619 sq. ft.

■ *Total living area 1,876 sq. ft.* ■ *Price Code C*

One Level Contemporary

An
EXCLUSIVE DESIGN
By Marshall Associates

■ *Total living area 1,266 sq. ft.* ■ *Price Code A* ■

No. 24327

■ This plan features:

— Three bedrooms

— Two full baths

■ A vaulted ceiling and elegant fireplace in the Living Room

■ An open layout between the Living Room, Dining Room and Kitchen gives a more spacious feeling

■ A well-equipped Kitchen with a double sink and a peninsula counter that may be used as an eating bar

■ A Master Suite that includes a walk-in closet and a private bath with a double vanity

■ Two additional bedrooms that have ample closet space and share a full hall bath

Main area — 1,266 sq. ft.
Garage — 443 sq. ft.
Basement — 1,266 sq. ft.

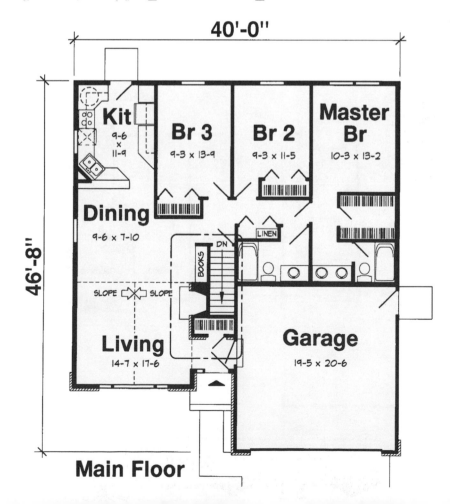

40'-0"

46'-8"

Kit
9-6 x 11-9

Br 3
9-3 x 13-9

Br 2
9-3 x 11-5

Master Br
10-3 x 13-2

Dining
9-6 x 7-10

LINEN

BOOKS

DN

SLOPE ⇨⇦ SLOPE

Living
14-7 x 17-6

Garage
19-5 x 20-6

Main Floor

For the Discriminating Buyer

■ *Total living area 1,710 sq. ft.* ■ *Price Code B* ■

No. 92625

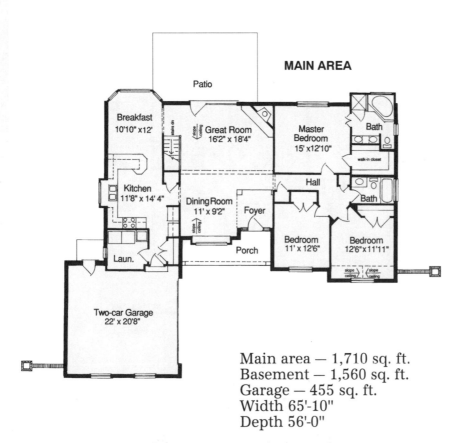

MAIN AREA

Main area — 1,710 sq. ft.
Basement — 1,560 sq. ft.
Garage — 455 sq. ft.
Width 65'-10"
Depth 56'-0"

■ This plan features:

— Three bedrooms

— Two full baths

■ An attractive, classic brick design, with wood trim, multiple gables, and wing walls

■ A sheltered entrance into the Foyer

■ A sloped ceiling adding elegance to the formal Dining Room which flows easily into the Great Room

■ A sloped ceiling and a corner fireplace enhancing the Great Room

■ A Kitchen with a garden window above the double sink

■ A peninsula counter joins the Kitchen and the Breakfast Room in an open layout

■ A Master Suite, equipped with a large walk-in closet and a private bath with an oval corner tub

■ No materials list is available for this plan

Split Bedroom Plan

No. 98224

This plan features:

— Three bedrooms

— Two full and one half baths

■ The elegant Dining Room crowned by a vaulted ceiling

■ The Living Room/Den highlighted by a vaulted ceiling, a fireplace and an entertainment center

■ The well-appointed Kitchen with a built-in pantry and ample storage and work space

■ The Breakfast Room adjoins the Kitchen and is naturally illuminated by a bay window

■ The extensive Master Suite has a private five-piece bath and a huge walk-in closet

■ Two additional bedrooms located at the opposite side of the home share a full bath

■ An optional basement, slab or crawl space foundation — please specify when ordering

■ No materials list is available for this plan

Main floor — 1,751 sq. ft.
Width 64'-0"
Depth 40'-6"

Total living area 1,751 sq. ft. ■ Price Code B

MAIN FLOOR

Brick Abounds

No. 98522

This plan features:

— Three bedrooms

— Two full baths

■ The covered front porch opens into the entry that has a 10-foot ceiling and a coat closet

■ The large Living room is distinguished by a fireplace and a front window wall

■ The Dining room features a 10-foot ceiling and access to the rear covered patio

■ The Kitchen is angled and has a pantry, and a cooktop island

■ The Master bedroom is located in the rear for privacy and boasts a triangular shaped walk in closet, plus a private bath

■ Two more bedrooms each have large closets and share a hallway bath

■ This home has a two-car garage that is accessed through the Utility room

■ No materials list is available for this plan

Main floor — 1,528 sq. ft.
Garage — 440 sq. ft.

Total living area 1,528 sq. ft. ■ Price Code B

Floor Plan

Centerpiece Circular Kitchen

No. 10514

■ **This plan features:**

— Three bedrooms

— Two full baths

■ Sheltered Entry opens to Living Room with a bar

■ Spacious Dining Room with built-in hutch and displace case, sliding glass door to Patio, adjoins Kitchen

■ Family Room with cozy fireplace and Sun space access, opens to Kitchen

■ Circular Kitchen with pantry, easily serves all areas indoors and out

■ Pampering Master Bedroom offers Patio access, two closets and a separate dressing area

■ Two additional bedrooms with ample closets, share a full bath and laundry

Main Floor — 1,870 sq. ft.
Garage — 434 sq. ft.

■ Total living area 1,980 sq. ft. ■ Price Code C ■

MAIN FLOOR

Brick & Siding Perfect Together

No. 99104

■ **This plan features:**

— Three bedrooms

— Two full baths

■ A covered entry and a front door with sidelights greets you

■ Walk in to the Living room enlarged by a cathedral ceiling, and also enhanced by a fireplace

■ The Dining room is open to the Living room.

■ The U-shaped eat in Kitchen opens to the Laundry room and the Garage beyond

■ The Master bedroom has a tray ceiling, a walk in closet, and a full bath

■ Two other bedrooms have large closets and share a bath in the hall

■ No materials list is available for this plan

Main floor — 1,370 sq. ft.
Basement — 1,370 sq. ft.

■ Total living area 1,370 sq. ft. ■ Price Code A ■

An
EXCLUSIVE DESIGN
By Ahmann Design Inc.

An Open Concept Home

■ *Total living area 1,282 sq. ft.* ■ *Price Code A* ■

No. 93021

■ This plan features:

— Three bedrooms

— Two full baths

■ An angled Entry creating the illusion of space

■ Two square columns that flank the bar and separate the Kitchen from the Living Room

■ A Dining Room that may service both formal and informal occasions

■ A Master Bedroom with a large walk-in closet

■ A large Master Bath with double vanity, linen closet and whirlpool tub/shower combination

■ Two additional bedrooms that share a full bath

■ No materials list is available for this plan

Main floor — 1,282 sq. ft.
Garage — 501 sq. ft.

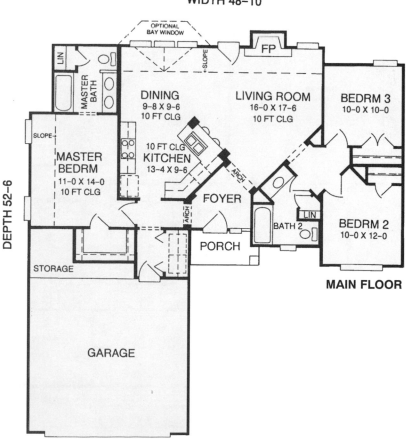

WIDTH 48–10

DEPTH 52–6

OPTIONAL BAY WINDOW

FP

DINING
9-8 X 9-6
10 FT CLG

LIVING ROOM
16-0 X 17-6
10 FT CLG

BEDRM 3
10-0 X 10-0

LIN

MASTER BATH

SLOPE

MASTER BEDRM
11-0 X 14-0
10 FT CLG

10 FT CLG
KITCHEN
13-4 X 9-6

FOYER

BATH 2

LIN

BEDRM 2
10-0 X 12-0

STORAGE

PORCH

GARAGE

MAIN FLOOR

Country Charmer

■ *Total living area 1,438 sq. ft.* ■ *Price Code A* ■

No. 96509

MAIN FLOOR

■ This plan features:

—Three bedrooms

—Two full baths

■ Quaint front Porch is perfect for sitting and relaxing

■ Great Room opening into Dining area and Kitchen

■ Corner deck in rear of home accessed from Kitchen and Master Suite

■ Master Suite with a private bath, walk-in closet and built-in shelves

■ Two large secondary bedrooms in the front of the home share a hall bath

■ Two-car garage located in the rear of the home

Main floor — 1,438 sq. ft.
Garage — 486 sq. ft.

Classic Columns

No. 93053 ®R

This plan features:

— Three bedrooms

— Two full and one half baths

■ Entrance framed by columns accesses Entry, Dining and Living rooms also defined by columns

■ Expansive Living Room with two-way fireplace and access to covered Porch

■ Formal Dining Room highlighted by a lovely arched window

■ Convenient Kitchen with work island, eating bar and nearby Breakfast area and Utility room

■ Master Bedroom wing offers a huge, walk-in closet and a pampering bath

■ Two additional bedrooms with ample closets, share a full bath

■ No materials list is available for this plan

Main floor — 2,329 sq. ft.
Garage — 582 sq. ft.
Width 86'-10"
Depth 51'-0"

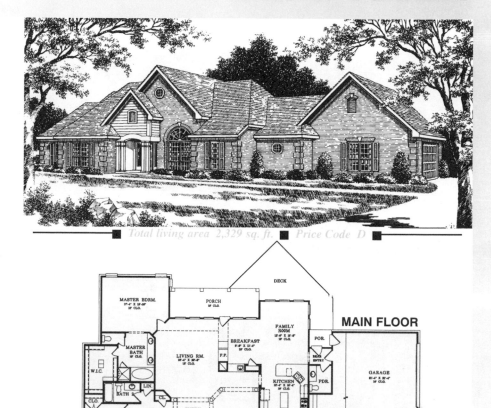

Total living area 2,329 sq. ft. ■ Price Code D

MAIN FLOOR

Great Room at the Heart of the Home

No. 99503

This plan features:

— Three bedrooms

— Two full baths

■ The Great room with it's cathedral ceiling, fireplace, and rear wall windows are at the center of the home

■ The Dining room also sports a cathedral ceiling as well as an arched window

■ The U-shaped country Kitchen has plenty of counter space and room for a kitchen table

■ A screen porch in the rear is accessed from the Great room and the Master bedroom

■ The Master bedroom features a vaulted ceiling, a plant shelf, a walk in closet and a private bath

■ Two additional bedrooms have a lot of closet space and share a bath

■ This home is completed by a two-car garage with a bonus room above it

■ No materials list is available for this plan

■ An optional slab or crawl space foundation — please specify when ordering

Main floor — 1,620 sq. ft.
Bonus room — 290 sq. ft.
Garage — 547 sq. ft.

An EXCLUSIVE DESIGN
By Georgia Toney Lesley.
Residential Designer

Total living area 1,620 sq. ft. ■ Price Code B

opt. entertainment room

21⁸ x 12⁶

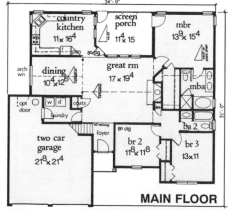

MAIN FLOOR

273

Fieldstone Facade

No. 92284

Total living area 2,261 sq. ft. ■ **Price Code D**

No. 92284

■ **This plan features:**

— Four bedrooms

— Two full and one half baths

■ Covered porch shelters entrance into Gallery and Great Room with a focal point fireplace and Patio access topped by a vaulted ceiling

■ Formal Dining Room conveniently located for entertaining

■ Cooktop island, built-in pantry and a bright Breakfast area highlight Kitchen

■ Secluded Master Bedroom with Patio access, large walk-in closet and corner spa tub

■ Three additional bedrooms with ample closets, share a double vanity bath

■ No materials list is available for this plan

Main floor — 2,261 sq. ft.
Garage — 640 sq. ft.

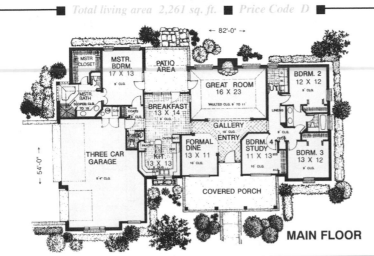

MAIN FLOOR

Cozy Three-Bedroom

No. 94800

■ **This plan features:**

— Three bedrooms

— Two full baths

■ Covered entry leads into Activity Room highlighted by a double window and a vaulted ceiling

■ Efficient Kitchen with work island, nearby laundry and Garage entry, opens to Dining area with access to Sun Deck

■ Plush Master Bedroom offers a decorative ceiling, walk-in closet and whirlpool tub

■ Two additional bedrooms, one with a vaulted ceiling, share a full bath

■ Garage with entry into Laundry Room serving as a Mud Room

■ An optional basement, crawl space or slab foundation — please specify when ordering

Main floor — 1,199 sq. ft.
Garage — 287 sq. ft.
Basement — 1,199 sq. ft.

Total living area 1,199 sq. ft. ■ **Price Code B**

MAIN FLOOR

ALT. PART FLOOR PLAN
(OMITTING BASEMENT STAIR)

■ *Total living area 1,368 sq. ft.* ■ *Price Code A* ■

No. 90357

■ This plan features:

— Three bedrooms

— Two full baths

■ Soaring ceilings to give the house a spacious, contemporary feeling

■ A fireplaced Great Room adjoining a convenient Kitchen, with a sunny Breakfast Nook

■ Sliding glass doors opening onto an angular deck

■ A Master Suite with vaulted ceilings and a private bath

Main area — 1,368 sq. ft.

Main Floor Plan

Traditional Brick with Detailing

Total living area 1,869 sq. ft. ■ Price Code D

No. 92536

This plan features:

— Three bedrooms

— Two full baths

- Covered entry leads into the Foyer, the formal Dining Room and the Den

- Expansive Den with a decorative ceiling over a hearth fireplace and sliding glass doors to the rear yard

- Country Kitchen with a built-in pantry, double ovens and a cooktop island easily serves the Breakfast area and Dining Room

- Private Master Bedroom suite with a decorative ceiling, a walk-in closet, a double vanity and a whirlpool tub

- Two additional bedrooms share a full bath

- An optional slab or crawl space foundation — please specify when ordering

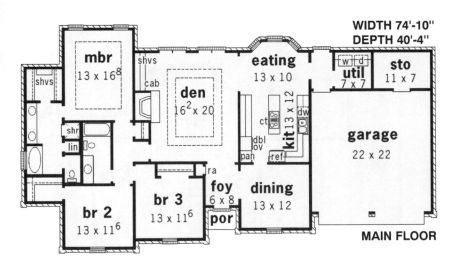

WIDTH 74'-10"
DEPTH 40'-4"

MAIN FLOOR

Main floor — 1,869 sq. ft.
Garage — 561 sq. ft.

Compact Design Packs Much In

No. 98804

This plan features:

- Three bedrooms
- Two full baths
- The covered front porch leads into a foyer that contains a coat closet
- The U-shaped Kitchen has it all, including a corner double sink, a pantry, a desk, and a nook with a bay window
- Direct access to the formal Dining room from the Kitchen
- The Living room is large and features access to the rear deck, and an open railed staircase to the basement
- The Master bedroom has double closets, a private bath, and a French door out to the deck
- Two bedrooms, identical in size share a bath in the hall with a skylight above it.
- This home has a Laundry/Utility room on the way out to the two-car garage
- No materials list is available for this plan

Main floor — 1,372 sq. ft.
Basement — 1,372 sq. ft.
Garage — 484 sq. ft.

An EXCLUSIVE DESIGN
By Weinmaster Home Design

Total living area 1,372 sq. ft. • Price Code A

MAIN FLOOR

L-Shaped Bungalow With Two Porches

No. 90407

This plan features:

- Three bedrooms
- Two full baths
- A Master Suite with a lavish Master Bath including a garden tub, shower, his-n-her vanities and separate walk-in closets
- Two additional bedrooms having ample closet space and sharing a full hall bath
- A large Family Room accentuated by a fireplace
- A U-shaped Kitchen with a built-in pantry, double sink and ample storage and counter space
- A sunny, bay Breakfast Nook for informal eating
- An optional basement, slab or crawl space foundation — please specify when ordering

Main floor — 1,950 sq. ft.

Total living area 1,950 sq. ft. • Price Code C

MAIN FLOOR

Room for More

■ This plan features:

— Two bedrooms

— Two full baths

■ A Living Room with a fireplace and access to two decks, expanding the outdoor living space

■ An efficient Kitchen opening to the Dining area

■ A Master Bedroom, including a private bath with a corner spa/tub

Main area — 1,127 sq. ft.

■ Total living area 1,127 sq. ft. ■ Price Code A ■

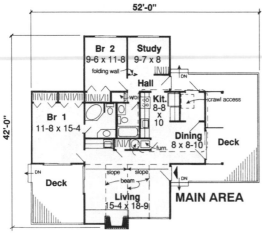

Basement Option

An
EXCLUSIVE DESIGN
By Marshall Associates

For the Young at Heart

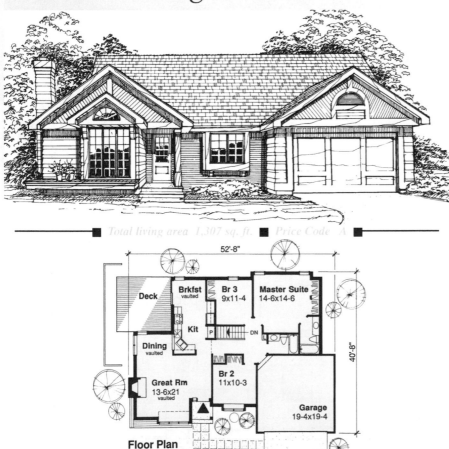

■ This plan features:

— Three bedrooms

— Two full baths

■ Half-round transom windows, divided-light windows, bay windows and a covered entry porch

■ A Great Room with a vaulted ceiling, a fireplace and a transom window

■ A Kitchen with a vaulted ceiling and a Breakfast area with sliding doors to the deck

■ A Master Suite with ample closet space and a private full Master Bath

Main area — 1,307 sq. ft.

■ Total living area 1,307 sq. ft. ■ Price Code A ■

Floor Plan

■ *Total living area 884 sq. ft.* ■ *Price Code A* ■

No. 90934

■ This plan features:

— Two bedrooms

— One full bath

■ An economical design

■ A covered sun deck adding outdoor living space

■ A mudroom/laundry area inside the side door, trapping dirt before it enters the house

■ An open layout between the Living Room with fireplace, Dining Room and Kitchen

Main floor — 884 sq. ft.
Width — 34'-0"
Depth — 28'-0"

An
EXCLUSIVE DESIGN
By Westhome Planners, Ltd.

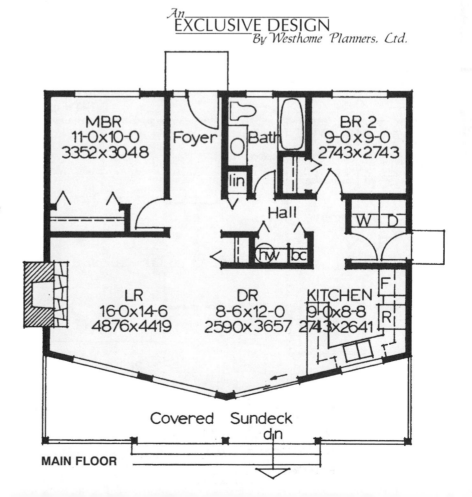

Charming Brick Home

■ *Total living area 1,868 sq. ft.* ■ *Price Code C* ■

No. 93107 ℞

■ This plan features:

— Three bedrooms

— Two full baths

■ A covered entrance leading into a spacious Living Room with a fireplace and an airy Dining Room with access to the Patio

■ An island Kitchen, open to the Dining Room, offering ample storage and easy access to the Laundry area and the Garage

■ A Master Bedroom with a walk-in closet, access to the Patio and a plush bath offering a window tub, a step-in shower and a double vanity

■ Two additional bedrooms, with decorative windows, sharing a full hall bath

■ No materials list is available for this plan

Main floor — 1,868 sq. ft.
Basement — 1,868 sq. ft.
Garage — 782 sq. ft.

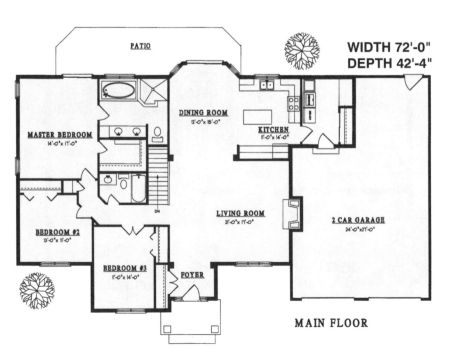

WIDTH 72'-0"
DEPTH 42'-4"

PATIO

MASTER BEDROOM
14'-0" x 17'-0"

DINING ROOM
17'-0" x 13'-0"

KITCHEN
11'-0" x 14'-0"

BEDROOM #2
13'-0" x 11'-0"

BEDROOM #3
11'-0" x 14'-0"

FOYER

LIVING ROOM
21'-0" x 17'-0"

2 CAR GARAGE
24'-0" x 27'-0"

DN

MAIN FLOOR

An
EXCLUSIVE DESIGN
By Ahmann Design Inc.

Vaulted Volume

No. 92564

This plan features:

— Three bedrooms

— Two full baths

■ A country styled sheltered front porch leads into the Great room

■ The Great room has a voluminous vaulted ceiling, and a fireplace

■ The U-shaped Kitchen has a pass through to the Dining room

■ The Dining room is open to the Great room for easy entertaining

■ The Master bedrooms has itís own full bath, plus two walk in closets

■ Two secondary bedrooms are identical in size and share a bath in the hall

■ A laundry closet is conveniently located near the bedrooms

■ An optional slab or crawl space foundation — please specify when ordering

Main floor — 1,263 sq. ft.
Garage — 572 sq. ft.

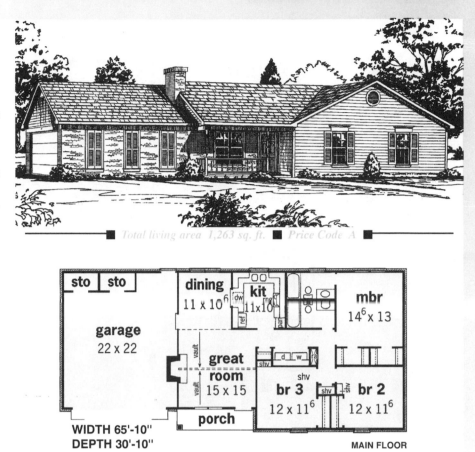

Total living area 1,263 sq. ft. ■ Price Code A

sto | sto

garage
22 x 22

dining
11 x 10⁶

kit
11x10

mbr
14⁶ x 13

great room
15 x 15

br 3
12 x 11⁶

br 2
12 x 11⁶

porch

WIDTH 65'-10"
DEPTH 30'-10"

MAIN FLOOR

Bay Windows and Fieldstone Accents

No. 34013

This plan features:

— Three bedrooms

— Two full baths

■ Recessed entrance framed by gracious bay windows leads into unique octagon foyer

■ Formal Dining Room highlighted by bay window below decorative ceiling

■ Sloped ceiling crowns Living Room with tiled, hearth fireplace and sliding glass door to Deck

■ Efficient Kitchen with angled snackbar counter easily accesses Breakfast area, Dining Room, Laundry area and Garage entry

■ Bright Breakfast area with access to covered Deck, built-in desk and expansive outdoor views

■ Corner Master Bedroom suite with decorative ceiling, boxed window and dressing area with a double vanity and walk-in closet

■ Two additional bedrooms with decorative windows and walk-in closets, share a full bath

Main floor — 1,803 sq. ft.
Garage — 499 sq. ft.
Basement — 1,803 sq. ft.

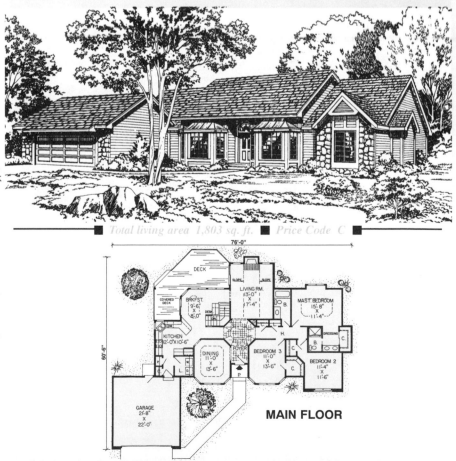

Total living area 1,803 sq. ft. ■ Price Code C

MAIN FLOOR

Great Starter or Empty Nester

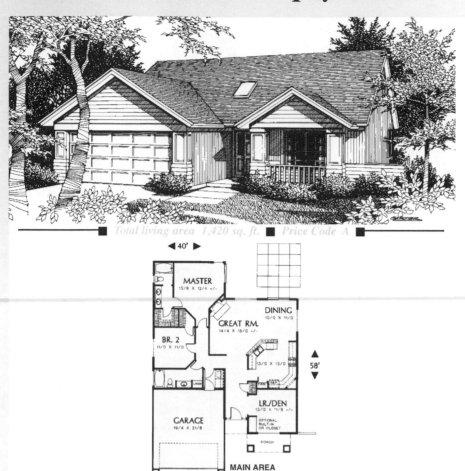

Total living area 1,420 sq. ft. • Price Code A

◀ 40' ▶

MASTER
13/8 X 12/4 +/-

DINING
10/0 X 11/0

GREAT RM.
14/4 X 15/0 +/-

BR. 2
11/0 X 11/0

13/0 X 13/0

58'

LR./DEN
13/0 X 11/8 +/-

GARAGE
19/4 X 21/8

OPTIONAL
BUILT-IN
OR CLOSET

PORCH

MAIN AREA

No. 91545

■ **This plan features:**

— Two bedrooms

— Two full baths

■ A formal Living Room or a cozy Den, the front room to the right of the Entry Hall adapts to your lifestyle

■ An efficient Kitchen with ample counter and storage space

■ A formal Dining Room situated next to the Kitchen and flowing from the Great Room

■ A corner fireplace highlighting the Great Room

■ A walk-in closet and a private double vanity bath in the Master Suite

■ An additional bedroom that easily accesses the full bath in the hall

■ This plan cannot be built in Clark County, WA

Main area — 1,420 sq. ft.

Charming Style

Total living area 1,372 sq. ft. • Price Code A

38'

MASTER SUITE
12 x 16

BATH

CLOSET

PORCH

BEDRM
11 x 12

DINING
10 x 9

LIVING RM
13 x 23

65'

BATH

KITCHEN
10 x 9

UTIL.

BEDRM
11 x 12

STORAGE

FOYER

PORCH

GARAGE
21 x 21

MAIN FLOOR

No. 96510

■ **This plan features:**

— Three bedrooms

— Two full baths

■ Tiled Foyer giving way to a welcoming Living Room highlighted by cozy fireplace

■ Living Room and Dining area adjoin creating the feeling of more space

■ An efficient galley-styled kitchen with direct access to the utility room and the dining area

■ Private Master Suite containing a walk-in closet and a private double vanity bath

■ Two additional bedrooms located in closet proximity to the full bath in the hall

Main floor — 1,372 sq. ft.
Garage — 465 sq. ft.

Inexpensive Ranch Design

■ *Total living area 1,500 sq. ft.* ■ *Price Code A* ■

No. 20062

■ This plan features:

— Three bedrooms

— Two full baths

■ A large picture window brightening the Breakfast area

■ A well planned Kitchen

■ A Living Room which is accented by an open beam across the sloping ceiling and wood burning fireplace

■ A Master Bedroom with an extremely large bath area

Main floor — 1,500 sq. ft.
Basement — 1,500 sq. ft.
Garage — 482 sq. ft.

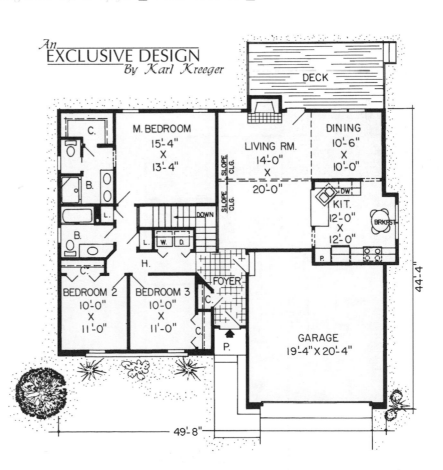

An
EXCLUSIVE DESIGN
By Karl Kreeger

Built-In Beauty

■ Total living area 1,687 sq. ft. ■ Price Code B

No. 91507

■ This plan features:

— Three bedrooms

— Two full baths

■ A sky-lit Foyer

■ A bump-out window enhancing the wide-open arrangement in the Living/Dining Room

■ An efficient island Kitchen with a built-in pantry, and a corner double sink

■ An informal Family Room with a lovely fireplace

■ A Master Suite with elegant double doors, and a luxurious private Master Bath

■ Two additional bedrooms flanking the laundry area

■ An optional basement or crawl space foundation — please specify when ordering

Main floor — 1,687 sq. ft.
Garage — 419 sq. ft.

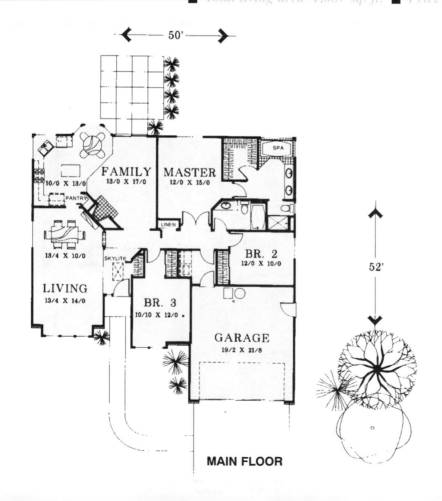

← 50' →

52'

FAMILY
13/0 X 17/0

MASTER
12/0 X 15/0

SPA

10/0 X 13/0

PANTRY

LINEN

13/4 X 10/0

SKYLITE

LIVING
13/4 X 14/0

BR. 2
12/0 X 10/0

BR. 3
10/10 X 12/0

GARAGE
19/2 X 21/8

MAIN FLOOR

Gourmet's Dream

Total living area 2,600 sq. ft. ■ Price Code D

No. 93183

This plan features:

— Three bedrooms

— Two full and one half baths

■ Formal Foyer invites guests into the comfort of the Great Room

■ Open Great Room has a centrally located fireplace flanked by built-in cabinetry, high ceilings and large windows

■ Formal Dining Room has arched entries and a large window

■ Kitchen includes a center island and an abundance of cupboard space

■ French doors open into the elegant master bedroom highlighted by a unique sitting area, two walk-in closets and a private master bath

■ Two additional bedrooms on the main level share a full bath in the hall

■ No materials list is available for this plan

■ This plan is not to be built within a 75 mile radius of Cedar Rapids, IA

Main floor – 2,600 sq. ft.

MAIN FLOOR PLAN

Flexible Floor Plan

Total living area 1,641 sq. ft. ■ Price Code B

No. 99657

This plan features:

— Three bedrooms

— Two full baths

■ Sheltering entrance Porch leads into an open Foyer, Living and Dining rooms

■ Comfortable Dining Room with an elegant bow window

■ Spacious Living Room enhanced by skylight, inviting fireplace and Terrace access

■ Country-size Kitchen offers a bright Dining area with Terrace access, laundry closet and Garage entry

■ Corner Master Bedroom offers a large walk-in closet and deluxe bath with a whirlpool tub

■ Two additional bedrooms share a double vanity bath

■ Convenient Den can be easily be converted to an Office or fourth bedroom

Main floor — 1,641 sq. ft.

Garage — 427 sq. ft.

Basement — 1,667 sq. ft.

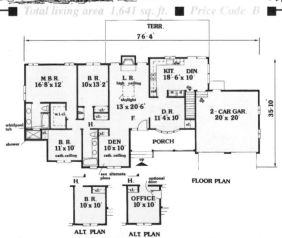

FLOOR PLAN

285

Great Traffic Flow

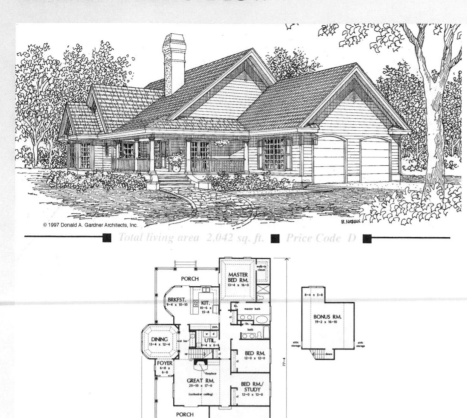

© 1997 Donald A. Gardner Architects, Inc.   B. NABAN.

Total living area 2,042 sq. ft. ■ Price Code D

FLOOR PLAN

© 1997 Donald A. Gardner Architects, Inc.

No. 96486

■ **This plan features:**

— Three bedrooms

— Two full baths

■ Perfect for narrow lots

■ Side porch leading to the Foyer giving access to the Great Room and the Dining Room

■ Great Room boasting a fireplace and built-in cabinets

■ Dining Room sporting an octagonal shape with a tray ceiling and columns

■ U-Shaped kitchen is open to the sunny Breakfast Bay with access to the back porch

■ Master Suite features a tray ceiling, back porch access, walk-in closet and an indulgent bath

■ Front bedroom doubles as a study, and the bonus room could make a fourth bedrooms upstairs

Main floor — 2,042 sq. ft.
Bonus room — 398 sq. ft.
Garage & storage — 514 sq. ft.

Welcome Home

© 1996 Donald A Gardner Architects, Inc.

Total living area 1,666 sq. ft. ■ Price Code C

FLOOR PLAN

© 1996 Donald A Gardner Architects, Inc.

No. 99819

■ **This plan features:**

— Three bedrooms

— Two full baths

■ Round-top window, gables, and all brick exterior say "welcome home"

■ Cathedral ceilings, a flexible Bonus space over the Garage, and a luxurious Master suite are only a few special features

■ The single Dining area works well for both casual family meals and formal events

■ The Kitchen is designed for easy meal preparation and service

■ A spacious Garage, with a designated workshop area and another separate area for storage

Main floor — 1,666 sq. ft.
Bonus — 335 sq. ft.
Garage — 609 sq. ft.

French Influenced One-Story

© 1990 Donald A. Gardner Architects, Inc.

■ *Total living area 2,045 sq. ft.* ■ *Price Code D* ■

No. 96421

■ This plan features:

— Three bedrooms

— Two full baths

■ Elegant details, arched windows, round columns and rich brick veneer creating curb appeal

■ Arched clerestory window in the foyer introduces natural light to a large Great Room with cathedral ceiling and built-in cabinets

■ Great room adjoins a skylit Sun Room with a wetbar which then opens onto a spacious deck

■ Kitchen with cooking island centrally located with easy access to a large pantry and utility room

■ Large Master Bedroom opening to the deck and featuring a garden tub, separate shower and dual vanity

■ An optional basement or crawl space foundation — please specify when ordering

Main floor — 2,045 sq. ft.
Garage & storage — 563 sq. ft.

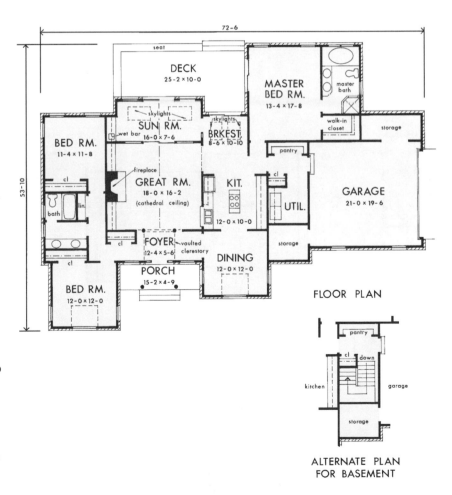

FLOOR PLAN

ALTERNATE PLAN
FOR BASEMENT

Tandem Garage

Total living area 1,761 sq. ft. ■ Price Code B

No. 93133

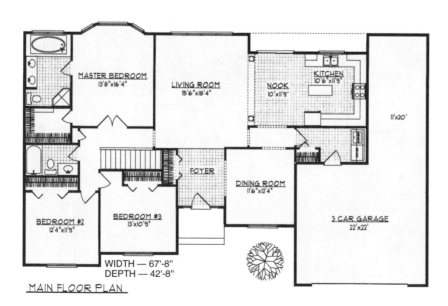

MASTER BEDROOM
13'8"x16'4"

LIVING ROOM
15'6"x18'4"

NOOK
10'x11'9"

KITCHEN
10'6"x11'9"

11'x20'

FOYER

DINING ROOM
11'6"x12'4"

3 CAR GARAGE
22'x22'

BEDROOM #2
12'4"x11'9"

BEDROOM #3
13'x10'9"

WIDTH — 67'-8"
DEPTH — 42'-8"

MAIN FLOOR PLAN

An
EXCLUSIVE DESIGN
By Ahmann Design Inc.

This plan features:

— Three bedrooms

— Two full baths

■ Open Foyer leads into spacious Living highlighted by a wall of windows

■ Country-size Kitchen with efficient, U-shaped counter, work island, eating Nook with back yard access, and nearby laundry/Garage entry

■ French doors open to pampering Master Bedroom with window alcove, walk-in closet and double vanity bath

■ Two additional bedrooms with large closets, share a full bath

Main floor —1,761 sq. ft.
Garage — 658 sq. ft.
Basement — 1,761 sq. ft.

One-Story Farmhouse

No. 99661

This plan features:

— Three bedrooms

— Two full baths

■ Main activity space grouped to the right of the Foyer

■ Large Living Room with a corner fireplace and a front-facing bow window

■ Dining room enhanced by three French doors to the rear deck

■ Eat-in Kitchen directly accesses the Dining Room

■ Two bedrooms off a short hall sharing a full bath

■ Master Bedroom Suite with a vaulted ceiling, a window with an elliptical top, a walk-in closet and a private bath

Main floor — 1,387 sq. ft.
Basement — 1,387 sq. ft.
Garage — 493 sq. ft.

Total living area 1,387 sq. ft. ■ Price Code A

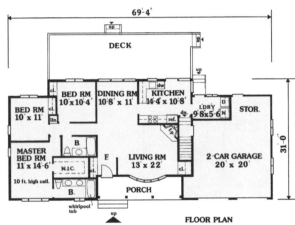

FLOOR PLAN

Desirable Split Bedroom Plan

No. 93419

This plan features:

— Three bedrooms

— Two full baths

■ A wrapping front porch has views into the home through windows with transoms

■ The foyer opens into the large Family room with an 11' ceiling and a fireplace

■ The Kitchen/Dining room has a center island, a long planning desk, and access to the rear deck

■ The Master bedroom is set away from the busy areas and features a walk in closet and a full bath

■ Two other bedrooms have bright front wall windows and ample closet space

■ The two-car garage has additional storage space

■ No materials list available for this home

Main floor — 1,595 sq. ft.
Garage — 470 sq. ft.

Total living area 1,595 sq. ft. ■ Price Code B

MAIN FLOOR

An EXCLUSIVE DESIGN *By Greg Marquis*

Ranch of Distinction

No. 99113

This plan features:

— Three bedrooms

— Two full and one half baths

■ The recessed entrance has an arched transom window over the door and a sidelight windows beside it

■ Once inside the Living room boasts a high ceiling and a warm fireplace

■ The large Kitchen area includes the open Dining area with a rear bay that accessed the backyard

■ There is a large utility room, garage access, and a half bath located off of the Kitchen

■ The Master and third bedrooms both have bay windows

■ All of the bedrooms have ample closet space and they are serviced by two full baths

■ This home has a three-car garage

■ No materials list is available for this plan

Main floor — 1,906 sq. ft.
Basement — 1,906 sq. ft.

Total living area 1,906 sq. ft. ■ *Price Code C* ■

MAIN FLOOR PLAN

An EXCLUSIVE DESIGN
By Ahmann Design Inc.

Compact Ranch

No. 99345

This plan features:

— Three bedrooms

— Two full baths

■ A Great Room and Dining area with vaulted ceilings

■ A Great Room with a fabulous fireplace

■ A Kitchen and sunny Breakfast area with access to a rear deck

■ A Master Suite with a private full bath and one wall of closet space

Main area — 1,325 sq. ft.

Total living area 1,325 sq. ft. ■ *Price Code A* ■

MAIN FLOOR

A Lovely Small Home

■ Total living area 1,402 sq. ft. ■ Price Code A ■

No. 93026

■ This plan features:

— Three bedrooms

— Two full baths

■ A large Living Room with a 10' ceiling

■ A Dining Room with a distinctive bay window

■ A Breakfast Room located off the Kitchen

■ A Kitchen with an angled eating bar to open that opens the room to the Living Room

■ A Master Suite with ten foot ceiling and his-n-her vanities, a combination whirlpool tub and shower, plus a huge walk-in closet

■ Two additional bedrooms that share a full bath

■ No materials list is available for this plan

Main floor — 1,402 sq. ft.
Garage — 437 sq. ft.

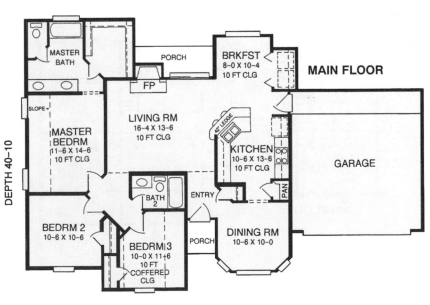

WIDTH 59–10

DEPTH 40–10

MAIN FLOOR

MASTER BATH

PORCH

BRKFST
8-0 X 10-4
10 FT CLG

FP

SLOPE

MASTER BEDRM
11-6 X 14-6
10 FT CLG

LIVING RM
16-4 X 13-6
10 FT CLG

42" LEDGE

KITCHEN
10-6 X 13-6
10 FT CLG

GARAGE

BATH 2

ENTRY

PAN

BEDRM 2
10-6 X 10-6

BEDRM 3
10-0 X 11-6
10 FT COFFERED CLG

PORCH

DINING RM
10-6 X 10-0

Exterior Shows Attention to Detail

■ Total living area 2,165 sq. ft. ■ Price Code D ■

No. 94811

■ This plan features:

—Three bedrooms

—Two full and one half baths

■ Privately located Master Suite is complimented by a luxurious bath with two walk-in closets

■ Two additional bedrooms have ample closet space and share a full bath

■ The Activity Room has a sloped ceiling, large fireplace and is accented with columns

■ Access to Sun Deck from the Dining Room

■ The island Kitchen and breakfast area have access to garage for ease when bringing in groceries

Main floor — 2,165 sq. ft.
Garage — 484 sq. ft.
Basement - 2,165 sq. ft.

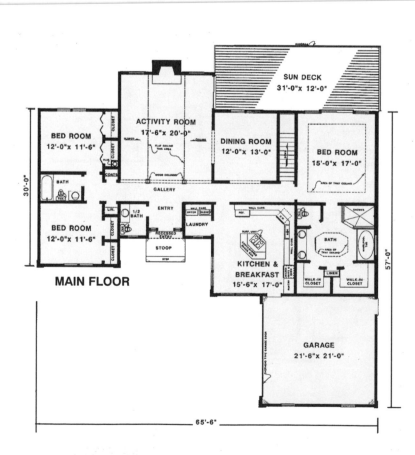

MAIN FLOOR

SUN DECK
31'-0"x 12'-0"

BED ROOM
12'-0"x 11'-6"

ACTIVITY ROOM
17'-6"x 20'-0"

DINING ROOM
12'-0"x 13'-0"

BED ROOM
15'-0"x 17'-0"

BATH

GALLERY

BED ROOM
12'-0"x 11'-6"

1/2 BATH

ENTRY

LAUNDRY

STOOP

BATH

KITCHEN & BREAKFAST
15'-6"x 17'-0"

WALK-IN CLOSET

LINEN

WALK-IN CLOSET

GARAGE
21'-6"x 21'-0"

30'-0"

57'-0"

65'-6"

Family Area is the Focal Point

No. 90867

This plan features:

— Three bedrooms

— Two full and one half baths

■ Designed for a hillside lot this plan features a walk-out basement

■ The large deck across the rear of the home extends your living area outdoors

■ The large Master bedroom has a unique front window and a private bath

■ The Living room features a bay window that overlooks the rear yard

■ The Dining room and the Family room both access the rear deck

■ The Kitchen has an angled serving bar and opens into the bay shaped Nook

■ There are two secondary bedrooms plus a bath and a half that complete this home

Main floor — 1,975 sq. ft.
Basement — 1,943 sq. ft.
Garage — 555 sq. ft.

An EXCLUSIVE DESIGN
By Westhome Planners, Ltd.

Total living area 1,975 sq. ft. ■ Price Code C

WIDTH 52'6"
DEPTH 70'

MAIN FLOOR

Didn't Waste An Inch of Space

No. 99834

This plan features:

— Three bedrooms

— Two full baths

■ Great Room with fireplace and built-in cabinets sharing a cathedral ceiling with angled Kitchen

■ Separate Dining Room allows for more formal entertaining

■ Master bedroom topped by a cathedral ceiling, walk-in closet, and well appointed bath

■ Front and rear Covered Porches encourage relaxation

■ Skylit Bonus Room making a great Recreation Room or Office in the future

Main floor — 1,575 sq. ft.
Bonus Area — 276 sq. ft.
Garage — 536 sq. ft.

© 1994 Donald A. Gardner Architects, Inc.

Total living area 1,575 sq. ft. ■ Price Code C

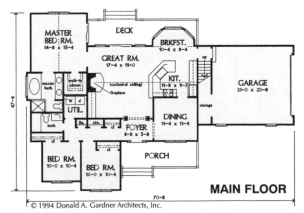

MAIN FLOOR

© 1994 Donald A. Gardner Architects, Inc.

Affordable to Build without Sacrificing Beauty

This plan features:

— Three bedrooms

— Two full baths

■ Simple clean lines making this ranch affordable to build

■ A large bay window, two car garage, straight forward roof lines and touches of decorative brick

■ A tiled Entry leading into the Living Room, which is enhanced by a gas fireplace

■ A Dining Room adjoining the Living Room, equipped with sliding glass doors to a rear deck

■ An efficient Kitchen with a breakfast bar separating it from the Dining Room

■ A Master Suite with a walk-in closet, bi-pass mirror doors, and a private Bath with an oversized shower

■ A Laundry Room/Mudroom convenient to the bedrooms

■ No materials list is available for this plan

Main floor — 1,250 sq. ft.

Total living area 1,250 sq. ft. • Price Code A

MAIN FLOOR

An
EXCLUSIVE DESIGN
By Independent Designs

Modern "Savior Faire"

This plan features:

— Three bedrooms

— Two full baths

■ Spacious country Kitchen has a built-in pantry, ample storage and work space

■ Great Room crowned in a vaulted ceiling and decorated by a fireplace, has convenient access to the kitchen

■ Master Bedroom highlighted by a private, full bath and a walk-in closet

■ Two additional bedrooms sharing a full hall bath

■ An optional crawl space or slab foundation available — please specify when ordering

■ No materials list is available for this plan

Main floor — 1,127 sq. ft.
Garage — 257 sq. ft.

Total living area 1,127 sq. ft. • Price Code A

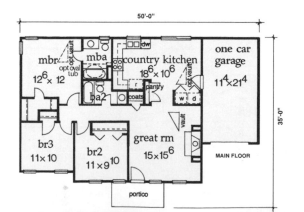

An
EXCLUSIVE DESIGN
By Georgia Toney Lesley,
Residential Designer

■ *Total living area 2,733 sq. ft.* ■ *Price Code F* ■

No. 92538

■ This plan features:

— Four bedrooms

— Three full baths

■ A central Den with a large fireplace, built-in shelves and cabinets and a decorative ceiling

■ Columns defining the entrance to the formal Dining Room, adding a touch of elegance

■ An island Kitchen that has been well thought out and includes a walk-in pantry

■ An informal Breakfast Room

■ A Master Bedroom with a decorative ceiling, a walk-in closet, and a luxurious Master Bath

■ Four additional bedrooms, each with private access to a full bath, two of which have walk-in closets

■ An optional crawl space or slab foundation available — please specify when ordering

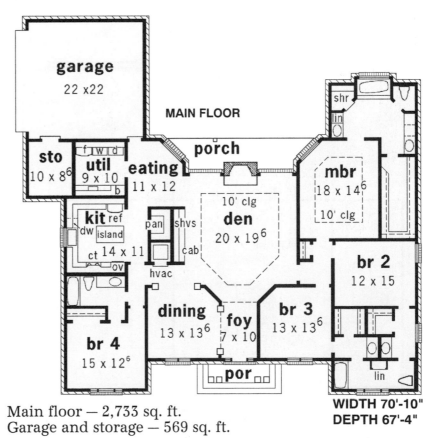

Main floor — 2,733 sq. ft.
Garage and storage — 569 sq. ft.

WIDTH 70'-10"
DEPTH 67'-4"

Exciting Ceilings Add Appeal

©1994 Donald A. Gardner Architects, Inc.

■ *Total living area — 1,475 sq. ft.* ■ *Price Code B* ■

No. 96452

FLOOR PLAN

DECK

spa

GARAGE
20-4 x 22-5

storage

BED RM.
11-4 x 10-0

fireplace
(cathedral ceiling)

GREAT RM.
15-4 x 16-0

KIT.
10-4 x 13-6

UTIL.

w
d

walk-in
closet

MASTER
BED RM.
13-4 x 14-4

cl

lin.

bath

cl

FOYER
15-4 x 3-8

DINING
10-4 x 12-0

master
bath

BED RM./
STUDY
11-4 x 10-4

PORCH

59-6

54-7

■ This plan features:

— Three bedrooms

— Two full baths

■ Open design enhanced by cathedral and tray ceilings above arched windows

■ Foyer with columns defining Great Room with central fireplace and Deck access

■ Cooktop island in Kitchen provides great cooks with convenience and company

■ Ultimate Master Bedroom suite offers walk-in closet, tray ceiling, and whirlpool bath

■ Front Bedroom/Study offers multiple uses with tray ceiling and arched window

Main floor — 1,475 sq. ft.
Garage & storage — 478 sq. ft.

Windows Create Horizontal Space

No. 96488

This plan features:

— Three bedrooms

— Two full and one half bath

■ Open floor plan and an abundance of windows creating horizontal spaciousness

■ Cathedral and tray ceilings adding vertical volume to home

■ Formal Foyer punctuated by elegant interior columns leading to a spacious Great Room and Dining Room

■ Great Room with a fireplace crowned in a cathedral ceiling

■ Octagonal Dining Room flowing from the Great Room and Kitchen

■ Kitchen receiving definition from columns having a pantry and an angled countertop with a liberal Breakfast Bar

■ Master Suite with double door entry, cathedral ceiling, patio access, walk-in closet, and lavish bath

■ Two additional bedrooms sharing a hall bath

■ Bonus space above the garage providing extra room for storage and expansion

Main floor — 1,695 sq. ft.
Bonus room — 287 sq. ft.
Garage & storage — 527 sq. ft

Total living area 1,695 sq. ft. ■ Price Code C

Comfortable Family Living

No. 99827

This plan features:

— Three bedrooms

— Two full baths

■ A stunning brick exterior with a columns supported triple arched front porch

■ The foyer opens into the Dining room as they are separated only by columns

■ The Great room has a cathedral ceiling, a fireplace, and access to the rear porch

■ The Kitchen features a island with a sink and a serving bar

■ A sunny Breakfast bay is open to the Kitchen

■ The Master bedroom has a tray ceiling, plus a private bath and a walk in closet

■ Two secondary bedrooms share a bath in their common hallway

■ This plan is completed by a two-car garage with storage and optional bonus space

Main floor — 1,972 sq. ft.
Garage — 600 sq. ft.
Bonus — 398 sq. ft.

Total living area 1,972 sq. ft. ■ Price Code C

A Contemporary Flair

■ *Total living area 1,491 sq. ft.* ■ *Price Code A* ■

MAIN FLOOR

No. 98806

■ **This plan features:**

— Three bedrooms

— One Full and One Three Quarter Bath

■ Striking bold elevation highlighted by an elevated entry canopy

■ Magnificent bayed Kitchen opens to the Breakfast Nook and the Family Room

■ Formal Dining Room includes a built-in china cabinet

■ Master Bedroom completed by a large walk-in closet and a three piece bath

■ Two additional bedrooms share a full bath in the hall

■ Patio with access from the Family Room

■ No materials list is available for this plan

Main floor – 1,491 sq. ft.
Basement – 1,491 sq. ft.
Garage — 408 sq. ft.

An
EXCLUSIVE DESIGN
By Weinmaster Home Design

Not Your Typical Ranch

© 1989 Donald A. Gardner Architects, Inc.

■ *Total living area 1,817 sq. ft.* ■ *Price Code C* ■

FIRST FLOOR

© 1989 Donald A. Gardner Architects, Inc.

No. 99855

■ **This plan features:**

— Three bedrooms

— Two full baths

■ The covered front entry reveals a door with sidelights

■ Past the foyer is the Great room that is highlighted by a cathedral ceiling, skylights, and a fireplace

■ The Dining room has windows that overlook the rear deck

■ The Kitchen has a center island with a cooktop and is open to the Breakfast bay

■ The Master bedroom has a walk in closet, a whirlpool bath, and a private covered deck

■ Two more bedrooms in the front of the home have access to a full bath in the hall

■ This home has a two-car garage

Main floor — 1,817 sq. ft.
Garage — 413 sq. ft.

■ Total living area 2,020 sq. ft. ■ Price Code C ■

No. 20099

■ This plan features:

— Three bedrooms

— Two full and one half baths

■ Angular windows and recessed ceilings separating the two dining areas from the adjoining island Kitchen

■ A window wall flanking the fireplace in the soaring, sky-lit Living Room

■ A Master Suite with a bump-out window and a double vanity bath

Main floor — 2,020 sq. ft.
Basement — 2,020 sq. ft.
Garage — 534 sq. ft.

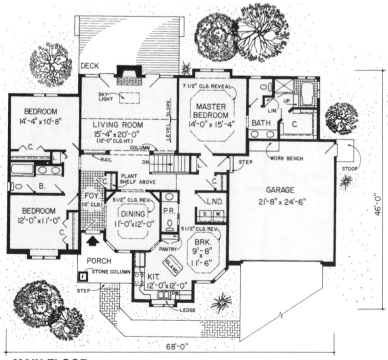

MAIN FLOOR

Multiple Gables and a Cozy Front Porch

Total living area 1,508 sq. ft. ■ Price Code B

MAIN FLOOR

Porch

Dining Area
11'6" x 14'2"

Kitchen
18' x 10'10"

Great Room
16'6" x 17'
slope ceiling

Master Bedroom
14' x 11'9"

Bath

Foyer

Bath

Hall

Laun.

Two-car Garage
20' x 22'

Porch

Bedroom
11' x 10'6"

Bedroom
10'6" x 10'6"

47'

60'

Main floor — 1,508 sq. ft.
Basement — 1,429 sq. ft.
Garage — 440 sq. ft.

No. 92649

This plan features:

— Three bedrooms

— Two full baths

■ Multiple gables and a cozy front porch

■ A Foyer area that leads to a bright and cheery Great Room capped by a sloped ceiling and highlighted by a fireplace

■ The Dining Area includes double hung windows and angles adding light and dimension to the room

■ Kitchen with additional room provided by a breakfast bar

■ A Master Bedroom Suite with a private bath

■ Two additional bedrooms share a full bath in the hall

■ No materials list is available for this plan

High Ceilings and Arched Windows

No. 98441

This plan features:

— Three bedrooms

— Two full baths

■ Natural illumination streaming into the Dining Room and Sitting area of the Master Suite through large, arched windows

■ Kitchen with convenient pass through to the Great Room and a serving bar for the Breakfast Room

■ Great Room topped by a vaulted ceiling accented by a fireplace and a French door

■ Decorative columns accenting the entrance of the Dining Room

■ Tray ceiling over the Master Suite and a vaulted ceiling over the sitting room and the Master Bath

■ An optional basement or crawl space foundation available — please specify when ordering

■ No materials list is available for this plan

Main floor — 1,502 sq. ft.
Garage — 448 sq. ft.
Basement — 1,555 sq. ft.

■ Total living area 1,502 sq. ft. ■ Price Code B

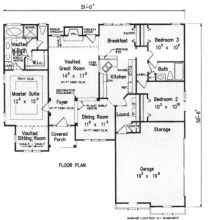

Traditional and Elegant

No. 99865

This plan features:

— Three bedrooms

— Two full and one half baths

■ The Master suite is extremely private in the back of the house and features skylights, a double vanity and a walk-in closet

■ The Great room with a cathedral ceiling and a fireplace, flows into the Kitchen and Breakfast area

■ The two other Bedrooms have access to the hall bathroom

■ The front of the house has an elegant Foyer and a formal Dining room

■ There is a large Bonus room available for future expansion

Main floor — 1,927 sq. ft.
Bonus — 536 sq. ft.
Garage — 669 sq. ft.

© 1994 Donald A. Gardner Architects, Inc.

■ Total living area 1,927 sq. ft. ■ Price Code C

301

Especially Unique

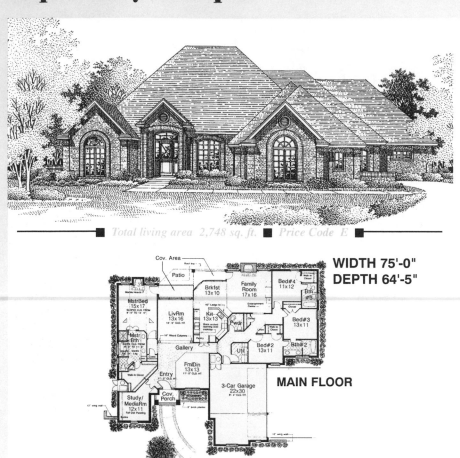

Total living area 2,748 sq. ft. ■ Price Code E ■

WIDTH 75'-0"
DEPTH 64'-5"

MAIN FLOOR

No. 98528

■ **This plan features:**

— Four bedrooms

— Three full and one half baths

■ An arch covered entry and arched windows add a unique flair to this home

■ From the entry with it's 11' ceiling turn left into the Study/Media room

■ The formal Dining room is open to the Gallery, and the Living room beyond

■ The Family room has a built in entertainment center, a fireplace, and access to the rear patio

■ The Master bedroom is isolated, and has it's own fireplace, bath, and walk in closet

■ Three additional bedrooms are on the opposite side of the home, and they share two full baths

■ This home has a three-car garage

■ No materials list is available for this plan

Main floor — 2,748 sq. ft.
Garage — 660 sq. ft.

Perfect for a Corner Lot

Total living area 1,494 sq. ft. ■ Price Code A ■

WIDTH 38'-0"
DEPTH 56'-0"

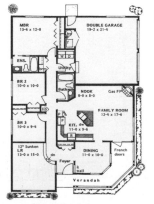

MAIN FLOOR

No. 99909

■ **This plan features:**

— Three bedrooms

— Two full baths

■ Covered porch providing a warm welcome

■ Sunken Living Room to the left of the Foyer

■ Formal and elegant Dining Room to the right of the Foyer

■ L-shaped Kitchen serving the Dining Room, Nook and Family Room with equal ease

■ Corner fireplace and French doors to the porch enhance the Family Room

■ Bedrooms arranged with easy access to a full bath

Main floor — 1,494 sq. ft.
Garage — 450 sq. ft.

An
EXCLUSIVE DESIGN
By Westhome Planners. Ltd.

Style All The Way Around

■ *Total living area 1,794 sq. ft.* ■ *Price Code B* ■

No. 94024

■ This plan features:

— Three Bedrooms

— Two full baths

■ Spacious entry leading to a modern Great Room with 12' ceilings naturally and a dormer window

■ Dining Room gaining its unique shape from the double bay windows

■ Center island/snack bar in the large Kitchen

■ Bay window in the front bedroom

■ Master suite enhanced by a bayed whirlpool tub area, a wrap around vanity

■ A grand covered deck with hot tub accessed from the Great room or the master suite

■ No materials list is available for this plan

Main floor — 1,794 sq. ft.
Garage — 766 sq. ft.

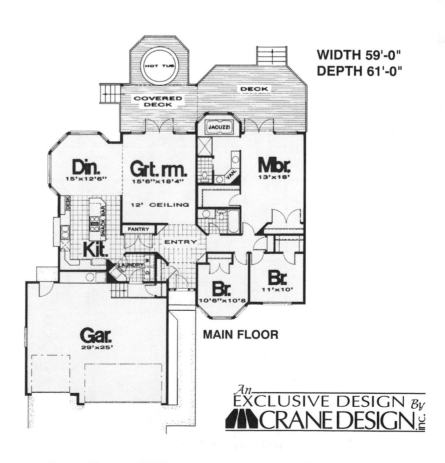

WIDTH 59'-0"
DEPTH 61'-0"

MAIN FLOOR

An EXCLUSIVE DESIGN By CRANE DESIGN inc.

A Modern Slant On A Country Theme

■ Total living area 1,648 sq. ft. ■ Price Code B ■

No. 96513

■ **This plan features:**

— Three bedrooms

— Two full baths

■ Country styled front porch highlighting exterior which is enhanced by dormer windows

■ Modern open floor plan for a more spacious feeling

■ Great Room accented by a quaint, corner fireplace and a ceiling fan

■ Dining Room flowing from the Great Room for easy entertaining

■ Kitchen graced by natural light from attractive bay window and a convenient snack bar for meals on the go

■ Master suite secluded in separate wing for total privacy

■ Two additional bedrooms sharing full bath in the hall

Main floor — 1,648 sq. ft.
Garage — 479 sq. ft.

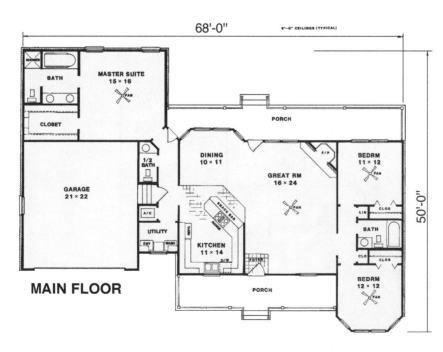

MAIN FLOOR

Ranch has Victorian Flair

■ This plan features:

— Four bedrooms

— Two full and one half baths

■ The quaint covered Porch has gables and gingerbread trim

■ The Living room has a massive fireplace and a cathedral ceiling

■ The formal Dining room is situated through French doors, off the Gallery

■ A country Kitchen with island and brick alcove abuts Breakfast area

■ An enormous Master suite has two walk-in closets and a spacious Bath

■ Three additional Bedrooms share a full Bath

■ No materials list is available for this plan

Main floor — 2,495 sq. ft.
Garage — 720 sq. ft.

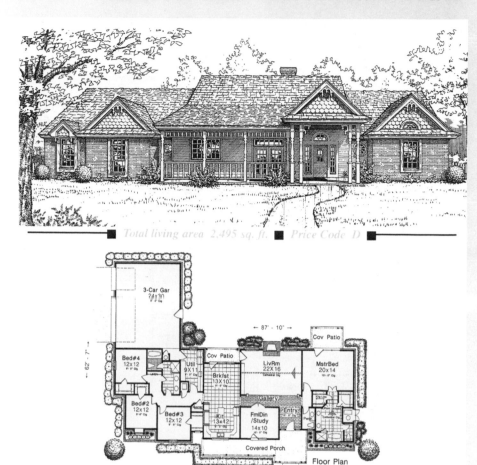

Total living area 2,495 sq. ft. ■ Price Code D

Build as You Need

No. 34064

■ This plan features:

— Three bedrooms

— Two full baths

■ Perfect home plan for expanding with a limited budget

■ Basic structure includes two bedrooms, bath, corner Kitchen with an open Family Room

■ Addition of front section expands home to a multi-window Dining and Living Room area, and Foyer with a closet

■ Two more sections add a Master Bedroom suite, and a Breakfast area with a fireplace, and a two-car garage

Starting module — 864 sq. ft.
All modules — 1,858 sq. ft.
Garage — 528 sq. ft.

Total living area 1,858 sq. ft. ■ Price Code C

MAIN FLOOR

Graceful Arches Accent Elevation

Total living area 2,517 sq. ft. ■ Price Code D

MAIN FLOOR

WIDTH — 69'-0"
DEPTH — 63'-6"

No. 93056

■ **This plan features:**

— Four bedrooms

— Two full and one half baths

■ Arched portico entrance leads into the raised Foyer, Dining and Living Rooms

■ Expansive Living Room with plant ledges and a wall of windows overlooks the Patio

■ Arched window below a sloped ceiling in the Dining Room

■ Ultimate Kitchen with a walk-in pantry and a peninsula snackbar that services the glass, octagon Breakfast area and the Family Room with a cozy fireplace

■ Double door entrance to the Master Bedroom suite with a cathedral ceiling, a lavish Master Bath with a garden tub and two walk-in closets

■ Versatile Bedroom/Study with a walk-in closet and a coffered ceiling over an arched window

■ Two additional bedrooms, with walk-in closets, share a full bath

■ An optional slab or crawl space foundation available — please specify when ordering

Main floor — 2,517 sq. ft.
Garage — 443 sq. ft.

Relax in the Cozy Den

Total living area 1,531 sq. ft. ■ Price Code B

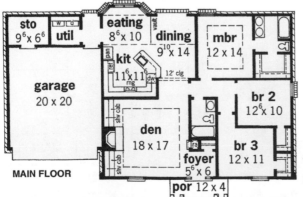

MAIN FLOOR

WIDTH 60'-10"
DEPTH 41'-5"

No. 92565

■ **This plan features:**

— Three bedrooms

— Two full baths

■ Attractive columns and a sheltering arched entry porch front this home

■ The foyer inside open to the Den that has a decorative ceiling, and a fireplace with built ins beside it

■ The Kitchen features an angled counter design and is open to both eating areas

■ The Master bedroom has a decorative ceiling, a full bath, and a walk in closet

■ Two additional bedrooms each have walk in closets

■ This home has a two-car garage with an attached storage room

■ An optional slab or a crawl space foundation available — please specify when ordering this plan

Main floor — 1,531 sq. ft.
Garage — 462 sq. ft..

■ *Total living area 1,338 sq. ft.* ■ *Price Code A* ■

No. 91544

■ This plan features:

— Three bedrooms

— One full and one three quarter baths

■ Skylight brightens entry into Living Room with vaulted ceiling, palladian window and an inviting fireplace

■ Convenient Dining area with decorative window extends from Living Room for easy entertaining

■ Efficient Kitchen with pantry, corner sink and eating Nook with an arched window and Patio access

■ Vaulted ceiling tops Master suite with a decorative window, double vanity and walk-in closet

■ Two additional bedrooms with ample closets, share a full bath and laundry

Main floor — 1,338 sq. ft.

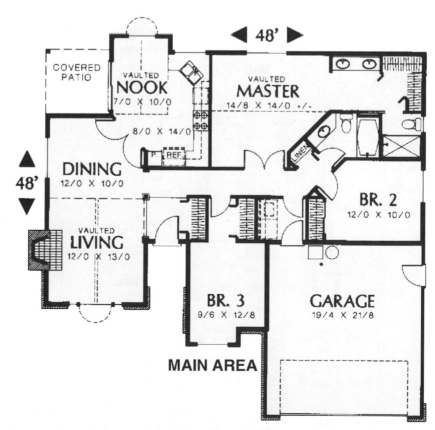

COVERED PATIO

VAULTED NOOK 7/0 X 10/0

8/0 X 14/0

◄ 48' ►

VAULTED MASTER 14/8 X 14/0 +/-

DINING 12/0 X 10/0

48'

VAULTED LIVING 12/0 X 13/0

LINEN

BR. 2 12/0 X 10/0

BR. 3 9/6 X 12/8

GARAGE 19/4 X 21/8

MAIN AREA

Cathedral Ceiling

■ *Total living area 1,346 sq. ft.* ■ *Price Code A* ■

No. 24402

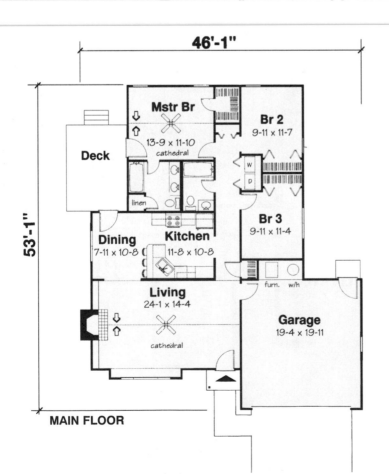

MAIN FLOOR

■ **This plan features:**

— Three bedrooms

— Two full baths

■ A spacious Living Room with a cathedral ceiling and elegant fireplace

■ A Dining Room that adjoins both the Living Room and the Kitchen

■ An efficient Kitchen, with double sinks, ample cabinet space and peninsula counter that doubles as an eating bar

■ A convenient hallway laundry center

■ A Master Suite with a cathedral ceiling and a private Master Bath

Main floor — 1,346 sq. ft.
Garage — 449 sq. ft.

An
EXCLUSIVE DESIGN
By Upright Design

Ideal for Formal Entertaining

No. 90421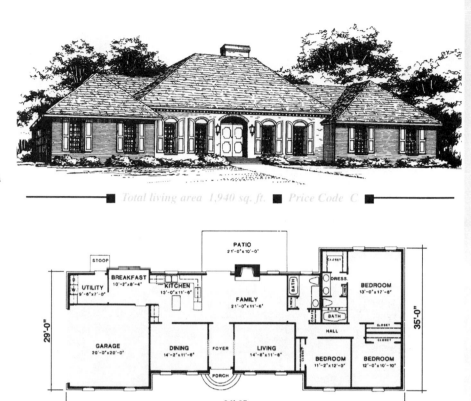

This plan features:

— Three bedrooms

— Two full baths

■ A lovely French Provincial design

■ A large Family Room with a raised hearth fireplace and double doors to the patio

■ An L-shaped, island Kitchen with a Breakfast Bay and open counter to the Family Room

■ A Master Suite including one double closet and a compartmentalized bath with walk-in closet, step-up garden tub, double vanity and linen closet

■ Two front bedrooms sharing a full hall bath with a linen closet

■ An optional basement, slab or crawl space foundation — please specify when ordering

Main floor — 1,940 sq. ft.

Total living area 1,940 sq. ft. ■ *Price Code C* ■

MAIN FLOOR

Great Starter Home

No. 91553

This plan features:

— Three bedrooms

— One full and one three quarter baths

■ This lovely starter home will fit perfectly on a narrow lot

■ The Living room features a corner fireplace and opens into the Dining room

■ The efficient Kitchen has plenty of counter space and a double sink with a window above

■ Two bedrooms have ample closet space and share a full bath

■ The Master bedroom has a walk-in closet, and a private three quarter bath

■ This plan has a two-car garage with an entry door into the home

■ No materials list is available for this plan

Main floor — 1,271 sq. ft.
Garage — 440 sq. ft.

Total living area 1,271 sq. ft. ■ *Price Code A* ■

◄ 40' ►

MAIN FLOOR

Attractive Ranch

■ Total living area 2,005 sq. ft. ■ Price Code C ■

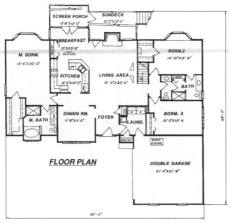

FLOOR PLAN

No. 93235

■ **This plan features:**

– Three bedrooms

– One full and one three quarter baths

■ The large Living room has a rear wall fireplace and access to the rear sundeck

■ The Kitchen straddles the formal Dining room and the Breakfast nook

■ Included in the Kitchen is a cooktop, and angled counter, and a pantry

■ The Master bedroom and the second bedroom both have bay windows on their rear walls

■ This home has been designed with plenty of closet space and a large laundry room

■ In the rear there is a screen porch and a sundeck for outdoor entertaining

■ No materials list is available for this plan

Main floor — 2,005 sq. ft.
Basement — 1,947 sq. ft.
Garage — 434 sq. ft.

An
EXCLUSIVE DESIGN
By Jannis Vann & Associates, Inc.

Classic Brick with One Floor Living

■ Total living area 1,330 sq. ft. ■ Price Code A ■

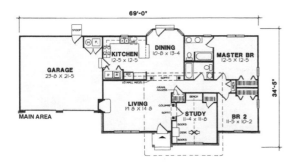

MAIN AREA

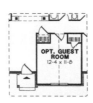

OPT. GUEST ROOM
12-4 x 11-8

No. 24709

■ **This plan features:**

– Two or three bedrooms

– Two full baths

■ Living room, enhanced by triple window and cozy fireplace opens to Dining Room through graceful columns

■ Quiet Study, with convenient built-ins and a sloped ceiling, can convert to third bedroom

■ Formal Dining Room highlighted by glass alcove and atrium door to rear yard

■ Efficient, U-shaped Kitchen with laundry closet, Garage entry and extended counter/eating bar

■ Corner Master Bedroom with double vanity bath

■ Second bedroom with large closet and access to a full bath

■ No materials list is available for this plan

Main floor — 1,330 sq. ft.
Garage — 523 sq. ft.

Varied Roof Heights Create Interesting Lines

■ Total living area 1,613 sq. ft. ■ Price Code B ■

No. 90601

■ This plan features:

— Three bedrooms

— Two full and one half baths

■ A spacious Family Room with a heat-circulating fireplace, which is visible from the Foyer

■ A large Kitchen with a cooktop island, opening into the dinette bay

■ A Master Suite with his-n-her closets and a private Master Bath

■ Two additional bedrooms which share a full hall bath

■ Formal Dining and Living Rooms, flowing into each other for easy entertaining

Main floor — 1,613 sq. ft.

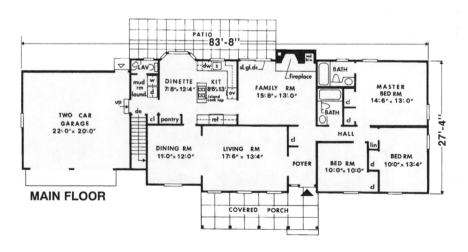

MAIN FLOOR

Southern Hospitality

Total living area 1,830 sq. ft. ■ Price Code C

No. 92220

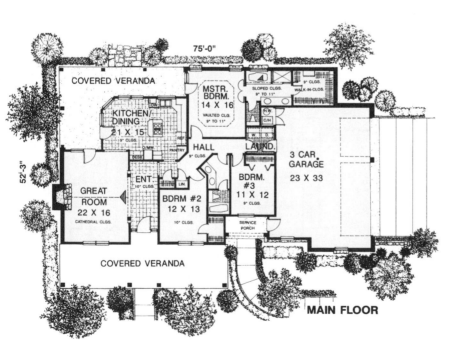

MAIN FLOOR

This plan features:

— Three bedrooms

— Two full baths

Covered Veranda catches breezes

Tiled Entry leads into Great Room with fieldstone fireplace, a cathedral ceiling and atrium door to another Covered Veranda

A bright Kitchen/Dining Room includes a stovetop island/snackbar, built-in pantry and desk

Vaulted ceiling crowns Master Bedroom that offers a plush bath and huge walk-in closet

Two additional bedrooms with ample closets share a double vanity bath

No materials list is available for this plan

Main floor — 1,830 sq. ft.
Garage — 759 sq. ft.

Compact and Appealing

No. 20075

■ This plan features:

— Three bedrooms

— Two full baths

■ A fireplaced Living Room and formal Dining Room with extra wide doorways

■ A centrally-located Kitchen for maximum convenience

■ A Master Bedroom with a vaulted ceiling and a private Master Bath and walk-in closet

Main floor — 1,682 sq. ft.
Basement — 1,682 sq. ft.
Garage — 484 sq. ft.

An

EXCLUSIVE DESIGN
By Karl Kreeger

Total living area 1,682 sq. ft. ■ Price Code B

MAIN FLOOR

European Flair in Tune with Today

No. 94804

■ This plan features:

— Three bedrooms

— Two full baths

■ European flavor with decorative windows, gable roof lines and a stucco finish

■ Formal Dining Room with floor to ceiling window treatment

■ Expansive Activity Room with decorative ceiling, hearth fireplace and Deck access

■ Open, efficient Kitchen with snack bar, Laundry, Breakfast area and Screened Porch beyond

■ Private Master Bedroom suite with a decorative ceiling, large walk-in closet and luxurious bath

■ Two additional bedrooms, one with a bay window, share a full bath

Main floor — 1,855 sq. ft.
Garage — 439 sq. ft.
Basement — 1,855 sq. ft.

Total living area 1,855 sq. ft. ■ Price Code C

MAIN FLOOR

Classy Stone and Stucco

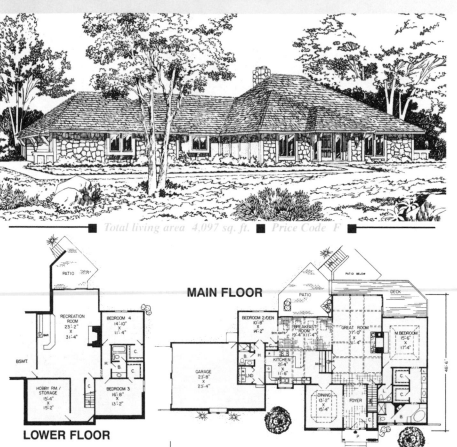

Total living area 4,097 sq. ft. ■ Price Code F

MAIN FLOOR

LOWER FLOOR

No. 10540

■ This plan features:

— Four bedrooms

— Three full and one half baths

■ A large, majestic foyer flowing into the formal Dining Room

■ A Great Room accented by a wetbar, a stone fireplace, and access to a spacious Deck

■ A spacious Kitchen highlighted by a writing area, work area, and a beamed Breakfast Room

■ A huge Master Bedroom with a dressing room and a separate whirlpool bath

■ A lower level featuring a Recreation Area and two additional bedrooms

Main floor — 2,473 sq. ft.
Lower floor — 1,624 sq. ft.
Basement — 732 sq. ft.
Garage & storage — 686 sq. ft.

An EXCLUSIVE DESIGN *By Karl Kreeger*

Dormers and Front Porch for Cozy Exterior

Total living area 1,843 sq. ft. ■ Price Code C

MAIN FLOOR

No. 96526

■ This plan features:

— Three bedrooms

— Two full and one half baths

■ A decorative ceiling treatment and a corner fireplace achieving a wonderful first impression

■ The Dining Room is open to the Great Room and the Kitchen creating the illusion of more space

■ Secondary bedrooms located to the right of the home are situated with a full bath between them

■ The Master Suite is topped by a decorative ceiling treatment and highlighted by a five-piece bath and two walk-in closets

Main floor — 1,843 sq. ft.
Garage — 531 sq. ft.

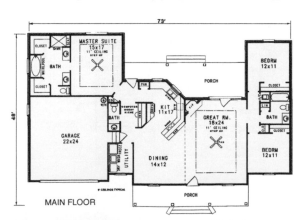

Spectacular Traditional

■ *Total living area 1,237 sq. ft.* ■ *Price Code B* ■

No. 92502

■ This plan features:

— Three bedrooms

— Two full baths

■ The use of gable roofs and the blend of stucco and brick to form a spectacular exterior

■ A high vaulted ceiling and a cozy fireplace, with built-in cabinets in the Den

■ An efficient, U-shaped Kitchen with an adjacent Dining Area

■ A Master Bedroom, with a raised ceiling, that includes a private bath and a walk-in closet

■ Two family bedrooms that share a full hall bath

■ An optional crawl space or slab foundation available — please specify when ordering

Main area — 1,237 sq. ft.
Garage — 436 sq. ft.

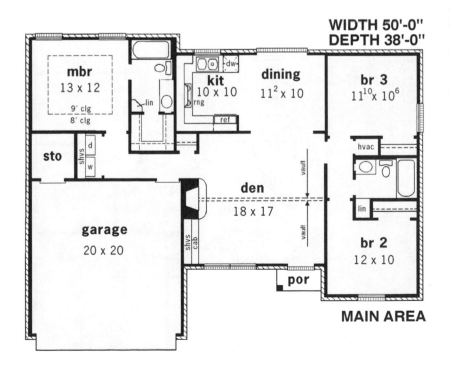

WIDTH 50'-0''
DEPTH 38'-0''

mbr
13 x 12

9' clg
8' clg

sto

garage
20 x 20

kit
10 x 10

dining
11² x 10

br 3
11¹⁰ x 10⁶

den
18 x 17

por

br 2
12 x 10

MAIN AREA

Attractive Roof Lines

Total living area 1,396 sq. ft. ■ Price Code A

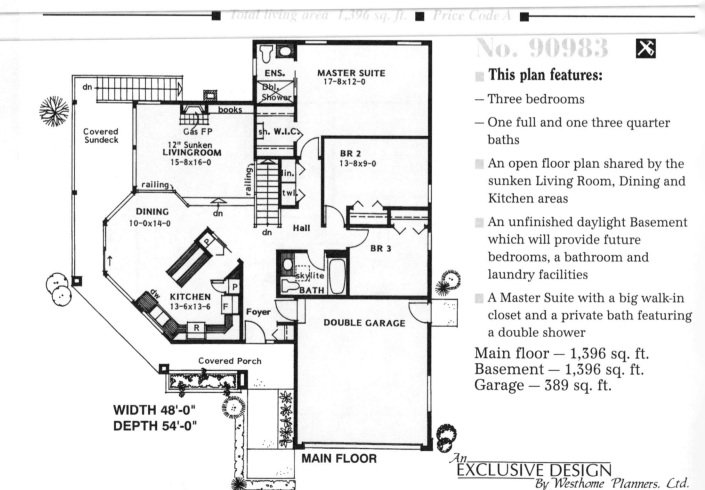

dn

Covered Sundeck

Gas FP

12" Sunken
LIVINGROOM
15-8x16-0

railing

railing

DINING
10-0x14-0

dn

KITCHEN
13-6x13-6

dw

P

F

R

Foyer

books

ENS.

Dbl.
Shower

sh. **W.I.C.**

in.

twl

Hall

dn

MASTER SUITE
17-8x12-0

BR 2
13-8x9-0

BR 3

skylite

BATH

DOUBLE GARAGE

Covered Porch

WIDTH 48'-0"
DEPTH 54'-0"

MAIN FLOOR

No. 90983

This plan features:

— Three bedrooms

— One full and one three quarter baths

■ An open floor plan shared by the sunken Living Room, Dining and Kitchen areas

■ An unfinished daylight Basement which will provide future bedrooms, a bathroom and laundry facilities

■ A Master Suite with a big walk-in closet and a private bath featuring a double shower

Main floor — 1,396 sq. ft.
Basement — 1,396 sq. ft.
Garage — 389 sq. ft.

An
EXCLUSIVE DESIGN
By Westhome Planners, Ltd.

Simple Style with Classic Accents

No. 92286

This plan features:

— Three bedrooms

— Two full baths

- Sheltered entry leads into busy living areas

- Spacious Living Room with cozy fireplace and access to rear yard

- An efficient Kitchen with a bright Dining area next to Utilities and Garage entry

- Two walk-in closets and a plush private bath offered in Master Bedroom

- Two additional bedrooms with ample closets share a double vanity sink

- No materials list is available for this plan

Main floor — 1,415 sq. ft.
Garage — 440 sq. ft.

Total living area 1,415 sq. ft. ■ Price Code A

Main Floor

Lots of Views and Breezes

No. 99284

This plan features:

— Three bedrooms

— Two full baths

- Garden entry and large windows appealing to all

- Kitchen directly off Foyer with work island/cooktop, serving counter/snackbar and adjoining Service Entry

- Sloped ceiling tops fireplace and sliding glass doors to Terrace in Living/Dining rooms

- Master Bedroom enhanced by outdoor access, his and her walk-in closets and a pampering bath with two vanities and a whirlpool tub

- Two additional bedrooms share a double vanity bath

Main floor — 2,189 sq. ft.
Garage — 480 sq. ft.

Total living area 2,189 sq. ft. ■ Price Code C

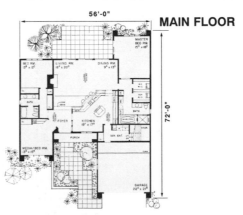

MAIN FLOOR

A Warm Welcome

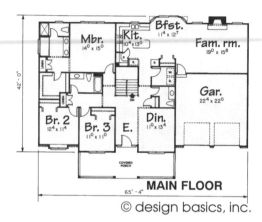

MAIN FLOOR

© design basics, inc.

■ *Total living area 2,042 sq. ft.* ■ *Price Code C* ■

No. 94984

■ **This plan features:**

— Three bedrooms

— Two full and one half baths

■ The quaint covered Porch has a front railing

■ The Entry opens into the formal Dining room

■ The L-shaped Kitchen with a center island opens into the Breakfast bay

■ The large Family room features rear wall fireplace and windows

■ The Master bedroom has a private bath and a large walk in closet

■ Two additional Bedrooms share a full bath

Main floor — 2,042 sq. ft.
Garage — 506 sq. ft.

Great Open Family Living Space

MAIN FLOOR

■ *Total living area 1,657 sq. ft.* ■ *Price Code B* ■

No. 96518

■ **This plan features:**

— Three bedrooms

— Two full baths

■ An open layout in the expansive family living area promotes family interaction

■ A cook top eating bar highlights the Kitchen and the Dining areas

■ A fireplace adds coziness to the Great Room

■ The Dining area directly accesses the porch expanding your choices to the outdoors

■ The Master Suite is crowned in a decorative ceiling and includes a private four piece bath

■ Two additional bedroom share the full bath in the hall

Main floor — 1,657 sq. ft.
Garage — 555 sq. ft.

Half-Round Window Graces Attractive Exterior

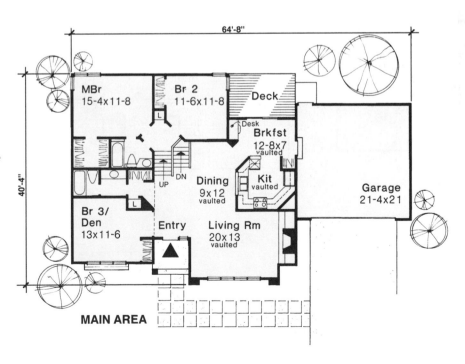

■ *Total living area 1,452 sq. ft.* ■ *Price Code A* ■

No. 90395

■ **This plan features:**

— Three bedrooms

— Two full baths

■ Soaring ceilings in the Kitchen, Living Room, Dining, and Breakfast Rooms

■ An efficient, well-equipped Kitchen with a pass-through to the Dining room

■ Built-in bookcases flanking the fireplace in the Living Room

■ A Master Suite with a private Master Bath and walk-in closet

Main floor — 1,452 sq. ft.

MAIN AREA

Cozy Country Ranch

■ *Total living area 1,576 sq. ft.* ■ *Price Code B* ■

No. 24708

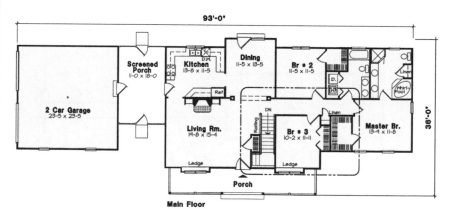

93'-0"

Screened Porch
11-0 x 18-0

2 Car Garage
23-5 x 23-5

Kitchen
13-8 x 11-5

Dining
11-5 x 13-5

Br # 2
11-5 x 11-5

Living Rm.
19-8 x 15-4

Br # 3
10-2 x 11-11

Master Br.
13-4 x 11-8

36'-0"

Porch

Main Floor

Main floor — 1,576 sq. ft.
Garage — 576 sq. ft.
Basement — 1,454 sq. ft.

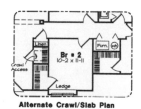

Br # 2
10-2 x 11-11

Alternate Crawl/Slab Plan

■ This plan features:

— Three bedrooms

— Two full baths

■ Front Porch shelters outdoor visiting and entrance into Living Room

■ Expansive Living Room highlighted by a boxed window and hearth fireplace between built-ins

■ Columns frame entrance to Dining Room which has access to back yard

■ Efficient, U-shaped Kitchen with direct access to the Screened Porch and the Dining Room

■ Master Bedroom wing enhanced by a large walk-in closet and a double vanity bath with a whirlpool tub

■ Two additional bedrooms with large closets, share a double vanity bath with laundry center

■ No materials list is available for this plan

Traditional Ranch Plan

No. 90454

This plan features:

- Three bedrooms
- Two full baths
- Large Foyer set between the formal Living and Dining Rooms
- Spacious Great Room adjacent to the open Kitchen/Breakfast area
- Secluded Master Bedroom highlighted by the Master Bath with a garden tub, separate shower, and his and her vanity
- Bay window allows bountiful natural light into the Breakfast area
- Two additional bedrooms sharing a full bath
- An optional basement or crawl space foundation available — please specify when ordering

Main floor — 2,218 sq. ft.
Basement — 1,658 sq. ft.
Garage — 528 sq. ft.

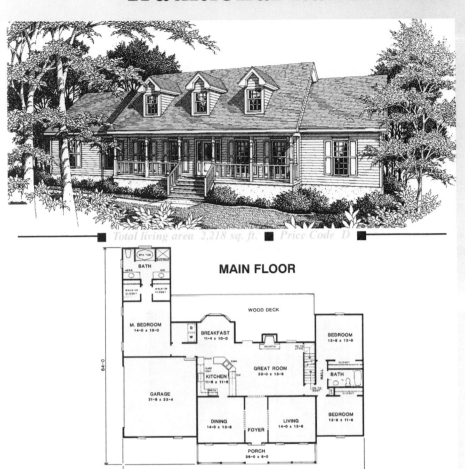

■ Total living area 2,218 sq. ft. ■ Price Code D ■

MAIN FLOOR

A Sweet Master Suite

No. 94916

This plan features:

- Three bedrooms
- Two full baths
- An arched covered stoop leads into Entry and Great Room beyond
- Spacious Great Room enhanced by a fireplace with windows on either side
- Boxed triple window naturally illuminating the Breakfast area
- Kitchen offers snackbar counter, built in pantry and adjoining laundry/Garage entry
- Master Bedroom suite enhanced by a decorative window, walk-in closet and plush bath with double vanity and well placed corner window tub
- Two additional bedrooms share a full bath

Main floor — 1,392 sq. ft.
Basement — 1,392 sq. ft.
Garage — 472 sq. ft.

■ Total living area 1,392 sq. ft. ■ Price Code A ■

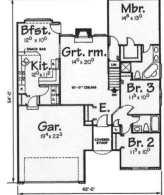

MAIN FLOOR

Unique Keeping Room

This plan features:

— Four bedrooms

— Two full and one half baths

■ Sheltered Porch and an open Foyer lead into the Dining and Living Rooms with 10' ceilings

■ Huge fireplace, built-ins and windows overlooking the rear yard highlight the Living Room

■ Open, efficient Kitchen with an island counter/serving bar, a walk-in pantry, a built-in desk, a Utility room and a Garage

■ Spacious Keeping/Breakfast Rooms adjoin the Kitchen and access the Covered Porch

■ Private Master Bedroom suite with his-n-her closets and a Master Bath with two vanities and a corner whirlpool tub

■ Two additional bedrooms with large closets, share a full bath

■ Walk-in closet in the Study/Bedroom offers options

■ An optional slab or crawlspace foundation available — please specify when ordering

■ No materials list is available for this plan

Main floor — 2,559 sq. ft.
Garage — 544 sq. ft.

Total living area 2,559 sq. ft. ■ *Price Code D* ■

MAIN FLOOR

Distinguished Styling

This plan features:

— Four bedrooms

— Two full and one three quarter baths

■ Brick quoins, segmented arches, plus oval and fan shaped windows create a distinguished style

■ The Family room has a cozy fireplace and flows into the Breakfast bay

■ The Living room and the Family room both access the rear Patio

■ The formal Dining room is steps away from the gourmet Kitchen

■ The Master bedroom features a vaulted ceiling, a walk-in closet, and a private bath

■ There are three additional bedrooms and a full and a three quarter bath

■ This plan has a three-car garage

■ No materials list is available for this plan

Main floor — 2,354 sq. ft.
Garage — 704 sq. ft.

Total living area 2,353 sq. ft. ■ *Price Code D* ■

MAIN FLOOR

Brick Detail with Arches

■ *Total living area 1,987 sq. ft.* ■ *Price Code D* ■

No. 92544

■ This plan features:

— Four bedrooms

— Two full and one half baths

■ Front and back porches expand the living space and provide inviting access to the open layout

■ Spacious Den with a fireplace flanked by built-in shelves and double access to the rear Porch

■ Formal Dining Room with an arched window

■ Efficient, U-shaped Kitchen with a snackbar counter, a bright Breakfast area and an adjoining laundry and Garage

■ Secluded Master Bedroom suite

■ Three additional bedrooms with walk-in closets, share one and half baths

■ An optional slab or crawl space foundation available — please specify when ordering

Main floor — 1,987 sq. ft.
Garage/Storage — 515 sq. ft.

67'-0'' Width
49'-0'' Depth

Easy Everyday Living and Entertaining

Total living area — 1,664 sq. ft. ■ Price Code B

No. 92238

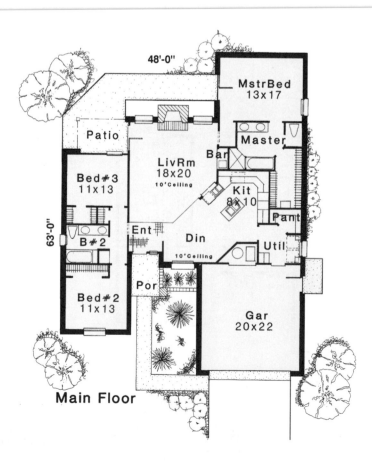

Main Floor

This plan features:

— Three bedrooms

— Two full baths

■ Front entrance accented by segmented arches, sidelight and transom windows

■ Open Living Room with focal point fireplace, wet bar and access to Patio

■ Dining area open to both the Living Room and the Kitchen

■ Efficient Kitchen with a cooktop island, walk-in pantry and Utility area with a Garage entry

■ Large walk-in closet, double vanity bath and access to Patio featured in the Master Bedroom suite

■ No materials list is available for this plan

Main floor — 1,664 sq. ft.
Basement — 1,600 sq. ft.
Garage — 440 sq. ft

Relaxed Style

No. 94985

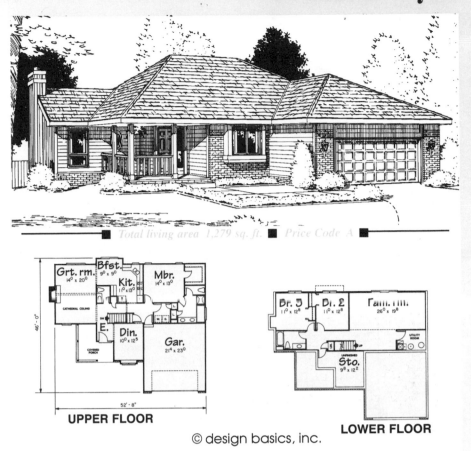

Total living area 1,279 sq. ft. ■ Price Code A

This plan features:

- Three bedrooms
- Two full and one half baths
- Lovely covered porch fostering the desire to relax and enjoy a cool breeze on the end of the day
- One bedroom for an empty nest lifestyle, with an option for two additional bedroom in the basement
- Kitchen, Breakfast area, and Great Room flowing into each other for ease in every day living
- Cathedral ceiling topping the Great Room while a fireplace enhances the atmosphere

Main floor — 1,279 sq. ft.
Bonus lower floor — 984 sq. ft.
Garage — 509 sq. ft.

UPPER FLOOR

© design basics, inc.

LOWER FLOOR

Foyer Isolates Bedroom Wing

No. 20087

This plan features:

- Three bedrooms
- Two full baths
- A Living Room complete with a window wall, flanking a massive fireplace
- A Dining Room with recessed ceilings and a pass-through for convenience
- A Master Suite tucked behind the two-car garage for maximum noise protection
- A spacious Kitchen with built-ins and access to the two-car garage

Main floor —1,568 sq. ft.
Basement — 1,568 sq. ft.
Garage — 484 sq. ft.

Total living area 1,568 sq. ft. ■ Price Code B

MAIN FLOOR

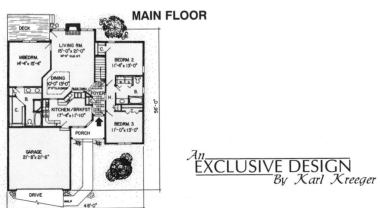

An EXCLUSIVE DESIGN
By Karl Kreeger

325

Energy Efficient Air-Lock Entry

Total living area 1,771 sq. ft. ■ Price Code B

MAIN FLOOR 54'-0"

No. 24714

■ **This plan features:**

— Two bedrooms

— Two full baths

■ The attractive covered Porch highlights the curb appeal of this charming home

■ A cozy window seat and a vaulted ceiling enhance the private Den

■ The sunken Great room is accented by a fireplace that is nestled between windows

■ A screened Porch, accessed from the Dining room, extends the living space to the outdoors

■ The Master bath features a garden tub, separate shower, his-n-her walk-in closets and a skylight

■ No materials list is available for this plan

Main floor — 1,771 sq. ft.
Basement — 1,194 sq. ft.
Garage — 517 sq. ft.

Great Room is Prominently Featured

Total living area 1,880 sq. ft. ■ Price Code C

No. 92566

■ **This plan features:**

— Three bedrooms

— Two full baths

■ A covered porch leads into a foyer that separates the Living and Dining rooms

■ The central Great room has a decorative ceiling, a fireplace, and access to the rear porch

■ The Kitchen is equipped with a double oven, a planning desk, a cooktop surface and plenty of counter space

■ The Eating nook is located right next to the Kitchen

■ The Master bedroom is set in the back of the home for privacy and features it's own full bath

■ Two secondary bedrooms on the other side of the home share a full bath

■ This home has a convenient utility room and a two-car garage

■ This plan is available with a slab or a crawl space foundation — please specify when ordering

Main floor — 1,880 sq. ft.
Garage — 489 sq. ft.

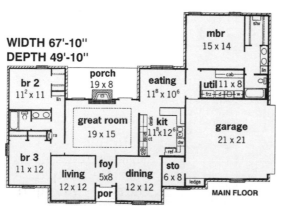

WIDTH 67'-10"
DEPTH 49'-10"

MAIN FLOOR

Dining in a Greenhouse Bay

■ *Total living area 1,476 sq. ft.* ■ *Price Code A* ■

No. 90620

■ This plan features:

— Three bedrooms

— Two full baths

■ Covered entrance into a bright Foyer highlighted by a skydome

■ Formal Living Room accented by a heat-circulating fireplace and sliding glass doors to the Terrace

■ Greenhouse Dining Room feels like eating outdoors

■ Efficient Kitchen with a peninsula counter and a bay window Dinette area convenient to the Laundry and Garage

■ Comfortable Master Bedroom with a private bath and walk-in closet

■ Two additional bedrooms share a full bath

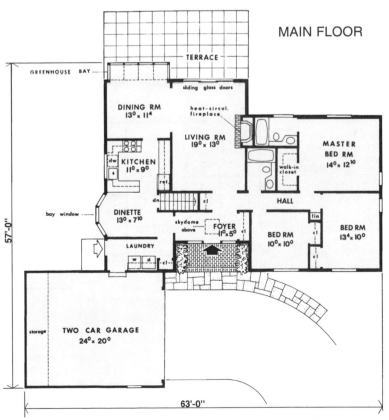

MAIN FLOOR

GREENHOUSE BAY

TERRACE

sliding glass doors

DINING RM
13⁰ x 11⁴

heat-circul. fireplace

LIVING RM
19⁰ x 13⁰

MASTER BED RM
14⁰ x 12¹⁰

walk-in closet

dw

KITCHEN
11⁰ x 9⁰

ref.

bay window

DINETTE
13⁰ x 7¹⁰

dn

cl

HALL

lin

BED RM
13⁴ x 10⁰

skydome above

FOYER
11⁰ x 5⁰

cl

BED RM
10⁰ x 10⁰

cl

LAUNDRY

w d

cl

57'-0"

storage

TWO CAR GARAGE
24⁰ x 20⁰

63'-0"

Main floor — 1,476 sq. ft.
Basement — 1,476 sq. ft.
Porch — 70 sq. ft.
Garage — 480 sq. ft.

Charming Southern Traditional

Total living area—1,271 sq. ft. ■ Price Code B

No. 92503

This plan features:

— Three bedrooms

— Two full baths

■ A covered front porch with striking columns, brick quoins, and dentil molding

■ A spacious Great Room with vaulted ceilings, a fireplace, and built-in cabinets

■ A Utility Room adjacent to the Kitchen which leads to the two-car Garage and Storage Rooms

■ A Master Bedroom including a large walk-in closet and a compartmentalized bath

■ An optional crawl space or slab foundation available — please specify when ordering

Main area — 1,271 sq. ft.
Garage — 506 sq. ft.

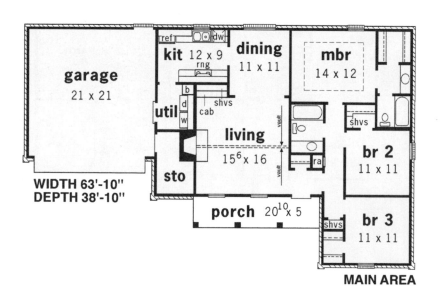

WIDTH 63'-10"
DEPTH 38'-10"

MAIN AREA

Accented Detailing

No. 98472

This plan features:

- — Three bedrooms
- — Two full baths
- The columned front Porch, keystones and shutters accent the exquisite detail of this home
- The foyer with a 14' high ceiling that continues into the Great Room
- The Great Room has a vaulted ceiling and a rear wall fireplace set between windows
- The Kitchen is conveniently arranged, and a covered porch is located nearby
- The Master Suite features a tray ceiling, a plant shelf, a walk in closet and French doors into the bath
- Two bedrooms with ample closet space share a full hall bath
- A two-car garage with storage space
- No materials list is available for this plan
- An optional a basement or a crawl space foundation — please specify when ordering

Main floor — 1,492 sq. ft.
Garage — 465 sq. ft.

Total living area 1,492 sq. ft. ■ Price Code A

FIRST FLOOR PLAN

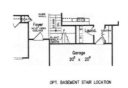

OPT. BASEMENT STAIR LOCATION

Huge Windows Create Cheerful Atmosphere

No. 91040

This plan features:

- — Three bedrooms
- — Two full baths
- A modern, efficient Kitchen layout flowing into the Nook and Living Room
- A Living Room, made spacious by an open layout, with a handsome fireplace
- A Master Suite with ample closet space and a private, full bath
- Two additional bedrooms that share a full hall bath

Main floor — 1,206 sq. ft.

Total living area 1,206 sq. ft. ■ Price Code A

MAIN FLOOR

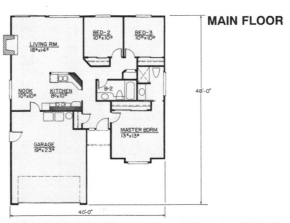

Outdoor Living Options

© 1997 Donald A. Gardner Architects, Inc.

■ Total living area 1,609 sq. ft. ■ Price Code C ■

■ **This plan features:**

—Three bedrooms

—Two full baths

■ Living areas that are open and casual

■ Great Room crowned by a cathedral ceiling which continues out to the screened porch

■ Kitchen opens to a sunny breakfast bay and is adjacent to the formal Dining Room

■ Master suite topped by a tray ceiling and enhanced by an indulgent bath with a roomy walk-in closet

■ Two additional bedrooms sharing a full bath

Main floor —1,609 sq. ft.
Garage & storage — 500 sq. ft.

Great Room Is Center of Attention

■ Total living area 1,972 sq. ft. ■ Price Code C ■

No. 96527

■ **This plan features:**

— Three bedrooms

— Two full baths

■ Foyer with vaulted ceiling to the dormer

■ The Great room has a rear wall fireplace, and opens to the rear Porch

■ The Kitchen features an eating bar and opens into the Dining bay

■ The Master suite has a tray ceiling and a whirlpool bath

■ Two secondary Bedrooms and a Study round out this plan

Main floor — 1,972 sq. ft.

Exciting Ceilings

■ Total living area 1,606 sq. ft. ■ Price Code B ■

No. 20191

■ **This plan features:**

— Three bedrooms

— Two full baths

■ A brick hearth fireplace in the Living Room

■ An efficient Kitchen, with an island and double sinks, that flows into the Dining Room, which features a decorative ceiling

■ A private Master Suite with a decorative ceiling and a pampering Master Bath

■ Two additional bedrooms that share a full bath

Main floor — 1,606 sq. ft.
Basement — 1,575 sq. ft.
Garage — 545 sq. ft.

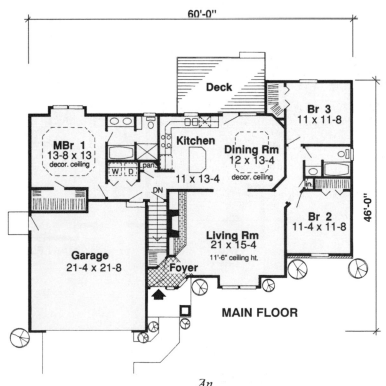

MAIN FLOOR

An
EXCLUSIVE DESIGN
By Karl Kreeger

Back Yard Views

Total living area 1,746 sq. ft. ■ Price Code B

No. 92655

Patio

Breakfast
10'10" x12'

Great Room
16'2" x 18'4"
slope ceiling

stairs dn

Master
Bedroom
15' x12'10"

Bath

walk-in closet

Kitchen
11'8" x 14' 4"

Dining Room
11' x 9'2"
slope ceiling

Foyer

Hall

Bath

Laun.

Porch

Bedroom
11' x 12'6"

Bedroom
12'6"x11'11"
slope ceiling / slope ceiling

WIDTH: 65' - 10"
DEPTH: 56' - 0"

MAIN FLOOR

Two-car Garage
22' x 20'8"

This plan features:

— Three bedrooms

— Two full baths

■ Front Porch accesses open Foyer, and spacious Dining Room and Great Room with sloped ceilings

■ Corner fireplace, windows and atrium door to Patio enhance Great Room

■ Convenient Kitchen with a pantry, peninsula serving counter for bright Breakfast area and nearby Laundry/Garage entry

■ Luxurious bath, walk-in closet and back yard view offered in Master Bedroom

■ No materials list is available for this plan

Main floor — 1,746 sq. ft.
Garage — 480 sq. ft.
Basement — 1,697 sq. ft.

Ranch Offers Attractive Window Facade

No. 10569

This plan features:

— Four bedrooms

— One full and two three quarter baths

■ A Living Room with sloping, open-beamed ceilings and a fireplace with built-in bookshelves

■ A Dining Room with a vaulted ceiling, adding a feeling of spaciousness

■ A Master Bath with ample closet space and a private bath

■ A two-car garage

Main floor — 1,840 sq. ft.
Basement — 1,803 sq. ft.
Garage — 445 sq. ft.

Total living area 1,840 sq. ft. ■ *Price Code C* ■

An EXCLUSIVE DESIGN *By Karl Kreeger*

MAIN FLOOR

Split Bedroom Floor Plan

No. 96519

This plan features:

— Three bedrooms

— Two full baths

■ A split bedroom floor plan gives the Master Bedroom ultimate privacy

■ The Great room is highlighted by a fireplace and a vaulted 10' ceiling

■ A snack bar peninsula counter is one of the many conveniences of the Kitchen

■ The Patio is accessed from the Dining Room and expands dining to the outdoors

■ Two additional bedrooms share the full bath in the hall

■ No materials list is available for this plan

Main floor — 1,243 sq. ft.
Garage — 523 sq. ft.

Total living area 1,243 sq. ft. ■ *Price Code A* ■

MAIN FLOOR

High Ceilings and Open Spaces

■ **This plan features:**

— Three bedrooms

— Three full baths

■ This home has long windows, high ceilings and open an layout between the rooms

■ A tiled Foyer leads into the Dining Area that flows uninhibited into the Great Room

■ A fireplace and built-in entertainment center accent the Great Room

■ The Kitchen has a snack bar, a built-in pantry, a breakfast area, and is adjacent to the Keeping Room with a fireplace

■ The Master Bedroom is pampered by a private bath and a walk-in closet

■ There is a double door entry into the office area

■ Two additional bedrooms are on the opposite side of the home, each with private access to the full bath

■ An optional basement, a slab or a crawl space foundation available — please specify when ordering

■ No materials list is available for this plan

Main floor — 2,330 sq. ft.
Basement — 2,330 sq. ft.
Garage — 416 sq. ft.

■ Total living area 2,330 sq. ft. ■ Price Code D ■

WIDTH 50'-0"
DEPTH 70'-0"

MAIN FLOOR

Delightful Detailing

■ **This plan features:**

— Three bedrooms

— Two full and one half baths

■ The vaulted ceiling extends from the Foyer into the Living Room

■ The Dining Room is delineated by columns with a plant shelf above

■ Family Room has a vaulted ceiling, and a fireplace with radius windows on either side

■ The Kitchen equipped with an island serving bar, desk, a wall oven, a pantry and a Breakfast Bay

■ The Master Suite is highlighted by a sitting room, a walk in closet, and a private bath with a vaulted ceiling

■ Two additional large bedrooms share a bath in the hall

■ There is an optional bonus room located over the garage

■ An optional basement or a crawl space foundation — please specify when ordering

Main floor — 2,622 sq. ft.
Bonus room — 478 sq. ft.
Basement — 2,622 sq. ft.
Garage — 506 sq. ft.

■ Total living area 2,622 sq. ft. ■ Price Code E ■

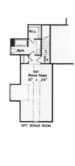

MAIN FLOOR

Total living area 1,670 sq. ft. ■ *Price Code B* ■

No. 90409

■ This plan features:

— Three bedrooms

— Two full baths

■ A massive fireplace separating Living and Dining Rooms

■ An isolated Master Suite with a walk-in closet and handy compartmentalized bath

■ A galley-type Kitchen between the Breakfast Room and Dining Room

■ An optional basement, slab or crawl space foundation — please specify when ordering

Main area — 1,670 sq. ft.

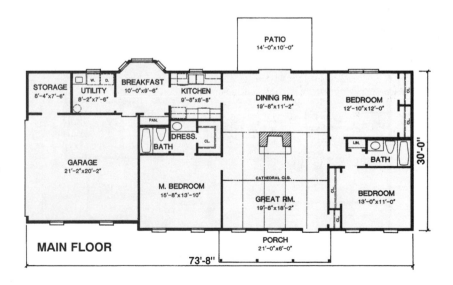

Country Style Charm

Total living area 1,857 sq. ft. ■ Price Code B

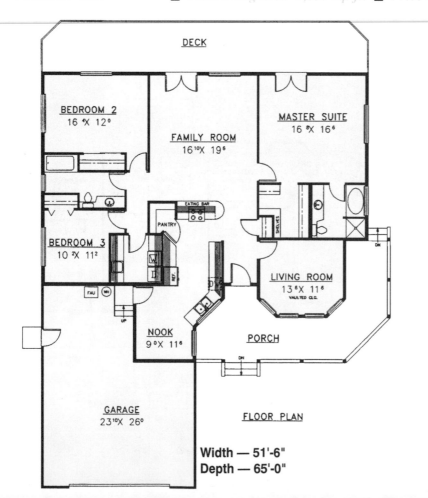

DECK

BEDROOM 2
16⁴X 12⁰

FAMILY ROOM
16¹⁰X 19⁵

MASTER SUITE
16⁸X 16⁶

EATING BAR

PANTRY

SHELVES

BEDROOM 3
10²X 11²

FAU

LIVING ROOM
13⁶X 11⁶
VAULTED CLG.

DN

UP

NOOK
9⁰X 11⁶

PORCH

DN

GARAGE
23¹⁰X 26⁰

FLOOR PLAN

Width — 51'-6"
Depth — 65'-0"

No. 91731

■ This plan features:

— Three bedrooms

— Two full baths

■ Brick accents, front facing gable,
and railed wrap-around covered
porch

■ A built-in range and oven in a
dog-leg shaped Kitchen

■ A Nook with garage access for
convenient unloading of groceries
and other supplies

■ A bay window wrapping around
the front of the formal Living
Room

■ A Master Suite with French doors
opening to the deck

Main area — 1,857 sq. ft.
Garage — 681 sq. ft.

Vaulted Ceilings Add Volume

No. 91554

This plan features:

— Three bedrooms

— Two full baths

■ The vaulted ceilings and an open plan create a larger feel to this compact plan

■ The Kitchen with it's center island is open to the Dining room and the Living room

■ The Living room is highlighted by a fireplace and a plant shelf

■ The large Master suite features a walk-in closet and a private five piece bath

■ Two other bedrooms have large closets and share a full bath in the hall

■ This plan is completed by a two-car garage

■ No materials list is available for this plan

Main floor — 1,467 sq. ft.
Garage — 400 sq. ft.

■ Total living area 1,467 sq. ft. ■ Price Code A ■

Varied Roof Lines Add Interest

No. 93255

This plan features:

— Three bedrooms

— Two full and one half baths

■ A modern, convenient floor plan

■ Formal areas located at the front of the home

■ A decorative ceiling in the Dining Room

■ Columns accenting the Living Room

■ A large Family Room with a cozy fireplace and direct access to the deck

■ An efficient Kitchen located between the formal Dining Room and the informal Breakfast Room

■ A private Master Suite that includes a Master Bath and walk-in closet

■ Two additional bedrooms that share a full hall bath

Main Area — 2,192 sq. ft.
Basement — 2,192 sq. ft.
Garage — 564 sq. ft.

■ Total living area 2,192 sq. ft. ■ Price Code C ■

FLOOR PLAN

An
EXCLUSIVE DESIGN
By Jannis Vann & Associates. Inc.

Charming Country Porch Entry

■ *Total living area 1,220 sq. ft.* ■ *Price Code A* ■

WIDTH 45'-0"
DEPTH 51'-6"

No. 94032

■ **This plan features:**

– Three bedrooms

– One full and one three-quarter baths

■ Attractive front Porch leads into tiled Entry and open Living/Dining room for ease in entertaining

■ An inviting fireplace, double window and sliding glass door to Deck enhance open space

■ Efficient Kitchen with a peninsula counter/snackbar, easily serves Dining area and Deck beyond

■ Roomy Master Bedroom features a walk-in closet and private bath

■ Two additional bedrooms with ample closets, share a full bath

■ Laundry facilities conveniently located near Garage and Entry

■ No materials list is available for this plan

Main floor — 1,220 sq. ft.
Garage — 440 sq. ft.

Master Retreat Welcomes You Home

■ *Total living area 1,486 sq. ft.* ■ *Price Code A* ■

Slab/Crawlspace
Option

No. 34154

■ **This plan features:**

– Three bedrooms

– Two full baths

■ Foyer opens into an huge Living Room with a fireplace below a sloped ceiling and Deck access

■ Efficient Kitchen with a pantry, serving counter, Dining area, laundry closet and Garage entry

■ Corner Master Bedroom offers a walk-in closet and pampering bath with a raised tub

■ Two more bedrooms, one with a Den option, share a full bath

Main floor — 1,486 sq. ft.
Garage — 462 sq. ft.

Surrounded with Sunshine

■ *Total living area 1,731 sq. ft.* ■ *Price Code B* ■

No. 90986

■ **This plan features:**

— Three bedrooms

— Two full and one half baths

■ An Italianate style, featuring columns and tile originally designed to sit on the edge of a golf course

■ An open design with pananoramic vistas in every direction

■ A whirlpool tub in the elaborate and spacious Master Bedroom suite

■ A Great Room with a corner gas fireplace

■ A turreted Breakfast Nook and an efficient Kitchen with peninsula counter

■ Two family bedrooms that share a full hall bath

An
EXCLUSIVE DESIGN
By Westhome Planners, Ltd.

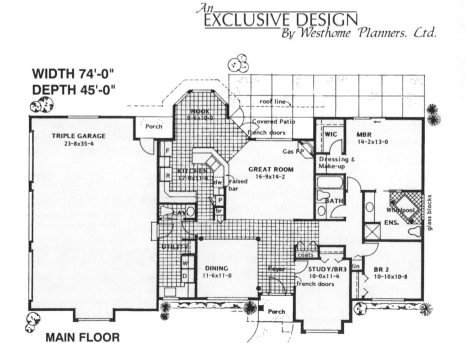

WIDTH 74'-0"
DEPTH 45'-0"

MAIN FLOOR

Main floor — 1,731 sq. ft.
Garage — 888 sq. ft.
Basement — 1,715 sq. ft.

Everything You Need...
...to Make Your Dream Come True!

You pay only a fraction of the original cost for home designs by respected professionals.

EXTERIOR ELEVATIONS

Elevations are scaled drawings of the front, rear, left and right sides of a home. All of the necessary information pertaining to the exterior finish materials, roof pitches and exterior height dimensions of your home are defined.

CABINET PLANS

These plans, or in some cases elevations, will detail the layout of the kitchen and bathroom cabinets at a larger scale. This gives you an accurate layout for your cabinets or an ideal starting point for a modified custom cabinet design. Available for most plans.

TYPICAL WALL SECTION

This section is provided to help your builder understand the structural components and materials used to construct the exterior walls of your home. This section will address insulation, roof components, and interior and exterior wall finishes. Your plans will be designed with either 2x4 or 2x6 exterior walls, but most professional contractors can easily adapt the plans to the wall thickness you require.

FIREPLACE DETAILS

If the home you have chosen includes a fireplace, the fireplace detail will show typical methods to construct the firebox, hearth and flue chase for masonry units, or a wood frame chase for a zero-clearance unit. Available for most plans.

You've Picked Your Dream Home!

You can already see it standing on your lot... you can see yourselves in your new home... enjoying family, entertaining guests, celebrating holidays. All that remains ahead are the details. That's where we can help. Whether you plan to build-it-yourself, be your own contractor, or hand your plans over to an outside contractor, your Garlinghouse blueprints provide the perfect beginning for putting yourself in your dream home right away.

We even make it simple for you to make professional design modifications. We can also provide a materials list for greater economy.

My grandfather, L.F. Garlinghouse, started a tradition of quality when he founded this company in 1907. For over 90 years, homeowners and builders have relied on us for accurate, complete, professional blueprints. Our plans help you get results fast... and save money, too! These pages will give you all the information you need to order. So get started now... I know you'll love your new Garlinghouse home!

Sincerely,

FOUNDATION PLAN

These plans will accurately dimension the footprint of your home including load bearing points and beam placement if applicable. The foundation style will vary from plan to plan. Your local climatic conditions will dictate whether a basement, slab or crawlspace is best suited for your area. In most cases, if your plan comes with one foundation style, a professional contractor can easily adapt the foundation plan to an alternate style.

ROOF PLAN

The information necessary to construct the roof will be included with your home plans. Some plans will reference roof trusses, while many others contain schematic framing plans. These framing plans will indicate the lumber sizes necessary for the rafters and ridgeboards based on the designated roof loads.

TYPICAL CROSS SECTION

A cut-away cross-section through the entire home shows your building contractor the exact correlation of construction components at all levels of the house. It will help to clarify the load bearing points from the roof all the way down to the basement. Available for most plans.

DETAILED FLOOR PLANS

The floor plans of your home accurately dimension the positioning of all walls, doors, windows, stairs and permanent fixtures. They will show you the relationship and dimensions of rooms, closets and traffic patterns. Included is the schematic of the electrical layout. This layout is clearly represented and does not hinder the clarity of other pertinent information shown. All these details will help your builder properly construct your new home.

STAIR DETAILS

If stairs are an element of the design you have chosen, then a cross-section of the stairs will be included in your home plans. This gives your builders the essential reference points that they need for headroom clearance, and riser and tread dimensions. Available for most plans.

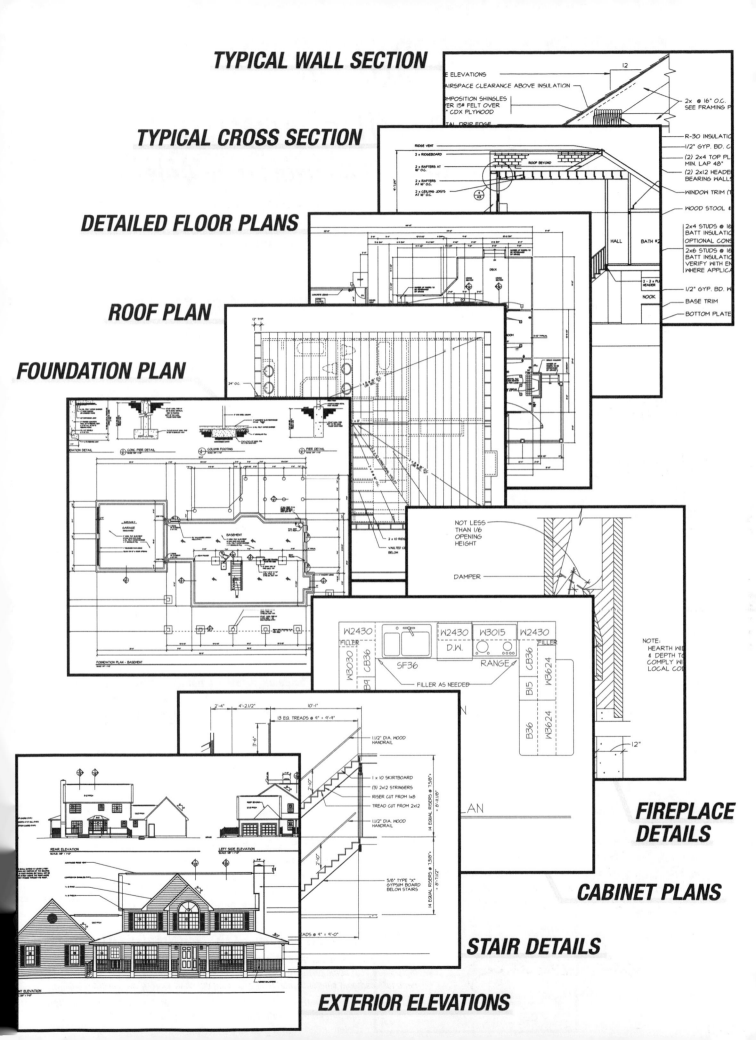

TYPICAL WALL SECTION

TYPICAL CROSS SECTION

DETAILED FLOOR PLANS

ROOF PLAN

FOUNDATION PLAN

FIREPLACE DETAILS

CABINET PLANS

STAIR DETAILS

EXTERIOR ELEVATIONS

Garlinghouse Options & Extras
...Make Your Dream A Home

Reversed Plans Can Make Your Dream Home Just Right!

"That's our dream home...if only the garage were on the other side!"

You could have exactly the home you want by flipping it end-for-end. Check it out by holding your dream home page of this book up to a mirror. Then simply order your plans "reversed." We'll send you one full set of mirror-image plans (with the writing backwards) as a master guide for you and your builder.

The remaining sets of your order will come as shown in this book so the dimensions and specifications are easily read on the job site...but most plans in our collection come stamped "REVERSED" so there is no construction confusion.

As Shown   Reversed

We can only send reversed plans with multiple-set orders. There is a $50 charge for this service.

Some plans in our collection are available in Right Reading Reverse. Right Reading Reverse plans will show your home in reverse, with the writing on the plan being readable. This easy-to-read format will save you valuable time and money. Please contact our Customer Service Department at (860) 343-5977 to check for Right Reading Reverse availability. (There is a $125 charge for this service.)

Specifications & Contract Form

We send this form to you free of charge with your home plan order. The form is designed to be filled in by you or your contractor with the exact materials to use in the construction of your new home. Once signed by you and your contractor it will provide you with peace of mind throughout the construction process.

$19.95 per set
(includes postage)

Remember To Order Your Materials List

It'll help you save money. Available at a modest additional charge, the Materials List gives the quantity, dimensions, and specifications for the major materials needed to build your home. You will get faster, more accurate bids from your contractors and building suppliers — and avoid paying for unused materials and waste. Materials Lists are available for all home plans except as otherwise indicated, but can only be ordered with a set of home plans. Due to differences in regional requirements and homeowner or builder preferences... electrical, plumbing and heating/air conditioning equipment specifications are not designed specifically for each plan. However, non-plan specific detailed typical prints of residential electrical, plumbing and construction guidelines can be provided. Please see below for additional information. If you need a detailed materials cost you might need to purchase a Zip Quote. (Details follow)

Detail Plans Provide Valuable Information About Construction Techniques

Because local codes and requirements vary greatly, we recommend that you obtain drawings and bids from licensed contractors to do your mechanical plans. However, if you want to know more about techniques — and deal more confidently with subcontractors — we offer these remarkably useful detail sheets. These detail sheets will aid in your understanding of these technical subjects. **The detail sheets are not specific to any one home plan and should be used only as a general reference guide.**

RESIDENTIAL CONSTRUCTION DETAILS

Ten sheets that cover the essentials of stick-built residential home construction. Details foundation options — poured concrete basement, concrete block, or monolithic concrete slab. Shows all aspects of floor, wall and roof framing. Provides details for roof dormers, overhangs, chimneys and skylights. Conforms to requirements of Uniform Building code or BOCA code. Includes a quick index and a glossary of terms.

RESIDENTIAL PLUMBING DETAILS

Eight sheets packed with information detailing pipe installation methods, fittings, and sized. Details plumbing hook-ups for toilets, sinks, washers, sump pumps, and septic system construction. Conforms to requirements of National Plumbing code. Color coded with a glossary of terms and quick index.

RESIDENTIAL ELECTRICAL DETAILS

Eight sheets that cover all aspects of residential wiring, from simple switch wiring to service entrance connections. Details distribution panel layout with outlet and switch schematics, circuit breaker and wiring installation methods, and ground fault interrupter specifications. Conforms to requirements of National Electrical Code. Color coded with a glossary of terms.

Modifying Your Favorite Design, Made *EASY!*

Modifying Your Garlinghouse Home Plan

Simple modifications to your dream home, including minor non-structural changes and material substitutions, can be made between you and your builder by marking the changes directly on your blueprints. However, if you are considering making significant changes to your chosen design, we recommend that you use the services of The Garlinghouse Co. Design Staff. We will help take your ideas and turn them into a reality, just the way you want. Here's our procedure!

When you place your Vellum order, you may also request a free Garlinghouse Modification Kit. In this kit, you will receive a red marking pencil, furniture cut-out sheet, ruler, a self addressed mailing label and a form for specifying any additional notes or drawings that will help us understand your design ideas. Mark your desired changes directly on the Vellum drawings. NOTE: Please use only a **red pencil** to mark your desired changes on the Vellum. Then, return the redlined Vellum set in the original box to The Garlinghouse Company at, 282 Main Street Extension, Middletown, CT 06457. **IMPORTANT**: Please **roll** the Vellums for shipping, **do not fold** the Vellums for shipping.

We also offer modification estimates. We will provide you with an estimate to draft your changes based on your specific modifications before you purchase the vellums, for a $50 fee. After you receive your estimate, if you decide to have The Garlinghouse Company Design Staff do the changes, the $50 estimate fee will be deducted from the cost of your modifications. If, however, you choose to use a different service, the $50 estimate fee is non-refundable.

Within 5 days of receipt of your plans, you will be contacted by a member of The Garlinghouse Co. Design Staff with an estimate for the design services to draw those changes. A 50% deposit is required before we begin making the actual modifications to your plans.

Once the preliminary design changes have been made to the floor plans and elevations, copies will be sent to you to make sure we have made the exact changes you want. We will wait for your approval before continuing with any structural revisions. The Garlinghouse Co. Design Staff will call again to inform you that your modified Vellum plan is complete and will be shipped as soon as the final payment has been made. For additional information call us at 1-860-343-5977. Please refer to the Modification Pricing Guide for estimated modification costs. Please call for Vellum modification availability for plan numbers 85,000 and above.

Reproducible Vellums for Local Modification Ease

If you decide not to use the Garlinghouse Co. Design Staff for your modifications, we recommend that you follow our same procedure of purchasing our Vellums. You then have the option of using the services of the original designer of the plan, a local professional designer, or architect to make the modifications to your plan.

With a Vellum copy of our plans, a design professional can alter the drawings just the way you want, then you can print as many copies of the modified plans as you need to build your house. And, since you have already started with our complete detailed plans, the cost of those expensive professional services will be significantly less than starting from scratch. Refer to the price schedule for Vellum costs. Again, please call for Vellum availability for plan numbers 85,000 and above.

IMPORTANT RETURN POLICY: Upon receipt of your Vellums, if for some reason you decide you do not want a modified plan, then simply return the Kit and the unopened Vellums. Reproducible Vellum copies of our home plans are copyright protected and only sold under the terms of a license agreement that you will receive with your order. Should you not agree to the terms, then the Vellums may be returned, **unopened,** for a full refund less the shipping and handling charges, plus a 15% restocking fee. For any additional information, please call us at 1-860-343-5977.

MODIFICATION PRICING GUIDE

CATEGORIES	ESTIMATED COST
KITCHEN LAYOUT — PLAN AND ELEVATION	$175.00
BATHROOM LAYOUT — PLAN AND ELEVATION	$175.00
FIREPLACE PLAN AND DETAILS	$200.00
INTERIOR ELEVATION	$125.00
EXTERIOR ELEVATION — MATERIAL CHANGE	$140.00
EXTERIOR ELEVATION — ADD BRICK OR STONE	$400.00
EXTERIOR ELEVATION — STYLE CHANGE	$450.00
NON BEARING WALLS (INTERIOR)	$200.00
BEARING AND/OR EXTERIOR WALLS	$325.00
WALL FRAMING CHANGE — 2X4 TO 2X6 OR 2X6 TO 2X4	$240.00
ADD/REDUCE LIVING SPACE — SQUARE FOOTAGE	QUOTE REQUIRED
NEW MATERIALS LIST	$.20 SQUARE FOOT
CHANGE TRUSSES TO RAFTERS OR CHANGE ROOF PITCH	$300.00
FRAMING PLAN CHANGES	$325.00
GARAGE CHANGES	$325.00
ADD A FOUNDATION OPTION	$300.00
FOUNDATION CHANGES	$250.00
RIGHT READING PLAN REVERSE	$575.00
ARCHITECTS SEAL (Available for most states.)	$300.00
ENERGY CERTIFICATE	$150.00
LIGHT AND VENTILATION SCHEDULE	$150.00

"How to obtain a construction cost calculation based on labor rates and building material costs in your Zip Code area!"

ZIP-QUOTE!
HOME COST CALCULATOR

ZIP QUOTE
HOME COST CALCULATOR

WHY?

Do you wish you could quickly find out the building cost for your new home without waiting for a contractor to compile hundreds of bids? Would you like to have a benchmark to compare your contractor(s) bids against? **Well, Now You Can!!,** with **Zip-Quote** Home Cost Calculator. Zip-Quote is only available for zip code areas within the United States.

HOW?

Our new **Zip-Quote** Home Cost Calculator will enable you to obtain the calculated building cost to construct your new home, based on labor rates and building material costs within your zip code area, without the normal delays or hassles usually associated with the bidding process. Zip-Quote can be purchased in two separate formats, an itemized or a bottom line format.

"How does **Zip-Quote** actually work?" When we receive your **Zip-Quote** order, we process your specific home plan building materials list through our Home Cost Calculator which contains up-to-date rates for all residential labor trades and building material costs in your zip code area. "The result?" A calculated cost to build your dream home in your zip code area. This calculation will help you (as a consumer or a builder) evaluate your building budget. This is a valuable tool for anyone considering building a new home.

All database information for our calculations is furnished by Marshall & Swift, L.P. For over 60 years, Marshall & Swift L.P. has been a leading provider of cost data to professionals in all aspects of the construction and remodeling industries.

OPTION 1

The **Itemized Zip-Quote** is a detailed building material list. Each building material list line item will separately state the labor cost, material cost and equipment cost (if applicable) for the use of that building material in the construction process. Each category within the building material list will be subtotaled and the entire Itemized cost calculation totaled at the end. This building materials list will be summarized by the individual building categories and will have additional columns where you can enter data from your contractor's estimates for a cost comparison between the different suppliers and contractors who will actually quote you their products and services.

OPTION 2

The **Bottom Line Zip-Quote** is a one line summarized total cost for the home plan of your choice. This cost calculation is also based on the labor cost, material cost and equipment cost (if applicable) within your local zip code area.

COST

The price of your **Itemized Zip-Quote** is based upon the pricing schedule of the plan you have selected, in addition to the price of the materials list. Please refer to the pricing schedule on our order form. The price of your initial **Bottom Line Zip-Quote** is $29.95. Each additional **Bottom Line Zip-Quote** ordered in conjunction with the initial order is only $14.95. **Bottom Line Zip-Quote** may be purchased separately and does NOT have to be purchased in conjunction with a home plan order.

FYI

An **Itemized Zip-Quote** Home Cost Calculation can ONLY be purchased in conjunction with a Home Plan order. The **Itemized Zip-Quote** can not be purchased separately. The **Bottom Line Zip-Quote** can be purchased seperately and doesn't have to be purchased in conjunction with a home plan order. Please consult with a sales representative for current availability. If you find within 60 days of your order date that you will be unable to build this home, then you may exchange the plans and the materials list towards the price of a new set of plans (see order info pages for plan exchange policy). The **Itemized Zip-Quote** and the **Bottom Line Zip-Quote** are NOT returnable. The price of the initial **Bottom Line Zip-Quote** order can be credited towards the purchase of an **Itemized Zip-Quote** order only. Additional **Bottom Line Zip-Quote** orders, within the same order can not be credited. Please call our Customer Service Department for more information. **Zip-Quote** will be available for plans 85,000 and above after September 1, 1998.

SOME MORE INFORMATION

The Itemized and Bottom Line Zip-Quotes give you approximated costs for constructing the particular house in your area. These costs are not exact and are only intended to be used as a preliminary estimate to help determine the affordability of a new home and/or as a guide to evaluate the general competitiveness of actual price quotes obtained through local suppliers and contractors. However, Zip-Quote cost figures should never be relied upon as the only source of information in either case. The Garlinghouse Company and Marshall & Swift L.P. can not guarantee any level of data accuracy or correctness in a Zip-Quote and disclaim all liability for loss with respect to the same, in excess of the original purchase price of the Zip-Quote product. All Zip-Quote calculations are based upon the actual blueprint materials list with options as selected by customer and do not reflect any differences that may be shown on the published house renderings, floor plans, or photographs.

Ignoring Copyright Laws Can Be
A $1,000,000 Mistake

Recent changes in the US copyright laws allow for statutory penalties of up to **$100,000** per incident for copyright infringement involving any of the copyrighted plans found in this publication. The law can be confusing. So, for your own protection, take the time to understand what you can and cannot do when it comes to home plans.

••• WHAT YOU CANNOT DO •••

You Cannot Duplicate Home Plans

Purchasing a set of blueprints and making additional sets by reproducing the original is **illegal**. If you need multiple sets of a particular home plan, then you must purchase them.

You Cannot Copy Any Part of a Home Plan to Create Another

Creating your own plan by copying even part of a home design found in this publication is called "creating a derivative work" and is **illegal** unless you have permission to do so.

You Cannot Build a Home Without a License

You must have specific permission or license to build a home from a copyrighted design, even if the finished home has been changed from the original plan. It is **illegal** to build one of the homes found in this publication without a license.

What Garlinghouse Offers

Home Plan Blueprint Package

By purchasing a single or multiple set package of blueprints from Garlinghouse, you not only receive the physical blueprint documents necessary for construction, but you are also granted a license to build one, and only one, home. You can also make simple modifications, including minor non-structural changes and material substitutions, to our design, as long as these changes are made directly on the blueprints purchased from Garlinghouse and no additional copies are made.

Home Plan Vellums

By purchasing vellums for one of our home plans, you receive the same construction drawings found in the blueprints, but printed on vellum paper. Vellums can be erased and are perfect for making design changes. They are also semi-transparent making them easy to duplicate. But most importantly, the purchase of home plan vellums comes with a broader license that allows you to make changes to the design (ie, create a hand drawn or CAD derivative work), to make an unlimited number of copies of the plan, and to build one home from the plan.

License To Build Additional Homes

With the purchase of a blueprint package or vellums you automatically receive a license to build one home and only one home, respectively. If you want to build more homes than you are licensed to build through your purchase of a plan, then additional licenses may be purchased at reasonable costs from Garlinghouse. Inquire for more information.

IMPORTANT INFORMATION TO READ BEFORE YOU PLACE YOUR ORDER

The Standard 8-Set Construction Package

Our experience shows that you'll speed every step of construction and avoid costly building errors by ordering enough sets to go around. Each tradesperson wants a set — the general contractor and all subcontractors; foundation, electrical, plumbing, heating/air conditioning and framers. Don't forget your lending institution, building department and, of course, a set for yourself.

The Minimum 4-Set Construction Package

If you're comfortable with arduous follow-up, this package can save you a few dollars by giving you the option of passing down plan sets as work progresses. You might have enough copies to go around if work goes exactly as scheduled and no plans are lost or damaged by subcontractors. But for only $50 more, the 8-set package eliminates these worries.

The Single Study Set

We offer this set so you can study the blueprints to plan your dream home in detail. As with all of our plans, they are stamped with a copyright warning. Remember, one set is never enough to build your home. In pursuant to copyright laws, it is _illegal_ to reproduce any blueprint.

All plans are drawn to conform to one or more of the industry's major national building standards. However, due to the variety of local building regulations, your plan may need to be modified to comply with local requirements — snow loads, energy loads, seismic zones, etc. Do check them fully and consult your local building officials.

A few states require that all building plans used be drawn by an architect registered in that state. While having your plans reviewed and stamped by such an architect may be prudent, laws requiring non-conforming plans like ours to be completely redrawn forces you to unnecessarily pay very large fees. If your state has such a law, we strongly recommend you contact your state representative to protest.

The rendering, floor plans, and technical information contained within this publication are not guaranteed to be totally accurate. Consequently, no information from this publication should be used either as a guide to constructing a home or for estimating the cost of building a home. Complete blueprints must be purchased for such purposes.

GARLINGHOUSE

Order Form

Plan prices guaranteed until 4/1/99 —After this date call for updated pricing

| Order Code No. **CHP03** |

____ set(s) of blueprints for plan #_____ $_____

____ Vellum & Modification kit for plan #_____ $_____

____ Additional set(s) @ $30 each for plan #_____ $_____

____ Mirror Image Reverse @ $50 each $_____

____ Right Reading Reverse @ $125 each $_____

____ Materials list for plan #_____ $_____

____ Detail Plans @ $19.95 each

     ❏ Construction ❏ Plumbing ❏ Electrical $_____

____ Bottom line ZIP Quote @ $29.95 for plan #_____ $_____

____ Additional Bottom Line Zip Quote

     @ $14.95 for plan(s) #_____

_____ $_____

____ Itemized ZIP Quote for plan(s) #_____ $_____

Shipping (see charts on opposite page) $_____

Subtotal $_____

Sales Tax   _{(CT residents add 6% sales tax, KS residents add 6.15% sales tax) (Not required for all states)} $_____

TOTAL AMOUNT ENCLOSED $_____

Send your check, money order or credit card information to:
(No C.O.D.'s Please)

Please submit all United States & Other Nations orders to:

Garlinghouse Company
P.O. Box 1717
Middletown, CT. 06457

ADDRESS INFORMATION:

NAME: _____

STREET: _____

CITY: _____ STATE: _____ ZIP: _____

DAYTIME PHONE: _____

TERMS OF SALE FOR HOME PLANS: All home plans sold through this publication are copyright protected. Reproduction of these home plans, either in whole or in part, including any direct copying and/or preparation of derivative works thereof, for any reason without the prior written permission of The L.F. Garlinghouse Co., Inc., is strictly prohibited. The purchase of a set of home plans in no way transfers any copyright or other ownership interest in it to the buyer except for a limited license to use that set of home plans for the construction of one, and only one, dwelling unit. The purchase of additional sets of that home plan at a reduced price from the original set or as a part of a multiple set package does not entitle the buyer with a license to construct more than one dwelling unit.

Payment must be made in U.S. funds. Foreign Mail Orders: Certified bank checks in U.S. funds only

Credit Card Information

Charge To: ❏ Visa   ❏ Mastercard

Card # | | | | | | | | | | | | | | | | |

Signature _____ Exp. _____ /_____

ORDER TOLL FREE — 1-800-235-5700
Monday-Friday 8:00 a.m. to 8:00 p.m. Eastern Time
or FAX your Credit Card order to 1-860-343-5984
All foreign residents call 1-800-343-5977

Please have ready: 1. Your credit card number   2. The plan number   3. The order code number ⇨ CHP03

Garlinghouse 1998 Blueprint Price Code Schedule

Additional sets with original order $30

PRICE CODE	A	B	C	D	E	F	G	H
8 SETS OF SAME PLAN	$375	$415	$455	$495	$535	$575	$615	$655
4 SETS OF SAME PLAN	$325	$365	$405	$445	$485	$525	$565	$605
1 SINGLE SET OF PLANS	$275	$315	$355	$395	$435	$475	$515	$555
VELLUMS	$485	$530	$575	$620	$665	$710	$755	$800
MATERIALS LIST	$40	$40	$45	$45	$50	$50	$55	$55
ITEMIZED ZIP QUOTE	$75	$80	$85	$85	$90	$90	$95	$95

Shipping — (Plans 1-84999)

	1-3 Sets	4-6 Sets	7+ & Vellums
Standard Delivery (UPS 2-Day)	$15.00	$20.00	$25.00
Overnight Delivery		$30.00	$35.00	$40.00

International Shipping & Handling

	1-3 Sets	4-6 Sets	7+ & Vellums
Regular Delivery Canada (7-10 Days)	$14.00	$17.00	$20.00
Express Delivery Canada (5-6 Days)	$35.00	$40.00	$45.00
Overseas Delivery Airmail (2-3 Weeks)	$45.00	$52.00	$60.00

Shipping — (Plans 85000-99999)

	1-3 Sets	4-6 Sets	7+ & Vellums
Ground Delivery (7-10 Days)	$9.00	$18.00	$20.00
Express Delivery (3-5 Days)	$15.00	$20.00	$25.00

Our Reorder and Exchange Policies

If you find after your initial purchase that you require additional sets of plans you may purchase them from us at special reorder prices (please call for pricing details) provided that you reorder within 6 months of your original order date. There is a $28 reorder processing fee that is charged on all reorders. For more information on reordering plans please contact our Customer Service Department at (860) 343-5977.

We want you to find your dream home from our wide selection of home plans. However, if for some reason you find that the plan you have purchased from us does not meet your needs, then you may exchange that plan for any other plan in our collection. We allow you sixty days from your original invoice date to make an exchange. At the time of the exchange you will be charged a processing fee of 15% of the total amount of your original order plus the difference in price between the plans (if applicable) plus the cost to ship the new plans to you. Call our Customer Service Department at (860) 343-5977 for more information. Please Note: Reproducible vellums can only be exchanged if they are unopened.

Important Shipping Information

Please refer to the shipping charts on the order form for service availability for your specific plan number. Our delivery service must have a street address or Rural Route Box number — never a post office box. (PLEASE NOTE: Supplying a P.O. Box number only will delay the shipping of your order.) Use a work address if no one is home during the day.

Orders being shipped to APO or FPO must go via First Class Mail. Please include the proper postage.

For our International Customers, only Certified bank checks and money orders are accepted and must be payable in U.S. currency. For speed, we ship international orders Air Parcel Post. Please refer to the chart for the correct shipping cost.

Plan#	Page#	Price Code	Square Footage
1074	55	A	1040
1078	45	A	1024
9850	91	D	2466
10220	90	A	888
10274	116	B	1783
10445	110	D	2466
10455	153	B	1643
10466	169	D	2285
10483	193	A	1025
10507	151	C	2194
10509	252	A	1464
10514	270	C	1980
10540	314	F	4097
10548	165	B	1688
10569	333	C	1840
10570	8	D	2450
10601	41	E	3025
10619	86	D	2352
10674	223	B	1600
10742	105	B	1617
10745	140	B	1643
10748	226	B	1540
10791	185	A	1092
10839	2	B	1738
20008	196	B	1545
20061	249	B	1674
20062	283	A	1500
20066	266	C	1850
20075	313	B	1682
20083	31	B	1575
20087	325	B	1568
20099	299	C	2020
20100	6	B	1737
20104	37	B	1686
20108	85	C	2120
20114	102	B	1652
20156	31	A	1359
20161	26	A	1307
20164	24	A	1456
20191	331	B	1606
20198	23	B	1792
20204	137	B	1532
20220	29	B	1568
20403	40	B	1734
22004	19	C	2070
22020	180	B	1772
24240	201	A	964
24250	84	B	1700
24256	244	C	2108
24259	122	C	2010
24302	138	A	988
24303	187	A	984
24304	203	A	993
24311	278	A	1127
24317	251	B	1620
24327	267	A	1266
24402	308	A	1346
24700	30	A	1312
24701	20	B	1625
24708	320	B	1576
24709	310	A	1330
24714	326	B	1771
24715	33	B	1771
24717	66	B	1642
24718	121	A	1452
24719	132	B	1702
24721	188	B	1539
24803	212	F	3947
26740	228	B	1512
34003	60	A	1146
34011	75	B	1672
34013	281	C	1803
34029	10	B	1686
34043	25	B	1583
34054	32	A	1400

Plan#	Page#	Price Code	Square Footage
34064	305	C	1858
34150	4	A	1492
34154	338	A	1486
34328	34	A	1092
35005	127	A	1484
84014	130	C	1901
84020	82	A	768
84056	101	B	1644
84330	174	A	1114
84357	145	A	1268
84426	73	B	1660
84505	54	B	1553
90001	219	C	2177
90288	172	A	1387
90324	231	A	1016
90325	188	A	988
90354	217	A	1478
90357	275	A	1368
90360	233	A	1283
90395	319	A	1452
90407	277	C	1950
90409	335	B	1670
90412	51	A	1454
90421	309	C	1940
90423	64	B	1773
90433	114	A	928
90441	159	C	1811
90454	321	D	2218
90461	215	D	2485
90467	54	D	2290
90476	224	C	1804
90478	69	D	2344
90479	106	A	1472
90502	258	B	1642
90601	311	B	1613
90620	327	A	1476
90638	148	A	1042
90680	35	A	1393
90682	92	A	1243
90683	177	B	1567
90684	220	B	1590
90689	118	A	1476
90691	147	B	1530
90692	183	A	1492
90697	236	B	1597
90857	260	A	1412
90867	293	C	1975
90905	195	A	1314
90926	246	B	1589
90934	279	A	884
90983	316	A	1396
90986	359	B	1731
90990	44	A	1423
91021	87	A	1295
91040	329	A	1206
91063	96	A	1207
91104	49	D	2126
91105	70	C	1908
91107	124	C	1199
91340	152	A	1111
91342	191	A	1345
91346	198	C	2185
91349	161	B	1694
91418	255	B	1665
91436	220	D	2591
91507	284	B	1687
91527	241	B	1565
91544	307	A	1338
91545	282	A	1420
91553	309	A	1271
91554	337	A	1467
91590	38	E	2755
91607	132	B	1653
91720	81	C	1870
91731	336	B	1857

Plan#	Page#	Price Code	Square Footage
91746	39	B	1717
91749	88	E	3051
91753	126	A	1490
91796	135	D	2280
91797	189	A	1485
91807	211	A	1410
92026	238	A	863
92127	108	D	2598
92132	98	C	1941
92209	263	F	3292
92220	312	C	1830
92238	324	B	1664
92239	153	A	1198
92257	164	D	2470
92265	52	F	3818
92268	209	B	1706
92275	83	E	2675
92279	100	E	3079
92281	225	A	1360
92283	157	B	1653
92284	274	D	2261
92286	317	A	1415
92289	322	D	2354
92400	166	A	1050
92404	214	D	2275
92405	253	B	1564
92501	264	F	2727
92502	315	B	1237
92503	328	B	1271
92509	43	E	2551
92515	72	D	1959
92516	53	D	1887
92517	65	D	1805
92523	125	B	1293
92525	150	B	1484
92527	160	C	1680
92528	216	B	1363
92531	227	C	1754
92536	276	D	1869
92538	295	F	2733
92544	323	D	1987
92546	47	E	2387
92550	68	F	2735
92552	103	D	1873
92554	97	D	1871
92555	155	C	1668
92556	156	C	1556
92557	170	B	1390
92558	180	B	1294
92560	197	C	1660
92561	217	D	1856
92563	233	C	1680
92564	281	A	1263
92565	306	B	1531
92566	326	C	1880
92617	247	C	1955
92625	268	B	1710
92630	18	B	1782
92649	300	B	1508
92655	332	B	1746
92657	13	F	4328
92658	82	B	1756
92660	36	C	1964
92685	49	A	1442
92688	102	D	2041
92694	156	B	1537
92705	95	C	1849
92803	99	B	1600
92902	141	E	2787
93000	190	C	1862
93015	200	A	1087
93017	245	A	1142
93018	209	A	1142
93021	271	A	1282
93026	291	A	1402

Plan#	Page#	Price Code	Square Footage	Symbols
93027	48	A	1500	
93030	67	C	1955	
93031	119	C	1955	
93033	228	D	2389	
93048	154	A	1310	
93053	273	D	2329	[R]
93056	306	D	2517	[X]
93059	322	D	2559	
93061	163	B	1742	
93073	218	A	1202	
93075	248	A	1170	
93100	50	B	1642	[X] [R]
93104	93	B	1756	[recycle] [R]
93107	280	C	1868	[R]
93130	121	B	1508	
93133	288	B	1761	[X] [recycle]
93143	56	C	1802	
93161	71	B	1540	[X] [recycle]
93165	137	A	1472	
93171	185	B	1642	
93183	285	D	2600	
00100	120	C	2106	[X] [recycle]
93191	182	B	1756	
93192	204	C	1868	
93193	252	C	1802	
93222	149	A	1292	[X] [recycle]
93231	257	B	1781	
93235	310	C	2005	
93255	337	C	2192	[X]
93261	205	B	1778	[X] [recycle]
93262	57	B	1708	
93279	229	A	1388	[X] [recycle]
93311	124	C	1810	
93414	177	A	1393	
93415	196	B	1714	
93416	249	A	1475	
93418	265	B	1631	
93419	289	B	1595	
93421	37	B	1507	
93425	85	C	1842	
93426	101	B	1655	
93427	140	B	1849	
93429	169	A	1496	
93430	204	B	1562	
93431	244	B	1572	
93702	164	B	1605	
93708	148	D	2579	
93906	294	A	1250	
93909	259	B	1716	
94024	303	B	1794	
94032	338	A	1220	
94041	59	A	1302	
94057	33	A	1403	
94066	74	A	1454	
94116	116	C	1546	[X]
94118	70	C	1724	
94130	145	C	1006	
94206	76	D	2214	
94220	107	F	3477	
94242	139	E	2978	
94307	184	A	786	
94602	212	B	1704	
94729	236	A	1417	[X]
94800	274	B	1199	[X]
94801	221	B	1300	[X]
94804	313	C	1855	[X]
94805	250	C	2079	[X]
94810	261	E	2690	[X]
94811	292	D	2165	[X]
94916	321	A	1392	[X] [R]
94917	63	B	1782	[X]
94921	38	B	1651	[X]
94922	69	B	1710	[X]
94923	12	B	1666	[X]
94926	34	C	1996	[X]
94959	78	C	2133	[X]
94966	79	C	1911	[X]
94967	113	D	2355	[X]
94969	179	B	1735	[X]
94970	129	A	1385	[X]
94971	172	C	2172	[X]
94972	201	B	1580	[X]
94973	241	D	2512	[X]
94979	260	D	2404	[X] [R]
94984	318	C	2042	[X] [R]
94985	325	A	1279	[X] [R]
94986	104	B	1604	[X]
96402	136	D	2027	[X]
96405	181	D	1903	[X]
96413	73	D	2349	[X] [recycle]
96417	199	C	1561	[X] [recycle]
96418	230	B	1452	[X]
96419	109	C	1514	[X]
96421	287	D	2045	[X]
96435	129	E	2526	[X]
96437	22	C	1858	[X]
96447	161	D	2207	[X]
96449	29	D	2211	[X]
96450	193	D	2090	[X]
96452	296	B	1475	[X]
96465	80	D	2050	[X]
96468	111	C	1864	[X]
96478	225	D	2203	[X]
96484	131	B	1246	[X]
96486	286	D	2042	[X]
96488	297	C	1695	[X]
96489	330	C	1609	[X]
96492	42	C	1829	[X]
96493	89	C	1770	[X]
96503	162	D	2256	[X]
96504	105	C	2162	[X]
96505	213	D	2069	[X]
96506	232	B	1654	[X]
96509	272	A	1438	[X]
96510	282	A	1372	[X]
96513	304	B	1648	[X]
96518	318	B	1657	[X]
96519	333	A	1243	
96521	41	E	3084	[X]
96522	86	B	1515	[X]
96523	109	B	1652	[X]
96525	265	B	1771	[X]
96526	314	C	1843	[X]
96527	330	C	1972	[X]
96529	46	C	2089	[X]
96530	94	D	2289	[X]
96531	106	D	2483	[X]
98224	269	B	1751	
98233	334	D	2330	
98408	128	C	1856	[X]
98411	178	A	1373	[X]
98414	202	B	1575	[X]
98415	113	A	1429	[X]
98421	235	C	2094	[X]
98423	256	B	1671	[X]
98424	50	D	2236	[X]
98425	112	C	1845	[X]
98426	334	E	2622	[X]
98430	133	C	1884	[X]
98434	173	A	1346	[X]
98435	257	C	1945	[X]
98441	301	B	1502	
98443	210	A	1359	
98456	53	B	1715	[X]
98460	234	B	1544	
98464	90	B	1779	
98468	65	A	1104	
98469	98	A	1042	
98472	329	A	1492	
98503	266	C	1876	
98504	305	D	2495	
98505	42	A	1405	
98510	81	C	1840	
98511	243	D	2445	
98512	262	C	2167	
98513	97	F	3352	
98522	269	B	1528	
98528	302	E	2748	
98733	115	D	2496	[X]
98742	61	B	1664	
98743	134	C	1958	
98746	66	B	1630	[X]
98747	167	A	1280	
98804	277	A	1372	
98805	207	A	1089	[X]
98806	298	A	1491	
98912	237	A	1325	[X]
99031	77	B	1598	[X]
99057	117	B	1720	[X]
99104	270	A	1370	
99106	144	A	1495	
99113	290	C	1906	
99208	58	C	1830	[X]
99284	317	C	2189	[X]
99308	45	B	1560	[X]
99318	89	A	1159	[X]
99321	168	A	1368	[X]
99324	278	A	1307	[X]
99345	290	A	1325	[X]
99448	57	E	2655	[X]
99469	77	D	2538	[X]
99503	273	B	1620	
99504	294	A	1127	
99610	222	B	1528	[X]
99614	58	D	2396	[X]
99639	239	A	1367	[X]
99651	74	B	1506	[X]
99657	285	B	1641	[X]
99661	289	A	1387	[X]
99802	123	C	1576	[X] [recycle]
99803	17	C	1977	[X] [recycle]
99804	21	C	1815	[X] [recycle]
99805	14	C	1787	[X] [recycle]
99806	46	B	1246	[X]
99807	15	C	1879	[X] [recycle]
99808	16	C	1832	[X] [recycle]
99809	143	B	1417	[X] [recycle]
99810	28	C	1685	[X] [recycle]
99811	171	B	1699	[X]
99812	206	B	1386	[X] [recycle]
99813	242	C	1959	[X]
99814	142	C	1800	[X] [recycle]
99815	175	D	1912	[X] [recycle]
99819	286	C	1666	[X]
99826	254	B	1346	[X]
99827	297	C	1972	[X]
99830	146	B	1372	[X] [recycle]
99831	78	C	1699	[X]
99834	293	C	1575	[X]
99835	61	C	1515	[X]
99838	176	D	2192	[X]
99840	194	C	1632	[X]
99844	240	C	1737	[X]
99845	158	C	1954	[X] [recycle]
99849	186	B	1322	[X]
99855	298	C	1817	[X]
99856	62	B	1310	[X]
99857	93	C	1865	[X]
99858	192	B	1253	[X] [recycle]
99860	208	B	1498	[X]
99865	301	C	1927	[X]
99871	62	C	1655	[X]
99878	27	C	1864	[X] [recycle]
99900	94	B	1592	[X]
99909	302	A	1494	[X]

CREATIVE HOMEOWNER PRESS®

How-To Books for...

ADDING SPACE WITHOUT ADDING ON

Cramped for space? This book, which replaces our old book of the same title, shows you how to find space you may not know you had and convert it into useful living areas. 40 colorful photographs and 530 full-color drawings.

BOOK #: 277680   192pp.   8½"x10⅞"

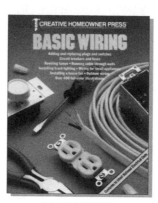

BASIC WIRING
(Third Edition, Conforms to latest National Electrical Code)

Included are 350 large, clear, full-color illustrations and no-nonsense step-by-step instructions. Shows how to replace receptacles and switches; repair a lamp; install ceiling and attic fans; and more.

BOOK #: 277048   160pp.   8½"x10⅞"

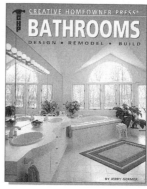

BATHROOMS: Design, Remodel, Build

Shows how to plan, construct, and finish a bathroom. Remodel floors; rebuild walls and ceilings; and install windows, skylights, and plumbing fixtures. Specific tools and materials are given for each project.

BOOK #: 277053   192pp.   8½"x10⅞"

Designing and Planning BATHROOMS

From the planning stage to final decorating, this book includes innovative and dramatic ideas for master baths, fitness bathrooms, powder rooms, and more. 200 inspirational color illustrations and photographs.

Book #: 287627   96 pp.   8½"x10⅞"

BUILD A KIDS' PLAY YARD

Here are detailed plans and step-by-step instructions for building the play structures that kids love most: swing set, monkey bars, balance beam, playhouse, teeter-totter, sandboxes, kid-sized picnic table, and a play tower that supports a slide. 200 color photographs and illustrations.

Book #: 277622   144 pp.   8½"x10⅞"

CABINETS & BUILT-INS

26 custom cabinetry projects are included for every room in the house, from kitchen cabinets to a bedroom wall unit, a bunk bed, computer workstation, and more. Also included are chapters on tools, techniques, finishing, and materials.

BOOK #: 277079   160 pp.   8½"x10⅞"

DECKS: Plan, Design, Build

With this book, even the novice builder can build a deck that perfectly fits his yard. The step-by-step instructions lead the reader from laying out footings to adding railings. Includes three deck projects, 500 color drawings, and photographs.

BOOK #: 277180   176pp.   8½"x10⅞"

FURNITURE REPAIR & REFINISHING

From structural repairs to restoring older finishes or entirely refinishing furniture: a hands-on step-by-step approach to furniture repair and restoration. More than 430 color photographs and 60 full-color drawings.

BOOK #: 277335   240pp.   8½"x10⅞"

HOUSE FRAMING

Written for those with beginning to intermediate building skills, this book is designed to walk you through the framing basics, from assembling simple partitions to cutting compound angles on dormer rafters. More than 400 full-color drawings.

BOOK #: 277655   240pp.   8½"x10⅞"

the Home Planner, Builder & Owner

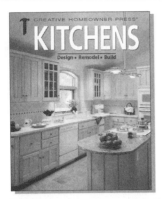

KITCHENS: Design, Remodel, Build

This is the reference book for modern kitchen design, with more than 100 full-color photos to help homeowners plan the layout. Step-by-step instructions illustrate basic plumbing and wiring techniques; how to finish walls and ceilings; and more.

BOOK #: 277065   192pp.   8½"x10⅞"

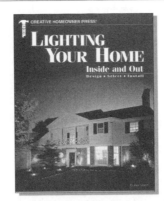

LIGHTING YOUR HOME: Inside and Out

Lighting should be selected with care. This book thoroughly explains lighting design for every room as well as outdoors. It is also a step-by-step manual that shows how to install the fixtures. More than 125 photos and 400 drawings.

BOOK #: 277583   160pp.   8½"x10⅞"

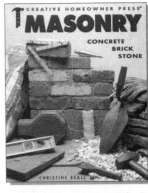

MASONRY: Concrete, Brick, Stone

Concrete, brick, and stone choices are detailed with step-by-step instructions and over 35 color photographs and 480 illustrations. Projects include a brick or stone garden wall, steps and patios, a concrete-block retaining wall, a concrete sidewalk.

BOOK #: 277106   176pp.   8½"x10⅞"

PLANNING A BETTER KITCHEN

From layout to design, no detail of efficient and functional kitchen planning is overlooked. Covers everything from built-in ovens and ranges to sinks and faucets. Over 260 color illustrations and photographs.

Book #: 287495   96 pp.   8½"x10⅞"

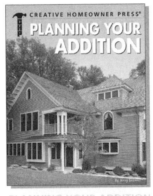

PLANNING YOUR ADDITION

Planning an addition to your home involves a daunting number of choices, from choosing a contractor to selecting bathroom tile. Using 280 color drawings and photographs, architect/author Jerry Germer helps you make the right decision.

BOOK #: 277004   192pp.   8½"x10⅞"

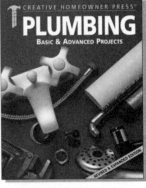

PLUMBING: Basic & Advanced Projects

Take the guesswork out of plumbing repair and installation for old and new systems. Projects include replacing faucets, unclogging drains, installing a tub, replacing a water heater, and much more. 500 illustrations and diagrams.

BOOK #: 277620   176pp.   8½"x10⅞"

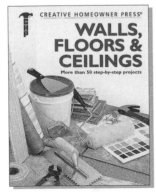

WALLS, FLOORS & CEILINGS

Here's the definitive guide to interiors. It shows you how to replace old surfaces with new professional-looking ones. Projects include installing molding, skylights, insulation, flooring, carpeting, and more. Over 500 color photos and drawings.

BOOK #: 277697   176pp.   8½"x10⅞"

WALLS, WALKS & PATIOS

Learn how to build a patio from concrete, stone, or brick and complement it with one of a dozen walks. Learn about simple mortarless walls, landscape timber walls, and hefty brick and stone walls. A special design section helps turn your dreams into reality. 50 photographs and 320 illustrations.

BOOK #: 277994   192 pp.   8½"x10⅞"

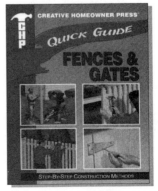

QUICK GUIDE: FENCES & GATES

Learn how to build and install all kinds of fences and gates for your yard, from hand-built wood privacy and picket fences to newer prefabricated vinyl and chain-link types. Over 200 two-color drawings illustrate step-by-step procedures.

BOOK #: 287732   80pp.   8½"x10⅞"

Place your Order ....

The Smart Approach to BATH DESIGN

Everything you need to know about designing a bathroom like a professional is explained in *this book*. Creative solutions and practical advice about space, the latest in fixtures and fittings, and safety features accompany over 150 photographs.

BOOK #: 287225   176pp.   9"x10"

COLOR IN THE AMERICAN HOME

Find out how to make the most of color in your American home with ideas for analyzing, selecting, and coordinating color schemes. Learn how differently light affects the colors you choose depending on where you live. Over 150 photographs of traditional and contemporary interiors.

BOOK #: 287264   176pp.   9"x10"

CHOOSING A COLOR SCHEME

Plan colorful and imaginative decorating schemes for your home with the style and flair of a professional interior decorator. Learn how color, light, pattern, and texture work together. Over 170 full-color illustrations and photographs of wallcovering, paint, fabric, and floor covering design schemes.

BOOK #: 287531   96pp.   8½"x10⅞"

BOOK ORDER FORM   *Please Print*

SHIP TO:

Name:

Address:

City: State: Zip: Phone Number:

(Should there be a problem with your order)

Quantity	Title	Price	CHP #	Cost
_____	Adding Space without Adding On	14.95	277680	_____
_____	Basic Wiring	14.95	277048	_____
_____	Bathrooms: Design, Remodel, Build	14.95	277053	_____
_____	Build a Kids' Play Yard	14.95	277662	_____
_____	Cabinets & Built-Ins	14.95	277079	_____
_____	Choosing a Color Scheme	9.95	287531	_____
_____	Color in the American Home	16.95	287264	_____
_____	Decks: Plan, Design, Build	14.95	277180	_____
_____	Designing and Planning Bathrooms	9.95	287627	_____
_____	Furniture Repair & Refinishing	19.95	277335	_____
_____	House Framing	19.95	277655	_____
_____	Kitchens: Design, Remodel, Build (New Ed.)	14.95	277065	_____
_____	Lighting Your Home Inside & Out	14.95	277583	_____
_____	Masonry: Concrete, Brick, Stone	14.95	277106	_____
_____	Planning a Better Kitchen	9.95	287495	_____
_____	Planning Your Addition	14.95	277004	_____
_____	Plumbing: Basic & Advanced Projects	14.95	277620	_____
_____	The Smart Approach to Bath Design	16.95	287225	_____
_____	Walls, Floors & Ceilings	14.95	277697	_____
_____	Walls, Walks & Patios	14.95	277994	_____
_____	Quick Guide - Attics	7.95	287711	_____
_____	Quick Guide - Basements	7.95	287242	_____
_____	Quick Guide - Ceramic Tile	7.95	287730	_____
_____	Quick Guide - Decks	7.95	277344	_____
_____	Quick Guide - Fences & Gates	7.95	287732	_____
_____	Quick Guide - Floors	7.95	287734	_____

Quantity	Title	Price	CHP #	Cost
_____	Quick Guide - Garages & Carports	7.95	287785	_____
_____	Quick Guide - Gazebos	7.95	287757	_____
_____	Quick Guide - Insulation & Ventilation	7.95	287367	_____
_____	Quick Guide - Interior & Exterior Painting	7.95	287784	_____
_____	Quick Guide - Masonry Walls	7.95	287741	_____
_____	Quick Guide - Patios & Walks	7.95	287778	_____
_____	Quick Guide - Plumbing	7.95	287863	_____
_____	Quick Guide - Ponds & Fountains	7.95	287804	_____
_____	Quick Guide - Roofing	7.95	287807	_____
_____	Quick Guide - Shelving & Storage	7.95	287763	_____
_____	Quick Guide - Siding	7.95	287892	_____
_____	Quick Guide - Stairs & Railings	7.95	287755	_____
_____	Quick Guide - Storage Sheds	7.95	287815	_____
_____	Quick Guide - Swimming Pools & Spas	7.95	287901	_____
_____	Quick Guide - Trim & Molding	7.95	287745	_____
_____	Quick Guide - Walls & Ceilings	7.95	287792	_____
_____	Quick Guide - Windows & Doors	7.95	287812	_____
_____	Quick Guide - Wiring, Second Edition	7.95	287884	_____

Number of Books Ordered _____ Total for Books _____

NJ Residents add 6% tax _____

Prices subject to change without notice.   Subtotal _____

Postage/Handling Charges
$2.50 for first book / $1.00 for each additional book

Make checks (in U.S. currency only) payable to: **Total** _____

CREATIVE HOMEOWNER PRESS®
P.O. BOX 38, 24 Park Way
Upper Saddle River, New Jersey 07458-9960